1912 – 2012

FAITH IN THE CITY

THE CHURCH FEDERATION OF GREATER INDIANAPOLIS

Rev. Dr. Angelique Walker-Smith
Executive Director,
The Church Federation of Greater Indianapolis;
Centennial History Project Director and Editor

David G. Vanderstel, Ph.D.
Managing Editor

Published & distributed by:

The Church Federation of Greater Indianapolis
1100 W. 42nd St.
Indianapolis, IN 46208
www.indyfaith.org

in association with:

IBJ Book Publishing
41 E. Washington St., Suite 200
Indianapolis, IN 46204
www.ibjbp.com

ISBN 978-1-934922-77-4
First Edition

Printed in the United States of America

Tribute to Federation historian Dr. Edwin Becker, author of *From Sovereign to Servant: The Church Federation of Greater Indianapolis, 1912-1987* (1987), 137:

The modern city does not have a single religious and moral monolith. Nor is it governed by a single oligarchy but by coalitions of persons responding to the interests and desires of people and their institutions. Economic and political leaders have more power than others, to be sure, but even they must wait for the tides and marshal support where they can. Religious and moral power curbs or abets the tidal movements but is not their source.

Churches that care about the city must have a Federation that is adaptive to the churning grinding environment of the city. It will listen and watch to learn what the city is doing to its poor, its children and youth, its aging, its minorities, its churches. It will look for those leaders of public spirit it can encourage and with whom it can link arms. It will confront those who abuse power and exploit one another.

This it can do only so long as there are ministers and lay leaders in the churches who claim the city as their home and who care enough to give their energy and substance to keep it a just and livable home for all its citizens, even its least. The Church Federation of Indianapolis arose from the efforts of people who embodied a commitment to a vision of a City of God, a commitment that has taken different forms across seventy-five years.

Recalling its history may lead to new expressions of that commitment in the decades ahead.

Contents

O N A WARM SUMMER AFTERNOON IN AUGUST 2010 I received a phone call from a colleague, asking me whether I might be interested in participating in a history project that would mark the centennial of a local religious organization. It sounded intriguing since I had spent four years as the assistant editor of *The Encyclopedia of Indianapolis* and then several years as senior research associate on the Project on Religion and Urban Culture, both projects located in The Polis Center at IUPUI and both of which allowed me to dig deeply into the history and culture of this city. So, when I learned that this new project was to commemorate the centennial of The Church Federation of Greater Indianapolis, I jumped at the opportunity. To participate in any project that seeks to mark a major milestone such as a centennial is truly significant. I am both honored and humbled to be serving in the capacity of "centennial historian" for The Church Federation of Greater Indianapolis, knowing full well that subsequent generations will be relying on this work – at least until the next anniversary volume is written – to learn about the work of the Federation over the decades.

To the reader, this is, in no way, the definitive history of The Church Federation of Greater Indianapolis. That will only be done by mining the collection of Federation records that is deposited in the William Henry Smith Memorial Library of the Indiana Historical Society in Indianapolis. Besides, it would take far more time to dig into, absorb, and assess the full content of nearly 200 archival boxes than the short seven months that we had for the authors to conduct their research and produce their essays. Rather than centering on individual people or individual congregations, this volume focuses on the Church Federation and examines how the organization evolved over the decades and under different leadership, how it impacted the city of Indianapolis and its residents, how it reacted and responded to local needs within the growing metropolitan area of Indianapolis, and ultimately how it participated in the expanding global ecumenical movement of the twentieth century. This is not a "leader- or congregation-centric" volume, but rather an examination of how people of faith sought to join together in their common Christian faith to address the needs of the modern city and impact the community in which they live.

I am truly grateful to The Lilly Endowment for providing the financial underwriting for this project without which it most likely would not have happened. Special thanks to N. Clay Robbins, President, Dr. Craig Dykstra, and the Reverend Jean Smith at the Endowment for their support and continuing the long tradition of Endowment support for the Church Federation.

I am particularly grateful to the Reverend Dr. Angelique Walker-Smith and the Board of Directors of The Church Federation of Greater Indianapolis for entrusting this project to my hands. It has been an honor to oversee the official centennial history of this noteworthy organization. That only happens ... every 100 years or so! That's clearly one way to guarantee one's name will enter into the history books!

I also am most appreciative to the contributing authors who participated in this project and who offered their insightful examinations of the rich Federation collection at the Indiana

Historical Society. I hope that the essays that are included within these covers offer some insight into the rich activities of the Church Federation and its impact on the city over the decades. If you are interested in learning more, visit the William Henry Smith Memorial Library of the Indiana Historical Society and spend some time reading through the boxes of archival material covering the history of this phenomenal organization.

I wish to extend my personal thanks to my colleague Steve Haller, Director of the William Henry Smith Memorial Library of the Indiana Historical Society, and his staff who proved to be most helpful to all of the authors and researchers who visited the Society's archives to dig into the Federation's past.

A very special thanks to Mary Risher who served as the project's photo researcher. Her expertise and deep experience in the field of publications provided us with excellent guidance in the development of the manuscript and the accompanying images. Thank you, Mary!

Special appreciation must go to Pat Keiffner, Publisher of IBJ Book Publishing, Jodi Belcher, Customer Service Representative, and the creative design staff of IBJ Book Publishing. It was a true pleasure to discuss the project with the staff and work with them to prepare a volume deserving of a centennial publication.

I am also grateful to the late Dr. Edwin Becker, Federation historian, for his 1987 history, which served as a valuable foundation upon which to build this centennial history. I am truly humbled that I can stand upon the shoulders and historical work of this individual.

And lastly, I am especially grateful to two individuals:

- Dr. James J. Divita of Marian University who, back in 2010, suggested my name to the Church Federation leaders and centennial committee to serve as the managing editor for this project. I appreciate the confidence that my long-time friend and colleague placed in me to lead this meaningful centennial project. His dedication to the value of local, and especially local religious, history has been an inspiration to me during my thirty year residence in Indianapolis. Given Dr. Divita's expertise in local ethnic and religious history, he was gracious to review the text for historical accuracy and context and offer critical comments and much needed advice, for which I am truly grateful. As always, Jim, I thank you!

- My wife (and fellow historian) Sheryl Dixon Vanderstel who saw me through every part of this project. Not only did she provide daily encouragement (and nourishment!) throughout the project, but she also participated as my research partner and veracity checker – researching numerous questions uncovered in the editing process, reviewing the essays, and assisting in the editorial and rewriting processes. I am so thankful that we share a mutual love of history! I guess that's why we have survived this long! As always, Sheryl, thank you!

As is customary, any opinions or historical assessments reflected in the essays are those of the essayists themselves and not those of the Church Federation. A project of this magnitude certainly could have used much more time. Any errors or oversights are mine alone, most likely because we did not have the time or the resources to extend the project to the desired length and coverage.

Happy 100th to The Church Federation of Greater Indianapolis! May you continue to prosper, flourish, and fulfill your mission over the next century – and until the next historian seeks to assess your accomplishments. It has been a distinct honor to participate in this chronicling of your first 100 years.

Soli Deo Gloria!

David G. Vanderstel, Ph.D.
Managing Editor
Indianapolis, Indiana
May 2012

Foreword

FAITH IN THE CITY: THE CHURCH FEDERATION OF *Greater Indianapolis 1912-2012* is a story about how the churches of Greater Indianapolis and their partners have sought to carry out a biblical mandate of unity and mission. Indeed, this story has sought to live out the prayer Jesus prayed just before the events leading up to His crucifixion and resurrection:

That they all may be one; as thou, Father, art in me, and I in thee, that they also may be one in us: that the world may believe that thou hast sent me. John 17: 21, KJV

At the same time, this is a story not only called to give expression and invitation to a biblical and theological vision of oneness of God's people but it is a story that has helped to shape and define the history of Greater Indianapolis, Indiana, the United States, and the world. While it is a story of the witness of the churches in Greater Indianapolis, it is also a story of brokenness and healing as well as challenge and joys. Most importantly, it is your story. If you, your church or group were a participant in this story, The Church Federation of Greater Indianapolis thanks you. If you were not, we welcome you to be a participant in this story that is still unfolding. We pray that this book will be a blessing to you and encourage you in your walk of faith.

Purpose

On 15 May 1987 Dr. Edwin L. Becker stated the following at the beginning of his book *From Sovereign to Servant: The Church Federation of Greater Indianapolis 1912-1987* on the occasion of the organization's seventy-fifth anniversary:

Seventy-five years ago white Anglo-Saxon Protestantism was the self-confident "establishment religion" of Indianapolis and the Federation was its expression. The Federation today is inclusive of a much wider constituency and is finding its way as servant both to its churches and to the city's people and their institutions in ways old and new.[1]

He concluded the book with the following after having related the Federation's seventy-five year history and posited what new experiences may lie ahead for the Federation:

Churches that care about the city must have a Federation that is adaptive to the churning grinding environment of the city. It will listen and watch to learn what the city is doing to its poor, its children and youth, its aging, its minorities, its churches. It will look for those leaders of public spirit it can encourage and with whom it can link arms. It will confront those who abuse power and exploit one another.[2]

On the occasion of the Centennial anniversary of The Church Federation of Greater Indianapolis, *Faith in the City: The Church Federation of Greater Indianapolis 1912-2012* is a book that seeks to: 1) continue the story of the Federation begun by Edwin Becker in his 1987 publication; 2) revisit and expand upon Becker's work with a group of scholars who bring a critical and deepened research agenda to the task of recalling the history of The Church Federation of Greater Indianapolis; and 3) propose what trends lie ahead not only for The Church Federation of Greater Indianapolis but the wider movement of Christian unity and mission in the future.

Content Overview

While the genesis of The Church Federation of Greater Indianapolis is located in the biblical call as cited at the outset of this foreword, it is also located within a larger national and global historical context and discussion about the merits of different institutional formulations of Christian unity and mission. In his book *A Tapestry of Justice, Service, and Unity: Local Ecumenism in the United States, 1950-2000,* Arleon L. Kelley identified the five historically prominent institutional expressions of local and regional expressions of Christian unity and mission:

- organizations of community ministries;
- local councils of churches;
- metropolitan councils/conferences of churches;
- state councils/ conferences of churches; and
- regional conferences/councils of churches which are multi-state.

The Church Federation of Greater Indianapolis began as a model of a local council and later became a metropolitan council as the churches and the city of Indianapolis began spreading out into suburban and exurban areas around Indianapolis. Indeed, the original name of The Church Federation of Indianapolis was changed to The Church Federation of Greater Indianapolis in 1954 because of this. This change was representative of what happened in many urban centers in the U.S. Such councils have been made up of member denominations, congregations, ministerial associations, and community ministries. Kelley further cited that while The Church Federation of Greater Indianapolis has had this membership, it has also been a council with a variety of services and programs, and has a focus on making neighborhoods viable communities. He further noted that the Church Federation has endeavored to be inclusive of all churches, meaning all races and ethnic groups as well as all theological persuasions, and to become an enabling bridge institution for community.

This book seeks not only to provide a historical story of faith in the area of Greater Indianapolis through the eyes of Christian unity and mission as markers of what it means to be the Church, but a story that has impacted models of Christian unity in other urban centers in the U.S. and abroad. At the same time, the story has been impacted by national and global trends as well. The introduction and chapter one of this book provide a substantive overview of the historic foundation for the global Christian unity and mission movement. The subsequent chapters unfold the joys and challenges of The Church Federation of Greater Indianapolis' impact on the city and its people and how the organization itself has been affected by local, national, and global trends.

Dr. David G. Vanderstel, managing editor of this book and Marion County (IN) Historian, stated the following about this volume:

This is a historical narrative that examines the growth and development of the Church Federation, its ministries throughout the community, its growing involvement in influencing public policy, and the increasingly Christian unity spirit that evolved over the decades. This book not only preserves the historical record of the Federation, but it also may be used to educate business, civic, community, and religious leaders as well as the interested public about how the Church Federation sought through its faith-based work and community outreach to address the changing needs of a growing urban center over the course of one hundred years.

The book is divided by decade with a thematic emphasis. This approach helps to provide the reader with user friendly entry points into this historical narrative and maintain the integrity of seasons of work of the organization. The following themes are examples of some of the thematic highlights: division and diversity; addressing a changing world; race relations; war and work; evangelism; strategies of expanding Christian unity; seeking common missions; shalom and hope.

As the chapters progress the reader will note an increasing participation of diversity of peoples, partners, and engagement of issues that reflect the changing social landscape of a particular period. The authors have taken care not only to make use of the extensive historical collection of The Church Federation of Greater Indianapolis at the Indiana Historical Society but also to include elements of Ed Becker's work, interviews, and other secondary texts that help to situate this story with scholarly resources and sensitivity to the time periods. At the same time, this historical account is captured in a way that shows both the coherence of the time periods as well as containment of a selected period or chapter.

Appreciation

This book is dedicated to the memory of those churches who gave us the fore-parents who answered the call to Christian unity and mission that was given local expression through the The Church Federation of Greater Indianapolis. In this regard, we are grateful to Dr. Edwin Becker, Paul McClure and Marian K. Towne who collaborated to provide the first historical book about The Church Federation of Greater Indianapolis. May this history be a tool for the celebration of Ed's memory and the dedicated service he gave over many years to The Church Federation of Greater Indianapolis as our historian. To God be the glory for what He has done through and with all in Greater Indianapolis!

Secondly, I would like to extend my appreciation to the leadership of Board President Maria Pimentel-Gannon and the rest of the board of directors and staff of The Church Federation of Greater Indianapolis who provided support to the vision for this book and who have supported the development of all Centennial observances. This includes the intensive work of our Centennial interns from IUPUI who devoted their staff time over a three-year period to the development of the Centennial: Ms. Amanda Koch, Mr. Rick Morris, and Ms. Sarah Lane. Special thanks to the Centennial History Committee and Centennial Committee chaired by the Reverend David Berry of Second Presbyterian Church and co-chaired by the Reverend Al Goertemiller of Pilgrim Lutheran Church, the former Board President during the envisioning period of the Centennial observances.

Thirdly, thanks must go to The Lilly Endowment, long-time partner with and supporter of the Federation, for providing financial support for the development and publishing of the book.

I also wish to acknowledge the managing editor of this book, Dr. David G. Vanderstel, Vice President of Institutional Advancement, Sponsored Programs, and Government Relations at Martin University; Ms. Mary Risher who served as the project's Visual Researcher; and the following scholars: the Reverend Dr. Paul A. Crow, Jr., Dr. James Divita, Dr. Jason S. Lantzer, Mrs. Marian K. Towne, Dr. Scott Seay, Dr. Jeffrey A. Duvall, the Reverend Dr. Ron Sommerville, the Reverend Dr. Thomas Best, Ms. Amanda Koch, Mr. John Warner, and the Reverend Dr. Richard Hamm. Special thanks are extended to the Indiana Historical Society staff, especially Library Director Steve Haller, who graciously worked with us and permitted us to obtain and use the photos for this book and visual exhibit as well as provide a place for our book dedication and initial book author talk. Our thanks to them for also being the place where our extensive archive is housed and for providing access to this treasure through the worldwide web.

Additional thanks go to the *Indianapolis Star* for providing access to their archive for this publication. Special thanks to the Second Presbyterian Church Fine Arts Committee and the Indiana Interchurch Center, home of The Church Federation of Greater Indianapolis, and its executive director, Mr. Mel Joliff, who have graciously worked with us to provide the visual history exhibit of the preview of the book.

Finally, thanks to my family, which has supported me through an extensive period of time working in preparation for the Centennial of

The Church Federation of Greater Indianapolis and the publication of this book. This includes my husband, the Reverend Dr. R. Drew Smith, and daughter Asha. I conclude with thanks to my parents, the Reverend Roosevelt V. Walker and Elder Geneva Walker who led me to Christ and taught me the virtues of humility, love, and hospitality required for the work of Christian unity and mission.

Rev. Dr. Angelique Walker-Smith
*Executive Director, The Church Federation of
Greater Indianapolis
Centennial History Project Director*

---

1   Edwin L. Becker, *From Sovereign to Servant: The Church Federation of Greater Indianapolis, 1912-1987* (Indianapolis: The Church Federation of Greater Indianapolis, 1987), ii.

2   Ibid., 137.

The Church Federation of Greater Indianapolis in the Global Context of Christian Unity and Mission

Paul A. Crow, Jr.

I T IS A POWERFULLY SIGNIFICANT FACT THAT THE Church Federation of Indianapolis was born in 1912, just two years after the historic World Missionary Conference at Edinburgh, Scotland in June 1910, an event that symbolized the birth of the modern Ecumenical Movement. The Reverend William Temple, who served as Bishop of Manchester and Archbishop of York and Canterbury and was one of the architects of the Ecumenical Movement in the early twentieth century, noted years after that conference, "In that year [1910] there occurred the most important event in the life of the Church for a generation." It quickly became clear that the Edinburgh Conference would impact the Protestant Christian movement for the ensuing decades.

Providentially, the vision of The Church Federation of Indianapolis was fed by reports from the Edinburgh Conference, which was led by prominent Protestant leaders such as John R. Mott, an American

Methodist layman and leader of the YMCA; Joseph H. Oldham, a Scottish missionary; and other visionaries who believed that the unity of Christians throughout the world was a mandate from Jesus Christ himself and was essential for effective mission. This vision of Christian unity and mission that inspired the Edinburgh Conference spread throughout the churches in the United States, including those in Indiana. One result of this vision was the formation of ecumenical bodies, such as The Church Federation of Indianapolis.

The Biblical Call for Unity

It was the biblical mandate for the unity of all Christians that motivated the churches in Indianapolis to seek an expression of their unity. In the Old Testament or the Hebrew Scriptures, the tradition of ancient Judaism was based on the concept of the one people of God. This unity was an expression of the oneness of God (Yahweh). As the Book of Genesis portrays, Yahweh created the world as one cosmos, a unity determined by one single Will where all creatures are responsive to the purposes of the Creator God. Then, when Yahweh chose Israel from all nations and entered into a covenant with it, Israel's sacred mission was to preserve the unity of God's people. When God's people broke the covenant, God sent prophets and preachers to call them back from division and unfaithfulness to their true vocation of unity and witness to all people of the world.

This vision of unity dominates the self-understanding of the Church in the New Testament. Indeed, the most constant affirmation of the Church in the New Testament is of one community of faith, one flock, one body. This oneness of all Christians was articulated by Jesus in the high-priestly prayer offered for his disciples at the Last Supper. Three times he prayed that his disciples might be and remain one, "so that the world may know that you have sent me and have loved them even as you have loved me." (John 17:20-23) Unity also became a powerful teaching of the Apostle Paul as he wrote to the Church in Rome, Corinth, Ephesus, and elsewhere: "For just as the body is one and has many members, and all the members of the body, though many are one body, so it is with Christ. For in the one spirit we were all baptized into one body – Jews and Greeks, slaves or free – and we were all made to drink of one Spirit." (I Corinthians 12:12-13).

Indeed, all of the writers of the New Testament affirmed the unity of the Church because to be "in Christ" was to belong to one fellowship *(koinonia)* composed of all who believed in Christ. The various biblical writers used similar metaphors to describe the Church: the Body of Christ (I Corinthians 12:17-20, Ephesians 4:11-15); the household of God (Ephesians 2:19); the temple of God (Ephesians 2:21, I Corinthians 3:16-17); God's building and the Bride of Christ (Ephesians 5:22-32, Revelation 21:9). All of these biblical texts witnessed to the Church as a visible community in the world, and its unity was of its essence, the being of the Church. In contrast, division within the Church was considered sinful since division among Christians signified that Christ had to be divided, which was an unthinkable distortion. (I Corinthians 1:10-17)

Struggles for Unity

The Church's history over twenty centuries can be told in terms of its struggles for unity amid tensions, disagreements, and costly divisions. Divisions took place in the second century over the date of Easter (Quartodecimanism) and over those who expected the imminent Second Coming of Christ (Montanism). In the fifth century a major division came between Christians in the Eastern world and those in Europe, primarily based on political and cultural differences, not theology. The greatest schism came in 1054 A.D. between the Eastern patriarch of Constantinople and the Western pope of Rome. While 1054 A.D. was the official date of separation, this agonizing division was six centuries in the making. The next dramatic Christian division came in the sixteenth century Protestant Reformation led by Martin Luther, John Calvin, and others.

During the seventeenth and eighteenth centuries voices in Great Britain and Continental Europe began to proclaim the visible unity of all Christians, hold conferences, and write proposals for unity, mutual recognition, and intercommunion. German Lutheran theologian George Calixtus called for a united Church between Lutherans and Reformed Christians based on the Apostles Creed and the patristic agreements of the first five centuries. Hugo Grotius, a Dutch philosopher and international lawyer, affirmed that "since all Christians are baptized into the same Christ, therefore, there ought to be no sects or divisions among them."[1] John Amos Comenius, a Czech educator and religious leader, lamented the disunity among the churches in Europe and produced a plan for world education based on the common knowledge of God and the community of human culture. This commonality, he believed, would unite the churches. Scots Presbyterian John Dury traveled to Sweden, Holland, Germany, and England to negotiate what he called "ecclesiastical pacification" among the churches based on the Apostles Creed and the theology of the early Church fathers. Richard Baxter, a Presbyterian Puritan minister, drafted proposals for church unity in England. Even German philosopher Gottfried Wilhelm Leibniz worked for union between Protestants and Catholics.

Nineteenth century America experienced various expressions of Christian unity. Non-denominational organizations arose, involving different traditions committed to evangelism, Christian education, and social witness. Among those were the American Board of Commissioners for Foreign Missions (1810), the American Home Missionary Society (1826), the American Bible Society (1816), the Sunday School Union (1824), the American Peace Society (1828), and two Christian youth movements, the Young Men's Christian Association (England, 1844; United States, 1851), and the Young Women's Christian Association (England, 1854; United States, 1872). The most significant voluntary ecumenical body in the nineteenth century was the Evangelical Alliance. Founded in London in 1846 the Alliance's primary purpose was "to bring individual Christians into close fellowship and cooperation on the basis of the spiritual union which already exists in the vital relation of Christ to the members of His body in all ages and all countries."

The second approach to Christian unity in the nineteenth

century involved the federation of denominations. More than just individuals with common commitments, different churches joined together in cooperative mission and witness. Two German-American theologians, Lutheran Samuel Simon Schmucker and Reformed Phillip Schaff, were major proponents of federation. In 1838 and 1870 Schmucker issued his "Fraternal Appeal to the American Churches," calling them to join in an alliance in which they would mutually recognize each other's ministries and practice intercommunion, all without affecting the authority, polity, worship, or discipline of the denominations involved.[2] Schaff called his concept "federal or confederative union."

The third type of unity proposed in nineteenth century America was known as "organic or corporate union." In such a union the traditions and practices of two or more divided churches were blended into a common identity. Two nineteenth century churches – the Disciples of Christ and the Episcopal churches – were committed to this ecumenical vision. The Disciples of Christ were born as a nineteenth century church in Great Britain and America, proclaiming the abhorrence of sectarianism and division among Christians and the necessity of the visible unity of all Christians. One of its leaders was Barton W. Stone, a Presbyterian minister in Kentucky who was a leader at the famous Cane Ridge Revival in 1801. This "sacramental meeting" brought Presbyterians, Methodists, Baptists, and other Christians together to overcome the divisive "partyism" and accept "the Bible alone as the only true standard of faith, practice, and discipline." Thomas Campbell and his son Alexander, both Scots-Irish immigrants from Ireland where they had been ministers in the Seceder strain of Presbyterians, led a second Christian/Disciples movement. Both decried the divisions among Christians as a scandal and gave effective voice to the biblical call to unity. Thomas Campbell's apologia for Christian unity, *Declaration and Address* (1809), is one of the classic modern ecumenical documents. Its central affirmation states: "The Church of Christ on earth is essentially, intentionally, and constitutionally one."[3] Their vision made the Disciples full partners in the eventual Ecumenical Movement.

American Episcopal priest William Reed Huntington wrote an essay in 1870 entitled *The Church-Idea: An Essay Towards Unity,* which proposed the Episcopal Church as the basis for a future united church. His four-point platform for ecumenism, known as the Chicago-Lambeth Quadrilateral, included the Holy Scriptures as the Word of God, the Apostles and Nicene creeds as the sufficient statements of the Christian faith, the sacraments of Baptism and the Lord's Supper, and the historic episcopate as "the keystone of governmental unity."[4]

Modern Pursuits for Christian Unity

The Ecumenical Movement of the twentieth century was characterized by four distinct movements: the Student Christian Movement, the International Missionary Movement, the Life and Work Movement, and the Faith and Order Movement. The latter three led to the creation of the World Council of Churches in 1948.

In 1886 American evangelist Dwight L. Moody helped to establish a worldwide Christian movement among university students at a conference in Mount Hermon, Massachusetts. During this meeting, 100 students made decisions to become overseas missionaries. As a result, John R. Mott, a young American Methodist layman, brought university students together in the Student Volunteer Movement. By 1895 Mott, Luther D. Wishard of the American YMCA, and student representatives from Great Britain, Germany, and Scandinavia had founded the World Student Christian Federation. Soon this global movement of university students proclaimed their goal to be "the evangelization of the world in our generation." Their purpose was to "lead students to become disciples of Jesus Christ as the only Savior and as God; to deepen the spiritual life of students; and to enlist students in the work of extending the Kingdom of God throughout the whole world."

Missionary cooperation among the churches became the second impulse of the modern Ecumenical Movement. The last half of the nineteenth century witnessed the growth of missionary societies with missionary expansion into Asia and Africa, often with colonial implications. One of the results was the convening of high level conferences of representatives of the missionary societies in Europe and North America. The World Missionary Conference at Edinburgh, Scotland in 1910 heralded a new era in Christian history. Over 1,200 delegates, primarily from North America and Europe, gathered for research and dialogue about the missionary witness around the world. One report noted, "The theme of Christian unity was running through the whole conference like a subterranean stream." The two principal leaders at Edinburgh were the American John R. Mott and Scotsman Joseph H. Oldham.

Those who participated in the Edinburgh conference contributed to the formation of the International Missionary Council (IMC) at Lake Mohonk, New York in 1921.[5] This initiative brought together in permanent counsel several missionary societies and the new ecumenical Christian Councils in Asia, Africa, and Latin America. Missionary planning quickly became ecumenical planning. Over the century, IMC conferences became the central expression of the emerging Ecumenical Movement. The council's first conference in Jerusalem in 1928 directed its attention to the threat of secularism and the impact of other world religions on the Christian mission. Racism, industrialization, and rural development were key mission issues addressed by attendees. The second IMC conference met in 1938 at Tambaram, near Madras, India and focused on the Church in mission and the authority of faith in the Church's witness. The third IMC conference took place in Whitby, Canada in 1947 and emphasized partnerships between sending and receiving churches. The fourth IMC conference in 1952 at Willingen, Germany took as its main theme the relationship between mission and Christian unity, giving attention for the first time to the understanding of mission as a sign of the presence of God in the secular world. Attendees at the fifth conference in Accra, Ghana in 1957 examined the sense of "lost direction" of mission due to a radically changing world.

Four years later, in 1961, the IMC became a part of the World Council of Churches at its meeting in New Delhi and changed its name to the Commission on World Mission and Evangelism

(CWME). Two years later, at its meeting in Mexico City, CWME admitted representatives of the Orthodox and Catholic Churches as full participants. In subsequent conferences in Bangkok (1972-1973) and Melbourne (1980), CWME delegates struggled with issues of exploitation, injustice, and churches existing in oppressed and impoverished conditions. Subsequent conferences also centered on reconciliation, God's grace, and a common experience of a wider ecumenism.

In addition to exploring ecumenical work, many churches, before World War I, began to develop a concern for moral and ethical issues facing the world. This movement, known as the Life and Work Movement and led by Nathan Söderblom, a Swedish Lutheran clergyman and Archbishop in the Church of Sweden, sought to promote church unity and emphasize Jesus' messages as relevant to social life. In the U.S. this movement was visible in the Federal Council of the Churches of Christ in America (FCC), formed in 1908 by twenty-nine churches with the goal "to express the fellowship and catholic unity of the Christian Church" and "to secure a larger combined influence of the churches of Christ in all matters affecting the moral and social conditions of the people."[6] The American Peace Union, committed to international goodwill and peace, was another expression of this movement. In 1925 the first Universal Christian Conference on Life and Work met at Stockholm, Sweden under the theme "Doctrine Divides, Service Unites" with Archbishop Söderblom presiding. Joseph H. Oldham was the moving force at this conference. One major American leader was William Adams Brown, distinguished professor at Union Theological Seminary in New York City.

The second Life and Work Conference met at Oxford, England in 1937. The clouds of World War II were gathering on the European continent as Adolf Hitler's National Socialism movement took power in Germany. At the Oxford Conference the major issue was the relation of the Church to the State. Attendees reflected deeply on the integrity of the Church and concluded to "Let the Church be the Church," thereby affirming the Church's role in the social, political, and international arenas of God's world.

The witness of the Life and Work Movement continued in two conferences sponsored by the World Council of Churches. In 1966 the Church and Society unit held a landmark meeting in Geneva, Switzerland under the theme "Christians in the Technical and Social Revolution of our Time." Attendees discussed Christian responses to developments in science and technology. In 1979 a World Conference on Faith, Science, and the Future brought together Christian scientists, technologists, and theologians together on the campus of the Massachusetts Institute of Technology in Cambridge, Massachusetts. This unique conference confronted four critical ecumenical concerns: ethical issues arising from new technological developments, such as the biological manipulation of life; care for the environment; the well-being of all peoples; and the encounter between faith and the contemporary technological worldview. WCC General Secretary Dr. Philip A. Potter presented the keynote address, "The Global Impact of Science and Technology – the Concerns of the Ecumenical Movement."[7]

Another critical phase of the Ecumenical Movement was the Faith and Order Movement. Charles Henry Brent, an Episcopal priest who attended the 1910 Edinburgh Missionary Conference and who later became the Episcopal bishop of the Philippines and of Western New York, was convinced that "a similar conference on matters of Faith and Order might be productive of good." Under Bishop Brent's influence the General Convention of the Protestant Episcopal Church met in Cincinnati, Ohio in October 1910 and adopted a resolution that called for a world conference "to be participated in by representatives of all Christian bodies throughout the world which accept our Lord Jesus Christ as God and Savior, for the consideration of questions pertaining to the Faith and Order of the Church of Jesus Christ." In one of those ironies of history, a similar action was taken on the same day, 19 October 1910, by the General Convention of the Disciples of Christ meeting in Topeka, Kansas. Peter Ainslie III, a minister of the Disciples congregation in Baltimore and an avid ecumenist, led the Disciples at their annual assembly to adopt a resolution calling for a "World Conference on Christian Unity." A seconding action regarding a Faith and Order conference came a few days later from the National Council of Congregational Churches gathered in Boston, Massachusetts. It is amazing that the origins of Faith and Order came from two such diverse American churches as the Episcopal Church and the Disciples of Christ.

Another prominent leader in the early Faith and Order Movement was Robert H. Gardiner, an Episcopal lawyer from Boston and colleague of Bishop Brent. His guidance was critical to the young movement. Under his and Brent's leadership deputations were sent to England to encourage the participation of Anglicans and the Free Churches, to Constantinople and Athens to invite Eastern Orthodox participation, and to Rome to inform Vatican leaders of the Catholic Church.

In a dramatic moment of ecumenical history the first World Conference on Faith and Order was held in 1927 at Lausanne, Switzerland. Representatives from 108 churches, including the full participation of the Eastern Orthodox Church, engaged in dialogue about the nature of the Christian Church, a common confession of faith, the ministry, and the sacraments. The greatest achievement of the Lausanne Conference was a statement on "The Call of Unity," unanimously approved, that placed the biblical call to Christian unity permanently on the churches' agenda. Faith and Order's methodology came to be called "comparative ecclesiology," whereby each church would state its teaching on the Church and its unity in comparison to that of other traditions, thus identifying the areas of agreement and disagreement.[8]

In 1937, ten years after Lausanne, the second Faith and Order Conference met in Edinburgh, Scotland. Bishop Brent's successor as chairman was William Temple, Archbishop of York. Temple's gifts of building consensus, ecclesial diplomacy, drafting documents, and humor were a great influence on the Ecumenical Movement.

The Edinburgh Conference marked a definite advance over the preceding decade of Faith and Order. Reports on the doctrine of grace as well as the ministry and the sacraments revealed exceptional progress towards the unity of the churches. The most memorable statement was an Affirmation agreed upon by the participants:

We are one in faith in our Lord Jesus Christ, the incarnate Word of God. We are one in allegiance to Him as Head of the Church, and as King of kings and Lord of lords. We are one in acknowledging that this allegiance takes precedence over any other allegiance that may make claims upon us. . . . This unity does not consist in the agreement of our minds or the consent of our wills. It is founded in Jesus Christ Himself, Who lived, died and rose again to bring us to the Father, and Who through the Holy Spirit dwells in His Church. We are one because we are all the objects of the love and grace of God, and called by Him to witness in all the world to His glorious gospel.[9]

It was also there where more than 400 participants and 122 churches agreed, despite some opposing voices, to unite Faith and Order with the movement for Life and Work to "form a council of churches." When the World Council of Churches was formed in Amsterdam in 1948, Faith and Order constituted a central part of the WCC's life and witness.

The third World Conference on Faith and Order met in 1952 at Lund, Sweden. Its central focus was upon ecclesiology, worship, and intercommunion. Attendees gave special attention to the so-called non-theological (i.e., social, political, cultural, and personal) factors that divide churches. Representatives of the younger churches of Asia and Africa where united churches were formed or were in the process of forming issued a powerful statement, appealing to older churches "to encourage similar schemes of union among yourselves and your kindred overseas." At Lund a dramatic shift in Faith and Order's methodology took place. The delegates confessed it was not effective to bring about visible unity among the churches merely to compare the various doctrines of the Church. It was essential "to penetrate behind [our] divisions to a deeper and richer understanding of the mystery of the God-given union of Christ and his Church."[10]

In 1963 the fourth World Conference on Faith and Order gathered at Montreal, Canada and devoted attention to the themes of Christ and the Church, Tradition and Traditions, Worship and

Institutionalism. Participants achieved a historic breakthrough in which they affirmed as authoritative Scripture and Tradition, that is, "the Gospel itself transmitted from generation to generation in and by the Church, Christ himself present in the life of the Church." The Montreal conference also marked the first official participation of the Catholic Church in the Faith and Order Movement, attributed to the reforms brought about by the Second Vatican Council.

Creating an Ecumenical Body

Throughout the history of ecumenism individuals have offered ideas to create a world ecumenical body. In the eighteenth and nineteenth centuries ministers such as Jonathan Edwards, William Carey, and Alexander Campbell offered proposals to unite Christians. During the early twentieth century Swedish Lutheran Archbishop Nathan Söderblom and the Ecumenical Patriarch of Constantinople of the Eastern Orthodox Church offered specific proposals for church unity. In 1920 representatives of the International Missionary Council, Life and Work, and Faith and Order proposed a world ecumenical organization of Protestant and Orthodox churches. A meeting of those bodies took place in 1933 at the initiative of American ecumenist William Adams Brown. In 1937 the World Conferences on Life and Work at Oxford, England and Faith and Order at Edinburgh, Scotland voted to pursue the vision of a world ecumenical body. The next year, representatives met in Utrecht, Holland and established a provisional committee of "the World Council of Church in Process of Formation." They elected Dr. Willem A. Visser 't Hooft, formerly the general secretary of the World Student Christian Federation, as the first general secretary of the World Council of Churches. He became one of the most celebrated ecumenical leaders of the twentieth century.

The first assembly of the World Council of Churches was originally planned for 1941. Delayed by World War II, the WCC met in Amsterdam 22 August to 4 September 1948 where 147 Protestant and Orthodox churches, representing all major Christian traditions except the Catholic Church, constituted the WCC. The theme of their first assembly was "Man's Disorder and God's Design." Leaders of the first Central Committee of the WCC included the Reverend George K. A. Bell, Anglican Bishop of Chichester, and the Reverend Franklin Clark Fry, President of the Lutheran Church in America. The WCC stated that it was "a fellowship of Churches which accept Jesus Christ as God and Savior," an international fellowship of churches, not individuals or councils, and that it was Christological and Trinitarian in focus.

Subsequent assemblies demonstrated the evolving international ecumenical spirit. The WCC held its second assembly 15-31 August 1954 in Evanston, Illinois with the theme "Christ — the Hope of the World." The assembly, consisting of 161 member churches, reflected upon "our oneness in Christ and our disunity as churches," the responsible society, churches amid racial and ethnic tensions, among other themes. Its third assembly with 197 member churches met in New Delhi, India from 19 November to 5 December 1961. Representatives ratified a major statement that described the future goal of the Ecumenical Movement as "the visible unity of all [Christians] in each place." The Eastern Orthodox presence was dramatically increased by the membership of Orthodox churches from the Eastern bloc countries of Bulgaria, Romania, and Poland as well as two Pentecostal churches from Chile. In an historic move the International Missionary Council was integrated into the World Council of Churches.

The fourth assembly of the WCC convened 4-20 July 1968 at Uppsala, Sweden under the theme "Behold, I Make All Things New." This assembly, consisting of 235 member churches, met amidst a dramatically changing world order marked by racial conflict, student protests against the Vietnam War, and a widening gap between rich and poor. The preacher for the opening service was to have been Dr. Martin Luther King, Jr., who was assassinated three months earlier.

Nairobi, Kenya was the site of the fifth WCC assembly, held 23 November to 10 December 1975. Meeting under the theme "Jesus Christ Frees and Unites," 285 member churches gathered in the WCC's first "developing world" venue to offer a new vision of the goal of Christian unity – the Church is "a conciliar fellowship of local churches which are themselves truly united." Such a unity, said the Nairobi assembly, would reconcile the divisions caused by racism, sexism, and the political struggles for liberation.

The sixth assembly met with 301 member churches at Vancouver, British Columbia, Canada, 24 July to 10 August 1983. The theme, "Jesus Christ – the Life of the World," linked the unity of the Church with the unity of humankind. Vancouver's message to the churches made this powerful affirmation: "Christ prays that we may all be one. We affirm that God's purpose is to restore all things into unity in Christ. The Church is called to be a sign of that unity which binds together all generations and all people." Members achieved a major theological consensus with a discussion on a historic theological document, *Baptism, Eucharist, and Ministry,* which explored the growing agreement and remaining differences among the churches' faith and life. The Nairobi Assembly decided to send the document to the churches for study, but regrettably did not achieve the desired reception.

The WCC met for its seventh assembly in Canberra, Australia, 7-20 February 1991, which brought Christians of all persuasions, cultures, and 317 member churches together under the theme "Come, Holy Spirit—Renew the Whole Creation." Canberra's theme was unique in that it was cast in a prayer and focused on the Holy Spirit. The Gulf War had begun three weeks before the assembly began, so there were deep differences among the participants on the justifiability of war. The assembly uniquely gave special attention to indigenous people around the world, especially Aboriginal Australians, and the presence of youth in the Ecumenical Movement.

The eighth assembly of the WCC met in Harare, Zimbabwe, 3-14 December 1998, under the theme "Turn to God – Rejoice in Hope." Marking its golden anniversary, the WCC, with 339 members, promised to remain in solidarity with its African hosts and establish a commission to explore the participation of the Orthodox churches in the WCC. Attendees also decided to extend the ecumenical outreach beyond WCC members.

The most recent WCC assembly was in Porto Alegre, Brazil, 14-23 February 2006. With the theme "God in your grace, transform the world," 348 member churches and 4,000 participants joined one of the most representative gatherings of Christians ever held. Representatives agreed on a text, "Called to be the One Church," which urged the WCC and its members to give priority to issues of unity, catholicity, baptism, and prayer. They also addressed issues of economic justice, religious pluralism, and youth and violence.[11]

Implications for Indianapolis

From this panorama of the twentieth century Ecumenical Movement, one can see that the call for a visible Christian unity was believed to be God's calling to *all* Christians of *all* traditions throughout the world. Not only was this found internationally and nationally, but also locally. Writing about the role of ecumenism in the U.S., the Reverend Arleon L. Kelley noted that the story of "local ecumenism" is "rarely told" and, if so, it is usually from a "denominational perspective."[12] At the end of the twentieth century, local ecumenism could be characterized by a variety of organizations, such as community ministries, local and metropolitan councils of churches, interfaith organizations, and "other ecumenical expressions." It is this tradition that gave birth to and sustained The Church Federation of Greater Indianapolis, now marking its centennial year in 2012.

So, what was the impetus for local ecumenism in Indianapolis? While not specifically focusing on the Hoosier capital, Kelley argued that there was a variety of forces that led people to seek the unity of all Christians. The biblical mandate for a united humanity as part of the Body of Jesus Christ. A belief in the inclusiveness of all believers. An affirmation that Christians must initiate change and speak for social justice. Kelley concluded that local ecumenism developed as "a hopeful spiritual and religious counterwitness to the excesses of the dominant cultural forces of nation-statism, industrialism, and materialism with their resulting global economic imperialism and domestic consumerism." He also argued that local ecumenism allowed people of faith to "transcend traditional boundaries of gender, race, patriarchy, super-patriotism, unemployment, income disparity, ecological degradation, misuse of power, and the so-called dysfunctional aspects of the machine era."[13]

The century-long story of The Church Federation of Greater Indianapolis is one that illustrates the development of ecumenism in the United States. It demonstrates efforts to create unity within the Protestant Christian Church. It shows how people built relationships with their fellow humans and, through that effort, restored their communion with God. It also demonstrates the commitment to service and the pursuit of social justice. Ultimately, it is a story of how people of faith pursued Christian unity in order to transform their urban community.

Endnotes

1   Hugo Grotius, *The Truth of the Christian Religion* (Leiden, 1627).

2   Simon Schmucker, *Fraternal Appeal to the American Churches on Christian Union* (Andover, 1838).

3   Thomas Campbell, *Declaration and Address of the Christian Association of Washington*. (Washington, Penn., 1809).

4   William Reed Huntington, *The Church-Idea: An Essay Towards Unity* (New York, 1870).

5   Frank Lenwood, "The International Missionary Council at Lake Mohonk, October 1921," *International Review of Mission* 11 (January 1922): 30-42.

6   Federal Council of the Churches of Christ in America Records, Presbyterian Historical Society, Philadelphia, PA. http://www.history.pcusa.org/collections/findingaids/fa.cfm?record_id=NCC18

7   Paul Albrecht, ed. *Faith, Science, and the Future*. (Philadelphia: Fortress Press, 1978).

8   Mary Tanner, "The First World Conference on Faith and Order, Lausanne, 3-12 August 1927: what difference has it made?" Paper given at the 75th Anniversary of Faith & Order, Lausanne, 25 August 2002.

9   Michael Kinnamon, *The Vision of the Ecumenical Movement and How It Has Been Impoverished by Its Friends* (Chalice Press, 2003), Appendix 4.

10 *Report of the Third World Conference on Faith and Order, Lund, Sweden, August 15-28, 1952.* (London, 1952).

11 World Council of Churches website, http://www.oikoumene.org/en/who-are-we/background/history/assemblies.html

12 Arleon L. Kelley, "Local Ecumenism in Historical and Cultural Context," in *A Tapestry of Justice, Service, and Unity: Local Ecumenism in the United States, 1950-2000*, ed. Arleon L. Kelley (Tacoma, WA: National Association of Ecumenical and Interreligious Staff Press, 2004), 1.

13 Ibid., 16.

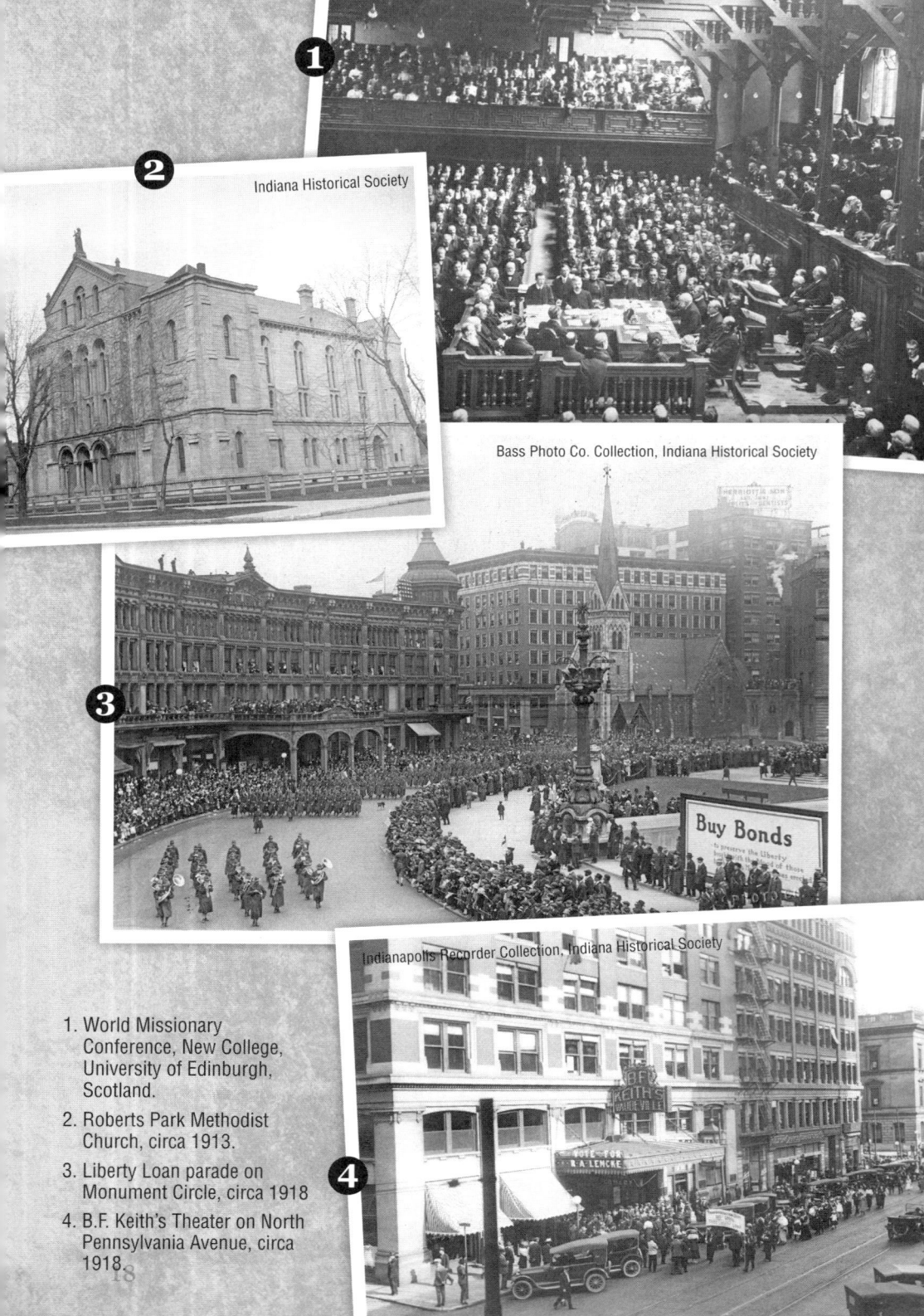

Indiana Historical Society

Bass Photo Co. Collection, Indiana Historical Society

Indianapolis Recorder Collection, Indiana Historical Society

1. World Missionary Conference, New College, University of Edinburgh, Scotland.

2. Roberts Park Methodist Church, circa 1913.

3. Liberty Loan parade on Monument Circle, circa 1918

4. B.F. Keith's Theater on North Pennsylvania Avenue, circa 1918.

18

1910s

The Church in the City

James J. Divita

T HE YEAR 1912 PROVED TO BE ONE OF GREAT challenges and significant accomplishments around the world. 1912 marked the opening of the First Balkan War. The small states of southeastern Europe sought freedom from foreign rule and to expand their territory. The Third Balkan War, better known as World War I, led to social change, the triumph of nationalism, and the creation of a new inter-continental balance of power. Out of the war came the first international peace organization, the League of Nations.

The year 1912 was the time that Americans at the national level talked about a Federal Reserve system, a graduated income tax, the popular election of U.S. senators, and public health care.

In 1912 Hoosiers were concerned about state regulation of stock and bond sales, supported workman's compensation, the regulation of railroads, public utilities, banking, and insurance, and called for primary elections. Socialist presidential candidate Eugene B. Debs of Terre Haute, Indiana, received 347,000 votes in the state, eighth largest Socialist vote in any state.

1912 is remembered for the sinking of the *Titanic*, which took 1,500 lives. The Girl Scouts organized; baseball stadiums opened in Detroit and Boston; the summer Olympics were held in Stockholm, Sweden; Roald Amundsen reached the South Pole; airplanes were deployed in warfare; and a diesel-powered submarine appeared on the high seas.

In Indianapolis clergy and laymen, aware of competition among Christians and the rise of immorality and secularism, proposed a new way for religion to make this a better world. In 1912 those religious leaders formed "The Church Federation of Indianapolis."

Religious Background for Christian Unity

I pray also for those who will believe in me through their word,
that all may be one as you, Father, are in me, and I in you;
I pray that they may be one in us, that the world may believe that
you sent me.
　　　— Gospel of St. John, 17, 20-21

The Church, having received this preaching and this faith,
although scattered throughout the whole world,
yet, as if occupying but one house, carefully preserves it.
　　　— Irenaeus of Lyons, 2nd century, A.D.[1]

Ecumenism is the name given to the movement toward greater unity and cooperation among Christians. One of the scandals of Christianity is that rivalry, bickering, and violence among Christian communities have reduced the spread and effectiveness of Jesus Christ's message of love and reconciliation for all humankind. This movement toward brotherhood and community is as old as Christianity itself, but it has taken two different approaches.

In ancient times, church overseers (bishops) met four times in worldwide ecumenical councils[2] to discuss the nature of Christ, and agree on what it believed about Christ's divinity and humanity. Each time they addressed controversial doctrine/practice (called *heresy* from the Greek word for *choice*). The bishops held that the Church was strong when it possessed unity of belief.

20

After the reduced threat of Islam, the settlement of newly arrived peoples in Europe, and the beginnings of capitalism during the Middle Ages, diverse religious approaches accompanied political, economic, and social change. Concern about how to obtain personal salvation when surrounded by the attractions of the world led to the rise of dissidents like Albigensians and Hussites, and the convocation of two councils[3] to deal with their ideas. Another two councils tried to effect union with the separated Eastern Orthodox churches.[4]

During the sixteenth century Protestant Reformation, individual interpretation of the Bible took the place of privileged clergy who wielded the Church's *magisterium* (teaching authority). Subsequently, many churches or denominations appeared, each with its own doctrine and differing forms of church governance. Even in this troubled century, some sought to restore Christian unity. Politicians and theologians, looking for common ground, produced the Augsburg Confession in 1530. Catholic bishops hoped that Protestant leaders would join them at Trento in 1545, but Christian unity remained illusive. In the next decades political ambition complicated by religious differences played a role in causing military conflict between Spain and England and in the destructive Thirty Years War (1618-1648).

Rise of Protestant Ecumenism

There is one Lord, one faith, one baptism.
— Letter of St. Paul to the Ephesians, 4: 5

There shall be one flock, one shepherd.
— Gospel of St. John, 10: 26

Christians of the eighteenth and nineteenth centuries witnessed the rise of science, secularism, demographic changes, and faltering religious commitment. Their thoughtful leaders pondered ways to counteract these forces. Would a united, coordinated Christian church have a greater influence on society than many small Christian churches? Might interchurch cooperation invigorate the spread of the Word through missionary activity at home and abroad? Could interchurch cooperation effectively address society's ills and maximize the impact of Christian notions of social justice?

I labor to see sectarianism abolished and all Christians of every name united upon the one foundation upon which the apostolic church was founded.
    — Alexander Campbell (1788-1866)[5]

In the United States, new denominations sought to bring people of good will together. After 1820 the Stone-Campbellite movement formed in Virginia and Kentucky, and the Church of Jesus Christ of Latter Day Saints (popularly called Mormons) arose in New York, Ohio, and Illinois. Unfortunately, rather than healing religious divisions, these two churches themselves split into two or three competing religious bodies: out of the Campbellites arose Disciples of Christ, Church of Christ, and Christian Church, while the Latter-day Saints divided into Utah and Missouri bodies.

Another effort at Christian unity was the Young Men's Christian Association (YMCA), which came to America from England in 1851. Its goal was to inculcate Christian principles into the youth by developing a healthy spirit, mind, and body. The Evangelical Alliance followed the YMCA from Britain in 1867. It provided a forum for individual Protestants to cooperate through social contact and intellectual exchange. The Federal Council of Churches, composed of thirty denominations, replaced the Evangelical Alliance in 1908 and worked to create a "Christian America."[6] The Federal Council strongly endorsed the formation of a federated movement in every state of the Union. As a result, the interdenominational Church Federation of Indiana organized in November 1909.

The kind of unity that is worth having is that rich and comprehensive unity which is attained not by ignoring differences, but by transcending them and taking up the element of truth involved in opposing views.
    — Joseph H. Oldham to John R. Mott, 21 May 1909[7]

In June 1910, after two years of study and work, eight commissions reported to the 1,200 Protestant and Anglican representatives attending the World Missionary Conference in Edinburgh, Scotland.[8] The conference's two chief organizers were John R. Mott, American secretary of the intercollegiate YMCA, and Joseph H. Oldham of the British Student Christian Movement and Scottish missionary to India. They decided that the conference agenda would be limited to missionary policy or church outreach, training, and strategy. Avoiding the stumbling blocks of the sixteenth century, they discouraged the discussion of theological issues and agreed not to sign any doctrinal statements. The spirit of Edinburgh was understood to be based on organizational unity with those who confessed Jesus Christ as Lord and Savior.

The Federal Council of Churches heartily accepted the goals of the Edinburgh conference, and confirmed its strong endorsement of local church federations. On 3 October 1910 the Reverend C. E. Bacon of the Methodist Church Indiana Conference[9] presented the Federal Council's recommendation for church cooperation to the Indianapolis Ministerial Association.

Interdenominational cooperation was not a novel idea to Indianapolis ministers. Since the Civil War, the city's white, mainline Protestant churches had cooperated in the Ministerial Association and the Marion County Sunday School Association. When the president and secretary of the Church Federation of Indiana addressed Ministerial Association members on the same topic in November 1911, the audience welcomed the ideas and voted to form a committee of 100 to study the possibility of federation.

At the same meeting laymen Caleb S. Denny and Albert B. Cornelius briefed the ministers on the work of social service and evangelism to be undertaken by the Men and Religion Forward Movement. Founded in New York State in 1911, this movement aroused religious enthusiasm among Protestant lay males, who looked to the hymn "Rise up, O men of God" as their "fight song."

Rise up, O men of God!
The church for you doth wait,
Her strength unequal to her task;
Rise up and make her great![10]

During the early months of 1912 the movement organized "community extension," or weekly religious meetings, for an estimated 5,000 workers at over thirty factories. The men gathered at noon in their workplace or a nearby church for a half-hour talk and hymn singing. Some of the participating factories and businesses were W. D. Allison & Co.; W. B. Burford Company; Bemis Bag Company; Fairbanks-Morse Company; Big Four Shops; Keyless Lock Company; Kingan & Co.; Atlas Engine Works; Eli Lilly & Company; and Nordyke and Marmon Company.[11]

In one newspaper account, the Movement's local members were credited with the formation of the Church Federation,[12] probably because of the large roles that Denny and Cornelius played in both organizations. Cornelius and Arthur H. Goddard were Movement members who worked with the Federation's evangelism committee for several years after its formation.[13]

The Birth of The Church Federation

On 6 May 1912 the committee of 100, chaired by Dr. Frederick E. Taylor, pastor of First Baptist Church and a former YMCA secretary, approved a report that recommended the formation of an interdenominational organization to foster church cooperation and outreach separate from the Ministerial Association.[14]

Then on 7 June 1912 the committee of 100 called a meeting at the YMCA to organize The Church Federation of Indianapolis. Representatives of forty churches chose as their first president Superior Court Judge Vinson Carter, a member of Tabernacle Presbyterian Church. The three vice-presidents were Taylor, YMCA secretary Goddard, and Arthur R. Baxter, head of Keyless Lock Company and member of Central Avenue Methodist Church. Federation secretary was Walter Howe, a member of Third Christian Church, and treasurer was Thomas L. Scott of the Society of Friends.

Indianapolis before World War I

Indianapolis is a part of the great world which is to be redeemed. Great forces are at work here which prophesy a better city – physically, morally and religiously. The churches are thoroughly united and were never so active and aggressive as now.

— Church Federation ad, *Indianapolis News*, 4 April 1914[15]

The clerical leadership and lay membership of the large and presumably wealthy downtown congregations were influential in the city's politics, business and economy, and religious life to such an extent that the city was seen as the quintessential American Protestant city of the future. Indeed, of all the industrial urban centers of the North in the early twentieth century, Indianapolis had one of the smallest non-Protestant populations. In 1906 almost 54 percent of the city's white and black church members were Protestant (about ten percent were African-American); 34.5 per cent were Catholic, and less than 1 percent were Jewish.

Evangelization as a goal of interdenominational cooperation fit this self-image of a Protestant city. A survey of Indianapolis's small immigrant population showed that a sizeable number of Germans, the city's largest immigrant group, were already Protestant. The rest were Catholics or Freethinkers. A minority of Irish were Protestant, the rest being Catholic. Methodist missionaries worked among Italian immigrants who were Catholic or apathetic in religious practice, while Presbyterian workers operated among Slovenian Catholics and socialists. The American Bible Society undertook an early Protestant effort among Italians and Slovenes when in 1908 it transferred a *colporteur* (distributor of Bibles) from Chicago to work among them. Protestant settlement houses reached the small numbers of Eastern Orthodox Greeks, Serbs, Romanians, Macedonians, and Bulgarians.

The real challenge to institutional Protestantism in Indianapolis, however, came from the in-migration of residents from predominantly rural Indiana and the Upper South who did not affiliate with any church. The city always had over half its population unaffiliated (not church members), and the 1906 statistics showed that only 40 percent of Indianapolis' residents was church-going.[16] Because of this low rate of church affiliation, religious leaders proposed offering a Bible study course in the public schools.

In 1913 two significant personalities occupied positions of responsibility and dominated the newly formed Church Federation of Indianapolis through the end of the decade. Elected second president was Caleb S. Denny, three-term mayor of the city (1886-1890, 1893-1895), elder of the Second Presbyterian Church, and a strong proponent of government enforcement of law and order. Joining him as full-time executive secretary was the Reverend Morton C. Pearson, former pastor of First Friends Church, fundraiser for Earlham College, a member of the Federal Council's permanent commissions on evangelism and interchurch federation, chairman of the Ministerial Association's public morals committee, and a board member of the Indiana Anti-Saloon League.[17]

It is not time now for men who believe in God, and Home,
and Country and Church to be resting in camp when so much
needs to be done to help right the world.
— Church Federation ad, *Indianapolis News*, 25 October 1919[18]

Individual Morality: Evangelism

The first goal of the Federation was to spread the Gospel, improve individual morality, and attract new members to local churches. Reaching this goal was so successful in the Denny/Pearson period that its approach became known nationally as "the Indianapolis plan of evangelism." Pearson worked with a strong committee that included well-known activist ministers and laymen like Bacon, Taylor, Goddard, and Cornelius, who arranged for religious speakers to appear before downtown workers in Keith's Theatre, located at 121 North Pennsylvania Street.[19] Attendance at Keith's in 1914 was estimated between 700 and 1,900 daily for ten days. Holy Week programs were scheduled at nearly 100 factories around the city.

Federation leadership considered these campaigns highly successful.

They estimated that 34,000 new members had joined the city's Protestant churches over a five-year period. Furthermore, almost 5,000 of their members had been trained and organized into evangelism teams. Underlying all this activity was a cordial feeling of unity among the participating churches.[20]

The Church Federation finally incorporated on 10 April 1916. The executive committee desired legal permanency as recognition of its most important activities: revivals at Keith's Theatre and some churches, the noon hour lunch meetings in factories, and its support for wholesome entertainments and opposition to questionable public events.[21] As if to confirm its efforts, the speaker at its fourth anniversary celebration at Second Presbyterian Church a few weeks later was Dr. Shailer Matthews of the University of Chicago and president of the Federal Council of Churches.[22]

Public Morality: Prostitution

Local religious leaders believed that a better moral atmosphere, appropriate to the city's Protestant calling, should accompany the spread of the message of Christ. In practical terms this meant that, although the Church Federation had established several committees, Denny and Pearson were primarily interested in the enforcement of existing laws.

Denny spelled out the major areas of concern in public morality: prostitution, the liquor traffic, and gambling. Pearson served as the "leg man," locating and gathering statistics on lawbreakers. Of special interest were north side prostitutes, saloonkeepers who did not close on time, and dance halls and pool halls that were considered to be attractive nuisances. Denny and Pearson reported their information to the mayor and the police for action. When government did not respond to their satisfaction, they took their case to the newspapers.

The Federation was wary of the influx of commercialized vice (houses of prostitution) due to a clean-up crusade in Chicago. Majority opinion among members was that the police were so lax as to invite human traffickers to operate in Indianapolis. Denny pressured Republican mayor Samuel Lewis Shank (1910-1913, 1922-1926) during

27

his first term to no avail. Shank appointed a commission to study vice, but Denny discovered that the police had typewritten instructions on how to handle vice cases in the "segregated districts." The mayor apparently believed that a "live-n-let-live" vice policy was desirable while he faced catastrophes like the great White River flood, major streetcar and teamster strikes, and a police mutiny when police refused to protect strikebreakers – all in 1913. Only when the Federation went public with its plan to impeach the mayor did he revoke the typewritten police order. At that point, "Mr. Shank repeatedly made dishonorable and scurrilous remarks about the ministers of the city."[23] After the mayor left office, Denny wrote the "Injunction and Abatement Law of Indiana,"[24] and the Federation successfully lobbied the state legislature to make commercial vice illegal. When Shank again sought the office of mayor, the Federation opposed his reelection "on moral grounds and also for a lack of fitness."[25]

Pearson was to Democratic mayor Joseph E. Bell (1914-1918) what Denny was to Mayor Shank. A deacon of Tabernacle Presbyterian Church, Bell established the city's first vice squad, but he did not take Pearson's reports of widespread crime seriously.[26] When Pearson sent the mayor a letter detailing immoral activities and received no response, he went public with his complaints. Bell took the offensive by charging that circulating the Federation letter to the *Indianapolis News* was disreputable because Pearson was in the employ of this Republican-leaning newspaper, had dishonored the Federation by sending out an anti-Catholic tract to the ministers of the city, and provided no solid evidence that the businesses which he listed by name had tolerated immoral activities.[27] The executive secretary denied that he was a *News* employee[28] and responded that a minister-friend had submitted the anti-Catholic material, requesting that it be included in a Federation mailing.[29] He also denied that the Church Federation was in any way responsible for the tract. Pearson concluded his letter by repeating his attacks on Mayor Bell.[30]

Reverend Pearson worked diligently during his tenure. He personally took to the pulpit of many member churches to preach and explain the work of the Federation. He publicized Federation activities by placing large advertisements in two Indianapolis newspapers. Editorials on religious subjects appeared in the Saturday edition of the *News* after late 1913, and his 500-word sermonette appeared in the Saturday edition of the *Star* beginning in early 1919. The Federation recommended political candidates for city and county offices and state legislative seats in 1914, 1916, and 1918. Candidates could be of either political party but must be of "good moral character and would enforce the law."[31]

Denny demanded the absolute suppression of open evil resorts that for years flourished under the protection of public authorities. At first only the prosecuting attorney and the county sheriff supported the Federation, but when the police joined the effort "complete victory followed in short order."[32]

Pearson continued his data gathering. His statistics of "girls over 16" showed the extent of young unmarried women contributing to the war economy. Of the 13,463 girls gainfully employed, 4,133 labored in manufacturing establishments, 2,067 worked in dry-goods and department stores, 1,395 had been hired by telephone/telegraph companies, 723 by bakeries and confections, and 716 by laundries. He found another 313 girls ages 14 to 16 employed: 150 worked in dry-goods and department stores and 91 in manufacturing establishments.[33]

Federation leadership soon tied the extent of young working girls from out of the city laboring at low wages to the growth of prostitution. Secretary Pearson sought to collect the names of all girls not earning eight dollars weekly and not living with their parents. In order for them to earn more legally, he encouraged high schools to offer the girls courses in salesmanship. A list of respectable boarding houses for young unmarried women was to be distributed to all employers. With Federation encouragement, the Indianapolis Police Department assigned eleven police women to specific street corners and public parks to monitor the girls so that they would not be led into private vice. Of special interest was night time in Riverside Park on the city's west side where police patrolled the river and park with searchlights.[34]

It should be noted that the Federation's struggle against prostitution was grounded in a respect for women and their rights. At a 1916 meeting where committee members discussed the morality of women dancing barefoot in public, the members expressed their sympathy for women suffrage.[35] In 1919 the Shriners, wearing red fezzes and costumes, and accompanied by their bands, held the largest convention ever held in the city until that time. The executive committee expressed protest and indignation over the Shriners' "vicious conduct" against women on downtown streets, and published a protest statement condemning the small minority of Shriners who lowered "the moral tone of the community."[36]

Public Morality: Liquor Traffic

The Federation strongly opposed the use of alcoholic beverages and always pressured local authorities to enforce whatever limits existed where drinking was illegal. During the previous decade, prohibition (e.g., stopping the manufacture, transportation, and consumption of alcoholic beverages) was possible through local option (e.g., voters could approve prohibition at the township, city, or county levels). The climax to the Federation's anti-alcohol efforts and lobbying for prohibition came on 2 April 1918, when a state-wide prohibition law, implemented on a one-year trial basis, closed some 650 saloons in Indianapolis. Federation leaders pointed out that legitimate businesses now operated in two-thirds of the former saloons; the remaining one-third were soda drink parlors or vacant.[37] Indiana's one-year trial limit was preempted by national prohibition when the prerequisite number of state legislatures ratified the Eighteenth Amendment to the U.S. Constitution in January 1919.

Sunday is Special

Remember to keep holy the sabbath day. Six days you may labor and do all your work, but the seventh day is the sabbath of the Lord, your God.

— Exodus 20: 8-10

The Church Federation closely monitored Sunday observance and argued that no paid entertainments, auto races, or prize fights should be permitted on Sundays and public holidays. The Federation applauded the mayor when he cut a picture film at the Circle Theatre "because of its objectionable character." Arguing that theatrical productions and moving pictures should be inspected for quality, the Federation formed a subcommittee to investigate the use of obscene words in theatre advertisements.[38] It successfully opposed the passage of the Sunday moving picture law, which would have allowed showings as entertainment, and favored the closing of groceries and barber shops as well as the State Fair on Sunday. When barber shops and groceries were ordered closed during summer months "to conserve man power, heat and light," the Federation's executive committee concluded that pool rooms should be added to the proscribed Sunday businesses.[39]

Strong concerns about Sunday sales came to the attention of the executive committee on 4 June 1918. Flushed with victory over groceries and barber shops, and just two months after Prohibition hit the state of Indiana, Federation leaders authorized a committee of three – Secretary Pearson, Methodist pastor Philip L. Frick, and businessman W. D. Allison – to approach the city's police chief and discuss the sale of popcorn on streets near church buildings on Sunday evenings, as well as the hawking of Sunday morning papers by newsboys in the city's residential sections early in the morning.[40]

Regulation of Church Development

A notable Federation activity originating in the Denny/Pearson years was the work of the Comity Committee. The purpose of this committee was to reduce interdenominational competition and better employ church resources by assigning specific neighborhoods to regularize the spread of religion in Indianapolis.

Denominations that wanted to establish or relocate churches brought their proposals to this committee and sought its approval. Denominations affiliated with the Federation were not to enter a neighborhood which the committee had assigned, and no churches could be located closer than three blocks from another. Documentation on this committee's work is spotty, but evidence indicates that the Baptists were assigned the West Michigan Street and Eagle Creek area in 1913, and the relocation of Churchman Avenue Baptist Church was limited to the two or three blocks around State and Minnesota streets in 1914.[41]

Another important issue before the Comity Committee was the competition of Methodist Episcopal work and the College Missions settlement among Italian immigrants along Georgia and Bates streets. "It is the desire of all," Pearson wrote, "that the matter be settled in the spirit of Christian love and unity and in the interests of the Kingdom."[42] At the next committee meeting, the College Missions representative offered to abandon their activities among the Italians on the southeast side in return for exclusive rights to work among the Slovenes and eastern Europeans in Haughville west of White River.[43] The committee heartily agreed to this generous offer on the part of College Missions (predecessor to Christamore House, located at Tremont and West Michigan streets in the early 1920s).

The Federation and Non-member Churches

So too we, though many, are one body in Christ and individually members one of another.
— Romans 12: 5

Indianapolis was one of the first cities in the U.S. to organize an interdenominational lay-dominated ecumenical organization. Among the Federation's first members were churches representing the Methodist, Baptist, Presbyterian, Christian, Congregational, Reformed, and Society of Friends denominations. Various smaller churches like United Brethren and English Lutherans were also represented.[44] The YMCA always was a strong supporter and provided the office space for the Federation from its beginning until 1960.[45]

In its first decade the Federation had limited contact with black Protestant congregations. The executive secretary informed black ministers of the existence of commercial vice in their neighborhoods, and the ministers reported any changes in the local situation. Also, when the Federation undertook a citywide religious census, the secretary called on the black ministers to provide volunteers to canvass their own neighborhoods.

Black ministers initiated closer relations with the Federation in 1919, when they called on Pearson to discuss ways to avoid Chicago-like race riots in the city. The secretary blamed racial tensions on well-financed, out-of-town propagandists; but, he agreed to call on white pastors to address issues involved to prevent any disturbances, and in the future he would work more closely with the black ministers.[46] The following year, in 1920, black ministers became involved in Federation committee work.

The Federation's connection with Catholics and Jews began slowly and with some difficulty. Although the first Catholic parish had roots before 1837 and the first Jewish congregation originated in 1856, neither presence was ever acknowledged in Comity Committee deliberations. In fall 1914, when proceeding with a religious census of the city, the Federation decided to inform Catholics and Jews of the initiative by publishing a letter in the newspaper. "Division appeared" to such a degree that the Federation made the canvass thoroughly interdenominational.[47] At the same time Pearson mailed out the anti-Catholic tract, which he claimed was inadvertent.

Two years later, in 1916, the Church Federation brought all three faiths into a major public manifestation of religion. As one of the events marking the 100th anniversary of Indiana statehood, the Federation organized the State Centennial Religious Parade on the night of 10 October. Congregations provided 100 floats, marchers, and 200 automobiles to carry church dignitaries. Protestants, Catholics, and Jews served on the arrangements committee. The report on the parade concludes: "Perfect harmony of action prevailed in all sessions of the committee."[48]

Another example of early interdenominational cooperation was "Christian Forces Mobilizing," a rally held at the Indiana Statehouse upon the U.S. entry into World War I in 1917. Rabbi Morris Feuerlicht of the Indianapolis Hebrew Congregation was one of the speakers, and the resolutions committee consisted of Earlham College President Robert L. Kelly; Rev. Frederick E. Taylor, pastor of First Baptist Church and a former YMCA secretary; and Father Francis H. Gavisk, pastor of St. John Catholic Church.[49]

The Church Federation During the War

World War I gave Indianapolis residents and churchgoers a greater awareness of individual and societal need. The daily newspapers saturated their readers with tales of hardship, violence, and death everywhere. The Federation and the churches supported social services and charity to help alleviate suffering for the short-term, including Red Cross work. One agency in the process of expansion was Wheeler Rescue Mission, founded in 1893. Denny and Pearson signed an official letter of support for Wheeler Mission and its work "among fallen men and women."[50]

During the war the Federation identified with the administration of President Woodrow Wilson and the national cause for peace. The military conflict's aim was to "save the Christian nations of the world from the domination of Prussian and Mahometan savagery." Similar to the popular idea that this was "the war to end all wars," the Federation proclaimed that with this conflict the "scourge of war will end, to be renewed no more upon the earth."[51] The Federation actively promoted Liberty Loan and war chest drives, and asked all churches to display the U.S. flag on Patriotic Sunday, 15 April 1918.

The Federation also sponsored lectures and conferences on the moral issues of the conflict. As in "Christian Forces Mobilizing," spiritual leaders presented views on the relation of religion and the problems of the great military conflict. People were encouraged to use the noon hour as a time of meditation and prayer for peace.

Just as during the Civil War a half-century earlier, immorality increased during the first World War. Pearson and the Federation worked to improve the religious and moral welfare of the soldiers stationed at Fort Benjamin Harrison located northeast of the city. Religious leaders asked the governor to order the careful policing of the reservation grounds and vicinity to control liquor sales and prostitution. For its part the Federation distributed Bibles and "furnished proper and refreshing entertainment" (like concerts) at the camp.[52]

The Federation demonstrated its concern for veterans following the war as well. Pearson lobbied for social hygiene courses in colleges, and the Federation encouraged the City Board of Health to enforce the ordinance on venereal diseases. Member churches were asked to poll employers who were members of their congregations to report to the Federation job vacancies for returning veterans.[53] The Federation also encouraged churches to sponsor frequent social events for returning veterans in order to facilitate their return to civilian life.[54]

Transition to the Postwar World

[Pearson's] strenuous activities in favor of the social well-being of the city through law enforcement have not merely helped greatly in advancing the cause of Christ, but in furthering the cause of civic welfare in Indianapolis. He has made our federation an organization without a superior in the nation.

— Indianapolis News, 28 October 1919[55]

At the end of the war the Church Federation underwent two major leadership changes. In April 1918 Thomas C. Day succeeded Denny as the third president. Day was an elder at First Presbyterian Church and the owner of a bond and insurance business that bore his name located near 16th and Meridian streets.

Pearson, elected president of the National Council of Federation Secretaries, in September 1918 became president of the Church Federation of Indiana. Thirteen months later, in October 1919, he accepted the position of executive secretary of the Detroit Church Federation. His reputation for effectiveness in federation work was well-known, as is shown by job offers from several cities, including the Atlanta federation in 1916. Mayor Charles W. Jewett (1918-1922), son of a Methodist minister, praised Pearson in farewell remarks. "I think now Indianapolis is the [morally] cleanest city of its class in the United States and a large share of the credit is due to Dr. Pearson."[56]

Reverend Charles H. Winders, former chairman of the committee that had developed the "Indianapolis Plan" and former pastor of Third (Downey Avenue) Christian Church, returned from a Missouri pastorate to succeed Pearson.

The change in Federation leadership was contemporary with changes in Indianapolis and the world. The number of Indianapolis residents, for instance, grew 86 percent (from 169,000 to 314,000) between 1900 and 1920. On the religious side, where around 50 percent of residents were unaffiliated with a church in 1900, that number increased to over 60 percent by 1920. So, Winders and the Federation would have pondered a city with a very large contingent of newcomers and unchurched people, residents who had few roots in local society and tradition.

Despite increasing individual freedom and general prosperity in the 1920s, economic competition, racial discrimination, and social disorganization were rampant. After the Denny-Pearson period the Federation adapted its mission to the troubled postwar world, recognizing that it needed to be attuned to local needs and guided by the principles drawn from the Social Gospel.

At the same time many in the city and state disliked "modernity" because its change created a new status quo. The Ku Klux Klan viewed Prohibition as a great victory for the righteous, but attempted to reduce the disrespect for moral values which accompanied Prohibition with its own "white sheet" lawlessness. It viewed certain unnamed foreign ideas – especially diversity and minority rights – imported during the war as un-American. So the Klan championed anti-immigrant, anti-Catholic, anti-black, and anti-Jewish discrimination to preserve a "100 percent American" Indiana. At the height of its power, the Klan controlled the offices of governor and mayor, and dominated the state legislature. It supported moves to segregate housing and the schools, require the same textbooks for all schools, and ultimately to outlaw private education.

In contrast to the Klan, the Federation strengthened its outreach to black Protestants and to Catholics. In 1920 the Federation established a "committee on racial relations" composed of five black and seven white members. Blacks were admitted to serve on its recreation and amusement, housing conditions, and law enforcement subcommittees, which became forums for black ministers to discuss their community's housing needs and employment problems. At first blacks could not serve on the Federation's standing committees,[57] but the situation changed rapidly. Five years later, black historian and civil rights activist Dr. W.E.B. DuBois spoke at a regular meeting of the Ministerial Association.

The Church Federation established a committee to foster international good will, and scheduled a "good will meeting" in Cadle Tabernacle on 15 December 1925. Earl Conder, fourth Federation president, gave the "warm-up" talk. Reverend S. Parkes Cadman, president of the Federal Council of Churches, told an audience of 9,000 that this great country was founded on religious freedom:

Tolerance is a word of cheap politics. We do not seek tolerance. We seek brotherhood, understanding, co-operation. It is the great business of religion to unite and not divide ... It is a unification in service and brotherhood and the job must be done by the church.
— Indianapolis Star, 16 December 1925[58]

Among those on the stage with the speaker were Methodist Bishop Frederick D. Leete, who introduced Rev. Cadman, Rabbi Morris Feuerlicht of Indianapolis Hebrew Congregation, and Msgr. Francis H. Gavisk, vicar general of the Catholic Diocese of Indianapolis and pastor of St. John's, who gave the benediction.

Conclusion

The Church Federation of Indianapolis was born of the desire to extend the Christian community through evangelization and ecumenism in 1912.

In its first decade the Federation fostered the cooperation of clergy and laymen to undertake religious outreach, increase church attendance, and strengthen private morality. Allied with government, the Federation sought to improve public morality by working to eliminate prostitution, protect women, and limit the use of alcoholic beverages. American society's acceptance of a greater role of religion was equated with the biblical concept of Sunday as the day of rest, prayer, and wholesome entertainment. Achieving these goals was complicated by the constant expansion of the city and a spiritually rootless population, which loosened morality during the World War.

It stands always for the coming of the Kingdom of God to our city and for wholesome, moral, spiritual and intellectual environment in which we may live and rear our families. It stands for a larger and better Indianapolis.

> *— Federation Accomplishments during Five Years,*
> September 1917

Counting its numerous successes during its formative decade, the Church Federation centered on the Social Gospel as the heart of its mission to extend the Christian community and address the challenges of the 1920s.

Endnotes

1   Irenaeus of Lyons, *Against Heresies*, Book 1, chapter 10, paragraph 2.

2   Arianism at Nicaea in 325, Nestorianism at Ephesus in 431, Monophysitism at Chalcedon in 451, and Monothelitism at Constantinople III in 680.

3   Albigensians at Lateran III in 1179, Hussites at Constance 1415.

4   Lyons II in 1174, Florence in 1445.

5   "Reply to 'T.T.,'" 17 January 1826, Alexander Campbell, editor, *The Christian Baptist*, III, section 17, 217.

6   "Federation," *The Church Federation of Indiana* (Indianapolis: Office Y.M.C.A., [1919], 5.

7   Letter of J. H. Oldham to John R. Mott, 21 May 1909, quoted in "Edinburgh 1910-1960," *Occasional Bulletin of the Missionary Research Library*, XI, 5 (14 June 1960), 7.

8   Catholic and Orthodox missionary representatives were not invited to the conference. However, Catholic Bishop Geremia Bonomelli of Cremona (1871-1914), at American Episcopal invitation, sent a lengthy letter of greeting to the Edinburgh Conference. The translated letter was read at the conference's 21 June 1910 afternoon session. Bonomelli told the young priest Angelo Roncalli in 1908 that the time was ripe for "a great ecumenical council." J.M. Delaney, "From Cremona to Edinburgh: Bishop Bonomelli and the World Missionary Conference of 1910," *Ecumenical Review*, 53, 3 (July 2000), 420. Roncalli was secretary to Bishop Giacomo Ratini-Tedeschi of nearby Bergamo (1905-14), an advocate of social justice, ecumenism, and peace, who the priest considered his mentor. When Roncalli was elected Pope John XXIII in

1958, he convoked the Second Vatican Council, established the Pontifical Council for Promoting Christian Unity, and was an advocate of social justice and peace.

9 Bacon also was superintendent, Indianapolis district. *Western Christian Advocate*, 13 January 1909, 19.

10 Music by W. H. Walter, published in 1872; words by William P. Merrill, published in 1911. This is the third verse of the hymn.

11 *Indianapolis News*, 17 February 1912, 11.

12 "Carter is Head of Church Union," *Indianapolis Star*, 8 June 1912, 10

13 See "Officers and Committees for Year Ending April 30, 1920," executive, evangelism, and social service committees, included with *Annual Report, Church Federation of Indianapolis 1918-1919*, 1-2.

14 Author unknown, typescript history of the leadership and legal status of the Church Federation, probably written for its silver anniversary in 1937, Church Federation Collection (hereafter CF), Box 190, Folder 1. Church Federation archives are preserved in the William Henry Smith Memorial Library of the Indiana Historical Society.

15 "Passion Week – Its Meaning," Church Federation advertisement, *Indianapolis News*, 4 April 1914, 20.

16 See graph "Religious Affiliation in Indianapolis: Selected Years, 1830 to 1990," in Jan Shipps' overview article on religion in the *Encyclopedia of Indianapolis*, eds. David J. Bodenhamer and Robert G. Barrows (Bloomington: Indiana University Press, 1994), 175.

17 C. E. Bacon, editor, *The Indiana Issue* (Indianapolis: Indiana Anti-Saloon League monthly), September 1907.

18 "Unattached Church Members," Church Federation advertisement, *Indianapolis News*, 25 October 1919, 29.

19 "Pearson resigns post in Church Federation," *Indianapolis News*, 28 October 1919, 10.

20 *Annual Report, Church Federation of Indianapolis 1918-1919*, 4.

21 Report of C. S. Denny, 4th annual meeting, 5 May 1916. For a list of Federation incorporators, see Ernest N. Evans, "Historical Sketch of Church Federation 1926." CF, Box 190, Folder 1.

22 *Indianapolis News*, 29 April 1916. Official certificate of incorporation in CF, Box 1, Folder 2.

23 "Shank did not close the immoral houses," newspaper clipping probably from 1913, CF, Box 190, Folder 2. For the Federation and Shank's impeachment, see *Indianapolis News*, 29 June 1912, 2, and 13 July 1912, 24.

24 Text of the act with a letter from Denny's successor T. C. Day in CF, Box 190, Folder 1.

25 Executive committee minutes, 4 September 1917, CF, Box 1, Folder 2.

26 *Indianapolis News*, 28 November 1914, 1.

27 Text of Bell's letter in *Indianapolis Star*, 2 December 1914, 9.

28 Ibid. Delavan Smith was the *News* publisher. After his death in 1922, he endowed the Indiana Historical Society library, which was renamed for William Henry Smith, Delavan's father. Ironically the Smith memorial library holds the Church Federation papers today.

29 Ibid. Pearson's minister-friend advised voters to refrain from supporting specific Catholic candidates and Catholic sympathizers. He quoted the fake Knights of Columbus oath as justification for his advice. The spurious Knights of Columbus oath first appeared in 1912 and was used successfully as election material in a Pennsylvania congressional race by a Quaker candidate against his Catholic opponent.

30 *Indianapolis News*, 2 December 1914, 6; 5 December 1914, 1, 11. *Indianapolis Star*, 4 December 1914, 16.

31 *President's Report* [1917?], CF, Box 190, Folder 1.

32 Ibid.

33 Handwritten list and tally in CF, Box 1, Folder 1.

34 "Girls in Employment", CF executive committee minutes, 20 May [1916?].

35 Social Service committee minutes, 11 December 1916. CF, Box 1, Folder 3.

36 "Vicious conduct" quotation in executive committee minutes, 12 June 1919. CF, Box 1, Folder 3. Reference to "moral tone" in "Suggestion to Shriners," *Indianapolis Star*, 15 June 1919, 21. In neither source is the conduct described, but given Federation interests it probably related to public drunkenness and sexual harassment.

37 *Annual Report, Church Federation of Indianapolis 1918-1919*, 5.

38 Ibid., 3-7. For Circle Theatre action, see executive committee minutes, 6 March 1918. CF, Box 1, Folder 2. Theatre ads discussed in executive committee minutes, 2 March 1920. CF, Box 1, Folder 3.

39 Executive committee minutes, 4 June 1918, CF, Box 1, Folder 3.

40 Ibid.

41 *Annual Report, Church Federation of Indianapolis 1918-1919*, 7-8.

42 Pearson in Committee on Comity minutes, 5 February 1914. CF, Box 1, Folder 1.

43 Ibid.

44 List of denominations and specific names of churches and their financial support in executive committee minutes, 20 June 1916. CF, Box 1, Folder 2.

45 *Annual Report, Church Federation of Indianapolis 1918-1919*, 7.

46 "Seek to avoid race trouble," *Indianapolis Star*, 2 August 1919, 20.

47 Executive committee minutes, 9 October 1914. CF, Box 1, Folder 1.

48 "State Centennial Religious Parade," 1-15 October 1916; President's Report, 30 April 1917. CF, Box 1, Folder 2. St. George Syrian Orthodox Church was apparently the first Orthodox congregation to apply for Federation membership. See *Church Federation Bulletin*, March 1925, 1. A search of Federation archives for the first decade did not reveal a relation with German Lutherans Missouri Synod.

49 "Churches of State to Plan Work in the War," and Church Federation advertisement, *Indianapolis News*, 12 May 1917, 23.

50 Executive committee resolution/letter, 10 May 1917. CF, Box 1, Folder 2.

51 Executive committee minutes, May 1917 [?], CF, Box 1, Folder 2, p. 8.

52 Executive committee minutes, 10 May 1917; "President's Report," CF, Box 190, Folder 1, and printed version for Sixth Annual Meeting, 16 April 1918, at First Baptist Church, CF, Box 190, Folder 2.

53 Executive committee minutes, 4 March 1919, CF, Box 1, Folder 3.

54 Executive committee minutes, 8 October 1918. 6th Annual Report of the President. CF, Box 1, Folder 3.

55 Rev. Philip L. Frick of the Meridian Street Methodist Church and Church Federation executive committee member, quoted in *Indianapolis News*, 28 October 1919, 10.

56 "Jewett gives Pearson praise," *Indianapolis Star*, 31 December 1919, 3.

57 Comity committee minutes, 30 April 1920, CF, Box 1, Folder 3. Also Secretary's report for the annual meeting, May 1921.

58 "Audience of 9,000 hears Good Will message stressed," *Indianapolis Star*, 16 December 1925, 1, 3.

Indiana Historical Society

1. Flanner House provided a free tuberculosis clinic to the African American population.

2. Police with distillation equipment confiscated in a raid at the height of Prohibition.

3. Slum housing existed for many in the poorest parts of the city during the 1920s and 1930s.

4. Ku Klux Klan members engage in cross burning during a nighttime rally.

Bass Photo Co. Collection, Indiana Historical Society

Bass Photo Co. Collection, Indiana Historical Society

Indianapolis Recorder Collection, Indiana Historical Society

1920s

Division and Diversity

Jason S. Lantzer

THE 1920S WAS A DECADE OF TRANSITION FOR Indianapolis, Indiana, and the nation. Religion professor and church historian Edwin L. Becker noted in his 1987 history of the Church Federation that as the Federation expanded its programs and involvement in the community, the city that it served was moving ahead and leaving the Federation behind. In part, this had to do with the overall growth of the modern city. In part, it also revealed the early stages of the decline of mainline Protestantism.

And yet, the Church Federation of Indianapolis pressed forward. Indeed, in many respects, the Roaring Twenties proved to be a boom time for the organization. Now an established part of the city's landscape, the Federation broadened its outreach at home and increasingly beyond Indianapolis's boundaries. It was actively engaged both in spreading the Gospel and reforming the city it served.

The Federation

The Church Federation made its headquarters at the YMCA at Illinois and New York streets. Both institutions, in their own ways expressions of the Social Gospel and Muscular Christianity movements, supported one another. The new Y building was an impressive place from which to lead the city's churches.[1]

The Federation was guided by its general secretaries. In 1920 the organization called the Reverend Charles H. Winders back to Indianapolis to become its executive secretary. Winders had helped found the Federation while serving as pastor at Downey Avenue Christian Church, before leaving the city to take a pastorate in Missouri. He would later lead Northwood Disciples of Christ (Christian) Church at 46th Street and Central Avenue.[2] In 1925 the Reverend Ernest N. Evans became the Federation's executive secretary. Evans had been pastor of the city's Second Reformed Church, before leaving the city to take a position within his denomination's hierarchy in Pittsburgh. The nominating committee that selected him was led by the Reverend Harry A. King, superintendent of the Indianapolis District of the Methodist Church. Evans's columns in the religion section of the *Indianapolis Star* became a major means for expressing the Federation's vision of a non-parochial, "co-operative evangelism" Christianity. He served the Federation until his death in 1939.[3]

By 1928, under the leadership of Evans and President Earl R. Conder, the Church Federation's organizational structure looked like this:

- the Financial Appeals Committee investigated religious groups raising money in the city;
- the Literature Committee worked with the public library to increase the number of religious books in its holdings;
- the Comity Committee had oversight of denominational relations in the city;
- the Public Morals Committee monitored conditions in the city;
- the Statistics Committee kept tabs on the growth of congregations and denominations;
- the Race Relations Committee examined ways of improving relations between whites and African Americans;
- the International Justice and Good Will Committee looked for avenues of global outreach for the Federation;
- the Social Service Committee looked for ways the Federation could aid the local community on its own and through joint action with other agencies and groups;

- the Publicity, Religious Education, and Evangelism Committees and the Women's Department.

Perhaps one of the most frustrating things for the Federation's leadership in its early years was that churches were often behind in their financial support of the organization. If there was any worry, the Federation was concerned with its budget. In 1928 the Financial Committee asked that member churches give 10 cents per member per year towards the operating budget, which for fiscal year 1928-1929 was targeted at $13,500. They were also interested in securing donations from some of the city's leading churchmen. Hence, in 1928, the Layman's Committee was honored that local businessman and philanthropist Josiah K. Lilly, Jr. offered to open his home for them to a retreat.

During the 1920s the Federation relied heavily on the four largest denominations in Indianapolis – Baptists, Disciples of Christ, Methodists, and Presbyterians – for leadership and support.[4] It also sought new ways for itself and member congregations to be active in the city. In 1926 the Federation supported the compilation of an Indianapolis Church Survey. One of the burning questions was whether the church was an ally of social service agencies. The problem with the question was that the Church was viewed more all-inclusive in terms of what people expected from it, which is different than how people viewed social agencies. The survey left little doubt that it would be up to Indianapolis's Protestant churches to shoulder burdens for the city, with white and black Protestants making up some 75 percent of Indianapolis religious adherents. It was a task the Federation felt prepared to do.

Public Evangelism

As an organized arm of Christianity, the Church Federation believed that its chief goal was to spread the Gospel of Christ. Doing so in a growing urban area proved to be easier said than done. In the mind of Secretary Evans, the city needed two things: "Christians who are more Christian, and more Christians." The guiding force of the

Federation believed that cooperative evangelism between the city's churches was the only means to achieve those goals.

How to do so was not an easy question to answer, and it was one the Federation wrestled with throughout the decade. In December 1928 Bishop Edwin H. Hughes, former president of DePauw University, noted that both visitation and mass evangelism had pros and cons. While society might change, he argued that the goal of the Church to win souls to Christ remained constant. Hughes was noted for his "deep faith and broad scholarship." At a special meeting held at Roberts Park Methodist Church in January 1929, ministers were encouraged to work together more in this spirit. The Church Federation also told them that while preaching was important, what they should be stressing to their congregations was "loyalty in attendance." The worry that Sunday was becoming too "liberal" was with the Federation throughout the 1920s. As a result, the Federation tasked the Reverend O.W. Fifer, senior pastor of Central Avenue Methodist Church, to encourage Sunday observance. He was noted for having a "broad vision" when it came to both creed and denomination working together.

As early as 1920, the Church Federation worked with the Indianapolis Ministerial Association to put Bibles in the city's public schools.[5] Twice, in 1925 and again in 1927, the Federation's Executive Committee endorsed a Religious Education Bill proposed in the state legislature by State Senator F. M. Dickerman of Indianapolis.[6] Though both efforts failed[7], the Federation still held out hope that such public expressions of faith could lead to a better city. In December 1927 the Church Federation announced its support for a Bible Sunday to fit into a wider "Family Circle Week" program.[8] The Evangelism Committee hoped to see better homes through the city's churches.[9]

Throughout the decade, the Federation sponsored speakers at the B.F. Keith's Theatre at 118 North Pennsylvania Street. With seating for over 1,600, the theater demanded big names who could deliver powerful, compelling addresses to the faithful and the public at large. So in 1927, for example, Chairman Dr. J.W. McFall announced that the Evangelism Committee had secured Dr. J.M. VanderMeulen, president of the Presbyterian Theological Seminary in Louisville and one of the most acclaimed pastors of the late 1920s, to be the speaker at Keith's. The idea was to provide a "forum and pulpit" event, not traditional revivalist campaigns, such as those that some churches and the Cadle Tabernacle sponsored. The Federation sought to make a large intellectual impact on the city.

These efforts at Keith's Theatre did not mean the Federation neglected large evangelistic campaigns, however. In 1921 it sponsored the Rodney "Gipsy" Smith crusade in the city. Smith had worked for the Salvation Army in the 1870s and 1880s until striking out as an evangelist. He was only one of the many evangelists that the Federation brought to the city. By the end of the decade, the Federation was more focused on "home evangelism," as pioneered by Dr. Guy Black, a Methodist minister who helped pioneer the National Home Visitation Program, and which fit into the Federation's status in the city and its other efforts, such as Bible distribution.[10]

There was other work to be done as well. The Evangelism Committee worked to streamline and coordinate mid-week church gatherings in the city in 1925. That year they also encouraged the public library to expand its religious holdings in an effort to help pastors as well as the community at large better understand theological issues.

Because of the growth of industry in the late nineteenth and early twentieth centuries, one area that Social Gospel-influenced groups like the Federation focused on were the conditions of the working class in cities. It was seen as both an outreach (since many of the working class were immigrants) as well as a means of Christian brotherhood. Unemployment was something that was a concern. But so too was the whole notion of industrialization. In 1922 the Federation's executive committee decided to invite the Reverend Worth M. Tippy, Methodist minister and graduate of DePauw University, who left the pulpit of Madison Avenue Methodist Church in New York City to dedicate himself full time to helping the Church solve social issues, to come to the city and speak on these topics. Towards the end of 1926, the Reverend Ulysses S. Clutton believed that there needed to be more outreach to the men working on the railroads, which helped to make Indianapolis the "crossroads of America" and fueled its industrial capability. Clutton was in a position to know. As pastor of Tuxedo Park Baptist Church on the city's industrial eastside, Clutton was a leader in both his neighborhood – Tuxedo Park Baptist was home to the first Boy Scout Troop in the city – and also in the state Baptist denominational leadership. A church builder in his own right (his congregation helped found several other congregations in Indianapolis), Clutton was an integral part of the Board of Weekday Religious Education in the city, and a strong voice within the Federation.

The Federation also was willing to try new approaches in its efforts to reach out to the community. In March 1929 it accepted an offer to work with First Presbyterian Church to broadcast on the radio, considering it the best way to get Christ's message to the masses in the modern age. The Evangelism Committee sponsored daily devotionals on WKBF, eventually part of the NBC radio network, in 1929. As the Reverend Ephraim D. Lowe of Olive Branch Christian Church explained, "the radio is here to stay and it is an asset to our civilization."

Outreach Both Near and Far Away

If evangelism was the goal, Christian service was seen as a means to that end. The Social Service Committee was the way for the Federation to be active and work with other organizations in the city to further both their individual and wider goals.

What this meant for the Federation was that it was constantly being asked to support efforts that perhaps fell outside the normal goals of the Church, but were considered important in the realm of social service. In 1920 the Church Federation supported the construction of a tuberculosis hospital for Marion County. On other issues, such as daylight savings time, it offered no opinion or guidance for the city's Christians. The Federation also decided in 1925 that, in addition to its support of Wheeler Mission, it would assume the responsibility for the spiritual needs of Protestant hospital patients at Riley, Long, and City hospitals. The Federation also became involved with and connected to the Indianapolis Community Chest, forerunner of the United Way, which utilized the federated fundraising model to raise money for community projects and organizations.

Other areas saw increased attention by the Federation as well. Considering all the changes the 1920s brought for women, including the right to vote, it is interesting to note the struggle that the Federation had in understanding what these changes meant for women in the Church.

In 1920 the Executive Committee took no action on a proposed "women's department." Five years later, however, Mrs. Charles A. Mueller was named the first chair of a new department aimed at the city's church women. And yet, the creation of a department did not end the internal debate. In 1928 there was considerable discussion on whether the Women's Department should be dissolved as an official part of the Federation or kept.

In some respects, the Federation's understanding of women was influenced by its working relationship with groups such as the Women's Christian Temperance Union (WCTU) as well as local congregational women's groups. As such, it often worried about duplication of effort. But, the Federation's understanding of the role women could and should play was also shaped internally by those who led the women's department as well as the Federation's own staff. Mrs. F. A. Metzer was the Federation's office secretary until 1924, making sure that the phones were answered, calls were made, and the men such as Winders and Evans were where they were supposed to be. Upon her retirement, Metzer was replaced by Natalie Coffin, who became something of an institution within the Federation. A DePauw graduate, Coffin was a member of Central Avenue Methodist Church. In 1927 she became the executive secretary of the Women's Department, a position she held until 1935, preserving it as part of the Federation.

The Church Federation also was interested in the world beyond Indianapolis. Even if it did not formally send out missionaries of its own, the Federation was interested in overseas work. In the wake of the First World War, the Federation became involved in relief work in Central Europe. It also had sympathy for other efforts, such as Near East Relief, but also realized that it could not support everything. The Federation was worried about the famine in China. It also sought to build a spirit of good will amongst the people of the world by supporting friendship projects in which Hoosier church members made a designated gift to be sent to children in another nation. In 1927 the project had been "dolls for Japan;" the following year it was "schoolbags for Mexico."

The Federation also decided to take a stance on world peace. Following the end of the Great War, the Executive Committee adopted a resolution in support of the Washington Naval Conference, a disarmament meeting of nine nations held November 1921 to February 1922, which set limits on sizes of battleships and fleets. The committee also supported U.S. participation in the Permanent Court of International Justice, predecessor of the present International Court of Justice. Thus, it is understandable why, in May 1925, the Federation formed a Committee on International Good Will. Executive Secretary Evans circulated a questionnaire among local ministers asking, "Do you believe in military preparedness as a means of achieving peace? Do you favor entrance of the United States into the World Court? Do you favor United States participation in the League of Nations?" Evans believed that responses would help pastors focus on "these important matters" and "furnish light and leading to the active peace forces."[11]

The Executive Committee also supported the idea of international disarmament. In 1928 the committee endorsed a "general pact for the renunciation of war." The Federation urged its members in November 1929 to commemorate Armistice Sunday in their churches. But, in addition to remembering the Great War, the churches were encouraged to speak to the higher cause of peace in sermons, including supporting the Kellogg-Briand Peace Pact. What members thought, no doubt, ran the gambit from general, if tepid, support, to wondering why the Federation was bothering with such an issue to begin with.

Interfaith Relations and Comity

Such weighty topics as world peace did not consume the Federation, however. Indeed, much of its time was spent in simple administration. The point of the Comity Committee was to avoid duplication of effort on the part of the city's churches. Its main task was to keep peace between the churches over expansion. Time and time again, the committee had to deal with one denomination wanting to build a new church close to another denomination's already existing church plant.

The Comity Committee was not just interested in where churches moved to, but also making sure that there were congregations available everywhere in the city. One of the challenges it faced was balancing the needs of smaller denominations against the wishes of larger, more established, populous, and numerous denominations. In 1928 one issue confronted by the Federation was the placement of a church in Mars Hill, a working class neighborhood on the southwest side of Indianapolis. The Lutherans expressed displeasure at the formation of a Christian church in the area. But upon investigation, the Federation discovered that this unapproved mission was not sponsored by the Disciples of Christ, and so there was little that could be done to prevent it from setting up a congregation. This incident highlighted one of the chief concerns facing the Federation, and why it felt its role was justified in approving church construction to begin with: "irresponsible missions" and evangelists who diverted attention and funds away from the work of the wider Church.

The Comity Committee also showcased other facets of the Circle City's Protestant establishment, including its uneven handling of immigrants. When a Syrian Church wanted to open near Fountain Street Methodist Church, it was argued that the Syrian congregation would push people out of the neighborhood. Still, the committee vowed to help the Syrians find an appropriate home for their congregation. Yet, in 1928, the Executive Committee voted to bring the Greek Orthodox Church into the Federation as a full member. Why some congregations were aided while others were not, and why some denominations seemed more inclined than others to press a case before the committee is not always easy to understand.

In 1929 the Comity Committee was pleased to reach a "gentleman's agreement" between the city's Baptists, Congregationalists, Evangelicals, Evangelical Synod, Friends, Lutherans, Methodists, Moravians, Reformed, and United Presbyterians on church plant construction and the placement of new congregations.[12] In many respects, the agreement was very reflective of what the Federation and the committee wanted and hoped to achieve in this area.

By far, the largest issue facing both the Comity Committee and the Church Federation in many ways during the 1920s was Protestant-Catholic relations. There was no dismissing the growth of Catholicism in both the state and nation. The relationship between Protestantism, as represented by the Federation and the Catholic Church was complex, both doctrinally and historically. It was a relationship that was made even more complex by the emergence of the second Ku Klux Klan.

Catholics and Protestants were far from ignorant of one another, and as individuals, often got along just fine. But, church hierarchies were another issue entirely. Both Protestant churches and the Catholic priests and bishops had a stake in keeping the two sides at least somewhat separate. The Protestant Reformation, in very real ways, still mattered, and so did the immigrant status of many Catholic parishioners. To the degree that there was a "Catholic ghetto" in Indianapolis, it was one constructed both by Protestant anti-Catholicism as well as Catholic anti-Protestantism. One issue that divided them was Prohibition, though even when they did agree on the need of a reform, such as dealing with the content of motion pictures, the two sides more often than not sought different means towards similar ends.

On top of all this, was the arrival of the second Ku Klux Klan in Indiana. While in the South, the hooded order's chief targets were African Americans. In the North, the Klan needed a new villain. In places like Indiana, the logical choice was Catholicism. A strong anti-Catholic sentiment was still a part of many Protestant churches, especially as it related to the institutional Catholic Church. Coupled with fears over immigration that many native-born Americans had in the 1920s, it proved a powerful issue for the Klan.[13]

The Church Federation took some steps to counter this development. In February 1927 the Federation announced that the city's Catholics had invited Indianapolis's Protestants to a public event at the Murat Temple about the situation in Mexico. The meeting was to be led by former Congressman Joseph Scott, and was to be informative, not a means by the Catholic Church to evangelize to non-Catholics.[14] Such steps at bridging the Reformation divide prompted the Federation, in 1928, to work with the city's Catholics on coordinated Good Friday services in the city.[15]

Indianapolis also had a vibrant Jewish community that the Federation sought to reach. Just before Christmas in 1924, the Executive Committee wanted to promote better relations with Jews in Indianapolis.[16] In November 1925 the Federation began working with Jewish and Catholic leaders on plans for Dr. S. Parkes Cadman's visit.[17] A native of England, Cadman was influenced by the Salvation Army and became a clergyman. He moved to New York City in the 1890s and led a Methodist congregation before becoming the head of a thriving Congregational church in Brooklyn. Along the way, he became a noted author, a pioneer in religious radio broadcasting, and a critic of both racism and anti-Semitism. Bringing him to the city was a statement by the Federation about the spirit of toleration within the Indianapolis community. Still, in 1926, the Executive Committee debated whether or not to include Catholics and Jews in the annual church directory.[18]

Race Relations and the Federation

If the Federation was bridging divides in many respects, there were also areas that proved troublesome. When it came to race relations prior to the 1920s, the Federation had remained largely ignorant of the concerns and issues faced by the growing population of African Americans in Indianapolis. This was despite the size and strength of several black churches in the city, including Bethel African Methodist

Episcopal Church, the historic mother church of African American Methodism in Indianapolis. The congregation, founded in 1836, was the oldest African American church in the Hoosier capital and believed to have been a stop on the Underground Railroad. Vibrant, yet largely unknown and untapped by the white leadership of the Federation up to this time, African Americans were about to make great strides with the organization, at least compared to where they had been.

In some respects, what the Federation accomplished in changing this was amazing. In 1920 the Federation formed the Committee on Racial Relations. Its membership soon had a "frank discussion" with the Federation proper.[19] What it found was that there was discrimination towards blacks in the city, poor housing in many areas, and crime in the "colored section of the city."[20] In 1926 a special committee, consisting of Faburn E. DeFrantz, member of St. Philip's Episcopal, Freeman B. Ransom, member of Bethel AME, and Henry L. Herod, minister at Second Christian Church, recommended placing one black member on each of the Federation's committees. The men also called upon the Federation to establish a "committee of sixteen of an equal number of each race to deal with matters and needs of the Negro race and make recommendations concerning same to the Executive Committee from time to time..."[21]

The Federation could hardly have hoped to do better in its membership selection for the committee. Herod, pastor of Second Christian Church since 1898, was interested in social welfare, the Marion County tuberculosis association, the YMCA, Flanner House, and temperance. He was known as a bridge builder between the races.[22] DeFrantz was a noted organizer, champion of civil rights, a vocal critic of the Klan, board member of the Madame C. J. Walker Company (the premier African American hair product producer in the nation), member of the Senate Avenue YMCA, and parishioner of St. Philip's Episcopal Church.[23] Ransom was a prominent African American attorney, corporate counsel and successful manager of the Madame C. J. Walker Company, active in Democratic politics, and the Senate Avenue YMCA, the School for the Blind, and Bethel AME

Church. He also was an early advocate of the construction of the Phyllis Wheatley YWCA to aid African American women.[24]

The work, even if small, of the Race Relations Committee was a slap at the Klan. Hoosiers did have pride in their role in winning the Civil War for the cause of union.[25] Indeed, the Klan proved to be problematic for Hoosier Protestant churches on multiple levels. It infiltrated the churches; it co-opted issues that American Protestantism held dear; and it diverted money away from church-based philanthropy and activities.[26] All the while, the Klan had to readjust its message from targeting African Americans almost exclusively, as was done in the South, to addressing the threats of Catholic immigration and the enforcement of Prohibition in the North.

By 1923 the Federation noted that there was a White Supremacy League operating in the city. They were making it hard for blacks to find work. The Federation believed that African Americans deserved "fair play" and hoped that holding a Race Relations Sunday would help in overcoming this trend. Equitable treatment and improved conditions for blacks were seen as both "Christian and patriotic."[27]

There were other examples. The Reverend Alva Taylor recommended that his fellow ministers read Joseph H. Oldham's *Christianity and the Race Problem*. Published in 1924, Oldham's book attacked notions of scientific or biological racism, and instead postulated that racism was steeped in economic considerations.[28] Taylor was a pioneer in promoting the value of social work within his own Disciples of Christ denomination with roots in temperance and social welfare advocacy – traits he displayed at the local level, as a member of Downey Avenue Christian Church, and as a denominational leader.[29] His example was followed by many in the Federation's leadership.

In 1925 the Federation reported that scholar and civil rights activist Dr. W.E.B. DuBois was slated to speak at Roberts Park Methodist Church as an expanded part of Interracial Sunday.[30] That this was at the height of the Klan's power and influence deserves to be noted. While the idea for Interracial Sunday originated with the Federal Council of Churches, the Indianapolis Federation had supported the idea, along with the city's Catholics and Jews, since 1923. The Federation sought "mutual understanding" between the races, noting that no one could be considered truly free until all were free from notions of racial superiority, and its member church pastors blasted "intolerance" from their pulpits and had the message spread in congregational Sunday schools under the banner of all mankind being brothers in Christ.[31]

As the decade went on, the Federation's work on the issue of race relations expanded. It sought to work with "colored pastors" more in 1926.[32] That same year, the Reverend Harry A. King was tasked with studying interracial issues.[33] By April 1927 the Federation supported the idea that the city's white churches should contribute financially to the construction of a YWCA for "colored girls."[34] In February 1928 an interracial meeting was held at Roberts Park Methodist Church, where Dr. Alain Locke, professor of philosophy at Howard University, was the speaker.[35]

Politics and Public Morals

By far, the Federation's chief concern was over the public moral welfare of Indianapolis. As such, it was very reflective of the city's churches in this regard. Congregations such as Central Avenue Methodist and Meridian Street Methodist railed often about dangers associated with movies and theaters, the need to enforce Prohibition, not patronizing businesses that were open on the Sabbath, and voting for those who upheld the laws of the land.[36]

Indeed, the effort at Sunday closings and public morals reached back to the 1890s and early 1900s. Methodists, for example, included in their list of "worldly traps" such things as dancing, cards, "shameless" clothes, and anything that might excite the "lusts of the flesh."[37] They, along with local WCTU chapters, urged the Federation to support a clampdown on Sunday amusements of all types.[38] The Federation was a very active part of Protestant attempts to influence the life of the city. In 1920, for example, it sent a delegation to visit Indianapolis government officials in order to prompt a vice crackdown. It urged ministers to preach against the "desecration" of Sunday.[39] The Executive Committee in 1926 noted that Sunday observance was slipping because church people were "without convictions" and others willing to take advantage of that. While they admitted that people could not be forced to go to church, they hoped laws could be passed and enforced that compelled people to rest.[40]

To the Federation, it was obvious that an "open Sunday" would prove ruinous to the souls of Indianapolis's citizens. At the heart of that fear were amusement parks, motion pictures, and the theatres that showed and displayed advertisements for the same. Along with the WCTU, it worried about Riverside Amusement Park. Complete with roller coasters, water rides, a dance and roller skating rink, the park on West 30th Street and the White River seemed to epitomize all the things that could distract good Christians from the work of the Lord.[41] Many of the Federation's Executive Committee believed that a censorship law needed to be passed in order to halt ads and shows that were "suggestive of impurity," "positively lewd and indecent," and downright "objectionable."[42] And yet, the Federation understood the power of movies. In November 1920 the Executive Committee authorized the purchase of a "motion picture machine."[43]

For much of the decade, this work was the area of expertise of Virgil H. Lockwood, chair of the Public Morals Committee. Lockwood was a prominent lawyer, a member of First Presbyterian Church, and a co-founder of the Indianapolis juvenile court.[44] Along with Ernest Evans, Lockwood worked hard to decide who the Federation would endorse in city elections and how to work with public officials, including the city's courts, in enforcing the laws and rehabilitating offenders.[45] In December 1925 the Federation announced that the Reverend F.A. Hayward, a leading local Baptist, would head the Public Morals Committee. The reason for the switch was that Lockwood was splitting his time between Indianapolis and Los Angeles, and could not devote his full energies to the work of the Federation.[46]

To those ends, the Federation was interested in politics. In 1920 the Executive Committee endorsed the Special Citizens Committee recommendations for primary election candidates.[47] The Federation sent letters out to its member churches in 1922, urging people in the congregations to vote "dry" in the upcoming elections and put pressure on elected officials to support Prohibition efforts.[48] In 1925 the Public Morals Committee drafted a letter to vet potential candidates. Methodist members of the Federation expressed worry about the state of public morality.[49] As a result, the Federation was active in supplying tips on vice hot spots to city officials.[50] In 1929, for example, it passed along information about bootlegging at the Van Cortland Apartments on North Meridian Street.[51]

In both advocating issues and influencing politicians, the Church Federation had a mixed record of success. Part of the reason was because the Federation was interested in a wide variety of public morals issues. Prize fighting and carnivals were things that the Federation hoped to do away with, as much as drinking alcohol. Additionally, the Executive Committee was extremely worried about gambling amongst the city's baseball players.[52] It also wanted to suppress obscene publications, limit business and special events (such as the Realtors' Home Show and car sales) on Sundays. The Public Morals Committee hoped the police would crackdown on street gangs, theater ads, and dog racing as well.[53]

Relations between Church and State, however, did not always work as the Federation hoped. Prostitution in the hotels of Indianapolis was a concern of the city's churches. In 1921 a delegation from the Federation met with Mayor Charles Jewett and the chief of police, both of whom laid the blame for lack of prostitution enforcement at the feet of the city judge. Very quickly, the Federation began to doubt if the mayor was in fact all that dedicated to enforcing the law.[54] In some ways, this was a surprise. A leading Republican, Jewett was the son of a Methodist minister who turned to the law and politics as his professions. But in power, Jewett tended to focus more on the city's finances and producing a balanced budget, as well as boosting Indianapolis's civic reputation, than he did with listening to the concerns of the Federation.[55] In another example of their testy relationship, the Federation wanted to make sure that potentially lewd or immoral dancing was prevented. Again, they were disappointed by Mayor Jewett. As New Year's Eve in 1921 approached, the mayor informed the Federation that he had no authority to close down establishments that hosted dances.[56]

Though the Federation did not have the best relationship with Jewett, they hoped to have a better one with Mayor Samuel Lewis Shank.[57] The new mayor, who had formerly held the post from 1910 to 1913, had a persona as a friend of the common man as well as a track record for supporting anti-vice and Sunday closing laws.[58] The Federation also had a much better relationship with Prosecutor William Remy, best known for his successful prosecution of Klan Grand Dragon D.C. Stephenson. Together, they went after pool rooms in 1926, which had long been a worry of the city's churches.[59]

Despite these political improvements, by 1926, the optimism of the past seemed to be fading. In the *Federated Church News*, the editors discussed what the role of Protestantism should or even could be in a democratic nation. Indeed, some had come to believe that Protestant Christianity was a minority view in the nation and, as such, it behooved them to ponder "how then shall the Christian group make its ideals count in the life of the city and the nation."[60]

The Federation and the Dry Crusade

Among the numerous issues pertaining to public morality, one that drew the Church Federation into the public square was Prohibition. Evangelical Protestants had long been advocates of temperance. Over the course of the nineteenth and early twentieth centuries, this cardinal Christian virtue had morphed in the minds of many American Christians from personal abstention to the outright banning of alcohol. In many ways, what occurred was a cultural clash over alcohol. It was more complex than simply categorization, but common themes of native-born vs. immigrant, American vs. European, Protestant vs. Catholic, and rural vs. urban were a part of the mix.[61] For most evangelical Protestants who belonged to Federation member churches, fighting for the "dry" cause was seen as doing the work of the Lord.

The driving force behind the coming of Prohibition both in the state and nationally was the Anti-Saloon League. While other organizations, such as the Women's Christian Temperance Union and the Prohibition Party, played important roles, it was the League that really captured the essence of a proactive Church in an era dominated by the Social Gospel and Progressivism.[62] The genius of the League was in painting the saloon, whether in a rural community or in a city, as a one-stop vice shop which, if removed, would create a virtual utopia in America.[63]

From 1907 until his death in 1929, the Reverend Edward S. Shumaker led the Indiana branch of the League. A Methodist minister, Shumaker was born in Ohio, raised in Illinois, and educated at DePauw University in Greencastle, Indiana. It was in the Hoosier State that Shumaker made both his ministerial career as well as his mark as a reformer. After holding several pastorates, including one in Terre Haute, in 1903 Shumaker was designated by the Methodist Church to work exclusively with the Anti-Saloon League. After a stint as the South Bend regional League representative, Shumaker took the helm of the state organization and never looked back. He helped engineer the passage of county local option in 1908, which was subsequently repealed, and then achieved victory with statewide prohibition in 1917. Throughout these and subsequent "dry" crusades, he worked closely with his fellow evangelical Protestants and with the various ministerial and church federations around the state.[64]

The League found a welcome helpmate in The Church Federation of Indianapolis.[65] The Federation worked along with the Anti-Saloon League in an effort to promote observance of the "dry" laws. It also believed it had a purpose in helping to think up new legislation and laws as well.[66] The Federation in 1925 wanted codification of "dry" laws. It supported the enactment of the Wright Bone Dry Law, which gave Indiana one of the strictest set of enforcement provisions in the nation. The Federation urged people to vote "dry," and called upon its membership to continue to support Prohibition and temperance.[67] To those ends, it often sponsored "dry" speakers. In March 1927 the Federation advertised that Dr. Clarence True

Wilson, perhaps the leading Methodist nationally in the cause of Prohibition, was coming to speak at Roberts Park Methodist Church on the subject of temperance.[68]

And then there was the Reverend Gerald L.K. Smith, who, as part of the Public Morals Committee, routinely blasted "wets."[69] Well before he departed for Louisiana where he became the "chief rabble rouser" for Huey Long and later a celebrated and reviled anti-Semitic and anti-Communist crusader, Smith was a Disciples of Christ minister in Indianapolis.[70] Known for his powerful oratorical style, Smith served the congregations of Seventh Christian Church and then University Place Christian Church. He also contributed to the work of the Federation.[71]

The Federation's ally in support of prohibition, the Reverend Edward Shumaker, soon found himself in serious legal trouble. He ran afoul of the Indiana Supreme Court as well as the state's Attorney General over comments he made about their enforcement (or lack thereof) of "dry" laws. Found in contempt of court after a protracted legal battle, Shumaker was sent to prison where he served out his sentence. Upon his release, the "dry" leader was proclaimed a martyr to the cause and a celebration was held in his honor, complete with representation from the Federation.[72] Shortly after the party in his honor, Shumaker grew ill and died.[73]

Shumaker would thus miss the decline of the "dry" cause. But, the Federation attempted to pick up the slack. The Executive Committee urged churches to fight the calls for repeal of Prohibition that increased with the onset of the Great Depression, fearing that the old times must not be allowed to come back.[74] Led by the Reverend William F. Rothenburger of Third Christian Church, the Public Morals Committee continued to advocate a non-partisan "dry" agenda through the end of the decade.[75]

Conclusion

In many ways, the Federation's experience with Prohibition and public morals showcased perfectly both where it had been and where it was headed. As an organization, the Federation was very influential,

61

and yet unable to guarantee victory for the causes it supported. Yet, regardless of the outcome of their endeavors, the Federation was an active and visible part of the reforms of the time.

Indeed, the Church Federation made some significant strides in the areas of race, women, and interfaith relations over the course of the decade. The Federation also made a principled stand against the Klan in ways that have not always been either recognized or appreciated. If the decade of the 1920s was not a golden age, neither was it a time that the Federation should look back on with a sense of regret. The city of which it was a part of and which it served was better for the Church Federation having been there.

Endnotes

1   *Indianapolis Star,* 14 February 1925.

2   *Indianapolis Star*, 29 March 1946.

3   *Indianapolis Star*, 4 November 1924 and 2 February 1925.

4   Church Federation of Greater Indianapolis Records, 1886-2002 (hereafter CF), Box 1, Folder 6, Indiana Historical Society, Indianapolis, Indiana.

5   CF, Box 1, Folder 3.

6   CF, Box 1, Folder 5.

7   *Indianapolis Star*, 6 February 1925.

8   CF, Box 139, Folder 1.

9   CF, Box 27, Folder 5.

10   Edwin L. Becker, *From Sovereign to Servant: The Church Federation of Greater Indianapolis, 1912-1987* (Indianapolis: Church Federation of Greater Indianapolis, 1987), 28.

11   Becker, 31-32.

12   CF, Box 25, Folder 1.

13   *Indianapolis Star,* 6 February 1925.

14   CF, Box 139, Folder 1.

15   CF, Box 1, Folder 6.

16 CF, Box 1, Folder 4.

17 CF, Box 1, Folder 5.

18 CF, Box 1, Folder 5.

19 CF, Box 89, Folder 1.

20 CF, Box 1, Folder 4.

21 CF, Box 1, Folder 4; Becker, 20-21.

22 *Indianapolis Star*, 25 July 1935.

23 *Indianapolis Star,* 25 September 1964.

24 *Indianapolis Star,* 7 August 1947.

25 Jason S. Lantzer, *"Prohibition is Here to Stay:" The Reverend Edward S. Shumaker and the Dry Crusade in America* (Notre Dame: University of Notre Dame Press, 2009), 101.

26 Lantzer, 113-131.

27 CF, Box 1, Folder 4.

28 CF, Box 139, Folder 1.

29 *Indianapolis News*, 26 September 1957.

30 CF, Box 139, Folder 1.

31 *Indianapolis Star,* 2 February 1925 and 9 February 1925.

32 CF, Box 1, Folder 5.

33 CF, Box 1, Folder 5.

34 CF, Box 139, Folder 1.

35 CF, Box 1, Folder 6.

36 *Dynamo,* newsletter of the Central Avenue Methodist Church; Meridian Street Methodist Church bulletins.

37 Lantzer, 26.

38 CF, Box 1, Folder 4.

39 CF, Box 1, Folder 4.

40 CF, Box 1, Folder 5.

41 CF, Box 1, Folder 4.

42 CF Box 1, Folders 3 and 6.

43 CF, Box 1, Folder 4.

44 *Indianapolis News*, 3 May 1932.

45 CF, Box 27, Folder 1 and Box 139, Folder 1.

46 CF, Box 139, Folder 1.

47 CF, Box 1, Folder 3.

48 *Indianapolis News*, 3 November 1922.

49 CF, Box 1, Folder 5.

50 CF, Box 1, Folder 4.

51 CF, Box 27, Folder 1.

52 CF, Box 1, Folder 4.

53 CF, Box 1, Folders 4 and 6; Box 27, Folder 1.

54 CF, Box 1, Folder 4.

55 *Indianapolis News*, 29 April 1961.

56 CF, Box 1, Folder 4.

57 CF, Box 1, Folder 4.

58 *Indianapolis News*, 24 September 1927.

59 CF, Box 1, Folders 4 and 5.

60 CF, Box 139, Folder 1.

61 Lantzer, 27.

62 Lantzer, 31-33.

63 Lantzer, 39.

64 Lantzer, 79-83.

65 Lantzer, 74-75.

66 CF, Box 1, Folder 4.

67 *Indianapolis Star*, 3 February 1925; CF, Box 1, Folder 4, and Box 139, Folder 1.

68 CF, Box 139, Folder 1.

69 CF, Box 1, Folder 6; Lantzer, 182-183.

70 *New York Times*, 16 April 1976.

71 *Indianapolis Times*, 23 July 1927.

72 Lantzer, 133-157; CF, Box 1, Folder 6.

73 Lantzer, 159-163.

74 CF, Box 1, Folder 6; Lantzer, 166-167.

75 CF, Box 27, Folder 1; *Indianapolis Star,* 9 September 1959.

1. Lockefield Gardens Public Housing Project.
2. Assemblyman and civil rights advocate, Henry J. Richardson
3. "Curtisville Bottom" on the west bank of the White River.

Indianapolis Star

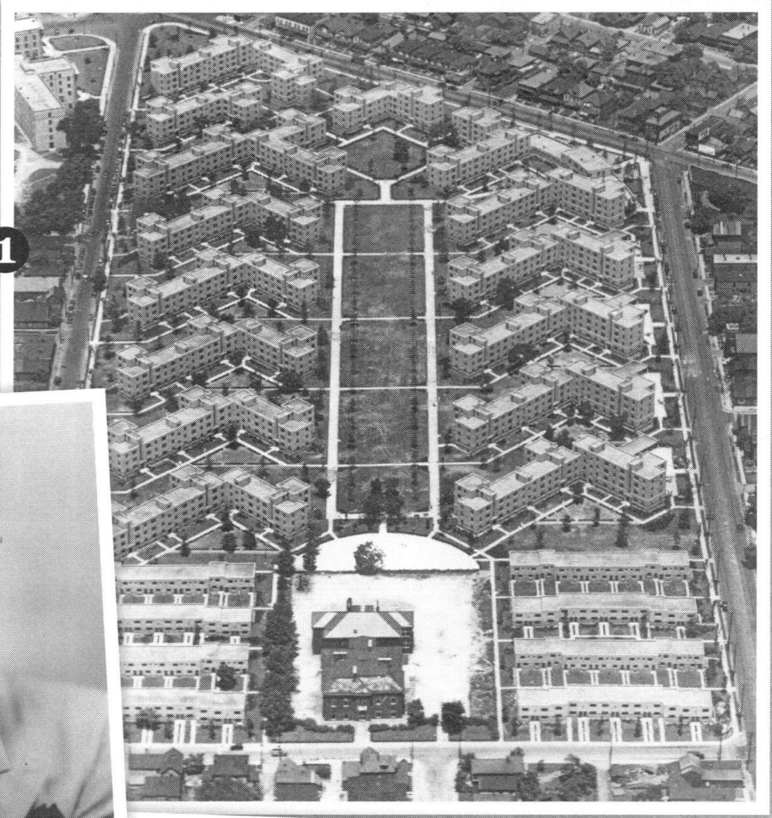

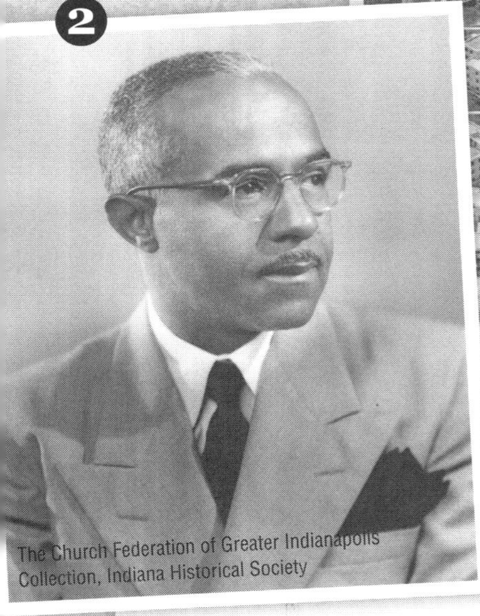

The Church Federation of Greater Indianapolis Collection, Indiana Historical Society

Bass Photo Co. Collection, Indiana Historical Society

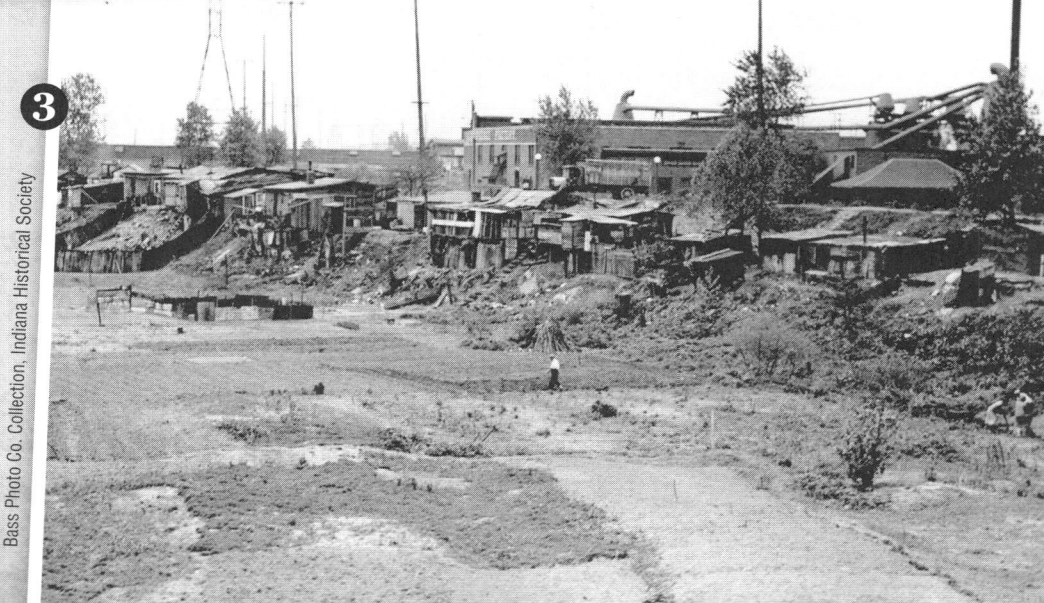

1930s

Addressing a Changing World

Marian K. Towne

T HE 1930S PROVED TO BE A MEMORABLE DECADE. It started with an economic crash that shook the world and ended in the outbreak of World War II, events that engulfed people around the globe. During the decade, the pastors and leaders of The Church Federation of Indianapolis became increasingly concerned about the relevance of the Church in society and the ability of people of faith to address the problems of the day. The collapse of the stock market in October 1929 brought on years of unemployment, poverty, and homelessness in the city, leading the Federation to explore ways of meeting the needs of those affected. The Federation and its member congregations also sought cooperative ecumenical action, particularly on evangelism, Sabbath observance, alcohol sales, racial discrimination, school desegregation, and public morals in general, believing that a united Christian front could solve those issues.

Yet, Federation leaders also encountered a downward trend in mainline Protestantism, something that had begun during the mid-1920s. Given these difficult economic times, many people expected that the nation would "return to religion." One professor at Chicago Theological Seminary, however, noted that "secularism had become so pervasive that a general revival was impossible."[1] Thus, things looked somewhat bleak for the Church in the U.S. and in Indianapolis, making the work of the Church Federation even more challenging during a decade of upheaval and uncertainty.

Federation Developments

When the Reverend Dr. Ernest N. Evans, executive secretary of the Church Federation since January 1925, convened the board for lunch at the YMCA, located at the corner of Illinois and New York streets, on 7 January 1930, he informed them that the financial status of the organization was precarious. The Federation's fiscal balance was only $63.76; outstanding notes totaled $1,750. Church contributions accounted for only 25-30 percent of the Federation's budget; about 15 percent came from individual donations, such as a $500 gift from local philanthropist Josiah K. Lilly Jr. Approximately half of the revenue came from the Community Chest Fund, an annual grant to the Federation since 1920, which had just been reduced from $6,000 to $5,500. Then, the Federation's International Good Will Committee, formed in 1925, announced that they had arranged a visit by Dr. Frederick William Norwood, pastor of City Temple, a nonconformist church in London, England, on Friday 31 January 1930. They needed $125 to cover the costs for the meeting. Fortunately, a large crowd generated an offering that more than covered expenses. Financial uncertainty remained a worry for leaders of the Federation throughout the decade.[2]

Officers for the Church Federation met in Room D of the downtown YMCA. Besides Executive Secretary Evans, there was Marshall D. Lupton, president, from Irvington Presbyterian; Perry R. McAnally, recording secretary, from the YMCA; Henry R. Danner, treasurer, from Second Presbyterian; Miss Natalie C. Coffin, assistant secretary and executive secretary of the Women's Department, from Central Avenue Methodist; and the Reverend Linn A. Tripp, a Disciples minister who led the Social Service Department.

In his annual report to the board, Executive Secretary Evans noted the extensive work of the Federation in 1931-1932. He discussed the impact of the Depression, the contributions of local leaders in advancing the Federation's mission, and the efforts of the Comity Committee to aid in "determining the needs of communities for churches, and the best way in which to supply churches for communities. But, he also had the foresight of understanding the growing role of the Federation by suggesting, "We are of the conviction that a change of the name of [the] organization to correspond with the actual situation would be in place, to read "The Church Federation of Indianapolis and Marion County" – a change that would not occur for another quarter century.[3]

In the midst of its third decade of existence, the Church Federation decided to revise its constitution and bylaws. The organization, in 1935, created an eighteen member Board of Directors and enlarged its Executive Committee to include all board members, committee chairs, presidential denominational heads, representatives from each cooperating denomination, and presidents of the Indianapolis Council of Church Women and Indianapolis Ministerial Association. By these actions, the Federation demonstrated the importance of ecumenism.

The Federation also began to encounter the growing trend toward unity within Protestantism. In the nineteenth century, Protestants were accustomed to working in denominationally-based voluntary societies. By the early twentieth century, increasing numbers of interdenominational agencies arose to coordinate home missions, foreign mission, Christian education, and other concerns such as public morality. Clearly, Protestants were beginning to realize the power in unified numbers as opposed to denominational divisions.

The Great Depression Hits Indianapolis

The stock market crash of October 1929 and the resulting years of economic depression came as a major shock to most Americans. It broke the exuberance of the 1920s, which had been characterized by economic prosperity, materialism, and "loose living." Now, as the Depression spread across the nation, people faced increasing challenges regarding daily survival. Likewise, the clergy were faced with the overwhelming task of paying the bills to keep their church

69

doors open, but also devoting time to care for their parishioners who had been affected by the economic downturn.

The Great Depression took its toll on Indianapolis. In the fall of 1930 the city's unemployment rate was less than 10 percent. It rose to more than 25 percent by November 1931 and peaked at 37 percent in the spring of 1933, rates that were still lower than other Midwestern industrial cities. By October 1933 more than ten thousand families out of the city's population of 364,000 were on relief. As businesses lost activity and the local construction industry dropped nearly 90 percent below pre-Depression levels, breadlines began to appear in the city.[4]

Facing the economic crisis of the day, Church Federation leaders were determined to address rising unemployment. In January 1931 they began to contact city agencies to see how local churches could help. By November the Federation, through its Industrial and Social Service committees, offered suggestions regarding unemployment. It called upon each church to care first for its own members, then refer members to the Family Welfare Society if they required additional assistance, and finally assist other families if the congregations had the resources. The Federation called for more social workers to assist in the crisis and encouraged churches to build morale "by working and praying together." Federation leaders suggested enlisting "every unemployed person in some definite church activity," opening church buildings for community use, creating an unemployment committee of two or three laymen in each church, preparing for immediate relief for "unemployed breadwinners and their families" who were willing to work, and arranging for "security for personal property and homesteads of unemployed workers whose resources are exhausted." Clearly, the Church Federation felt called to offer its services to help the growing unemployed population of the city and even advocated a study "to prevent future Depressions."[5]

Federation leaders decided in 1931 that the *Federated Church News*, originally the *Church Federation Bulletin*, would be printed instead of mimeographed, but only if finances permitted. They decided to publish information regarding unemployment and agencies that could assist the unemployed. The *News* also included a request from the Emergency Work Committee of the Indianapolis Commission for the Stabilization of Employment, asking local ministers to encourage members of their own congregations to make work available in their homes for the unemployed.

The Reverend Linn A. Tripp, Director of Social Service for the Federation from 1927-1945, reported on 5 January 1932, that homeless men were sleeping in the waiting room at Union Station. Tripp noted that he had contacted agencies in the city and "that adjustment had been made, and agencies that care for transient men were taking care of such homeless men." He also reported that street begging in the downtown was an increasing problem.[6]

Addressing the problem of housing in the city, the *Indianapolis Star* of 27 May 1935 printed a story, "Depressionvilles to Go." It focused on "Hooverville," a shanty town named after President Herbert Hoover, located along White River, and "Curtisville Bottom," another cluster of homeless and unemployed, named after Vice President Charles Curtis, that arose opposite the Kingan Meat Packing Plant. The paper reported that Mayor John Worth Kern Jr. and the Board of Public Works intended to inspect the area, settled nearly four years previous, and present plans to remove over 120 huts along the river south of Washington Street as part of a larger flood prevention plan.[7] By October 1935 the *Star* reported that these settlements would be destroyed soon in order to implement the flood plan of the Works Progress Administration. Mayor Kern recommended that areas further south between Morris Street to Raymond Street along White River could accommodate more than sixty families that would be displaced. Despite their concern for housing, there is no evidence that the Church Federation took a stand on this proposed displacement.

Another program that helped the poor came to Indianapolis in 1930. Goodwill Industries, founded in Boston in 1902, began in the Hoosier capital with the support of the Methodist Church. A small program began at Fletcher Place Methodist Church, located at the intersection of South and East Streets and Virginia Avenue, and served the local neighborhood. It gathered used clothing, toys, and household items that were repaired and sold by Goodwill employees. Revenue generated from the sales of the goods provided jobs for residents of the neighborhood. The Reverend Howard Lytle, pastor of Fletcher Place Methodist Church, became executive secretary of the program in 1934 and held the position until 1969. The Federation endorsed this project as one way of reaching the poor.

In the midst of the Depression, the Church Federation also expressed concern about increasing dropouts from local schools. Social Service Director Tripp reported in late 1933 that Arsenal Technical High School had requested help from the Federation to address the increased number of dropouts. By January 1934 Tripp noted that the "project at Technical High School [is] coming along well." Throughout the year, Tripp reported that while boys and girls were dropping out, the efforts of the Federation were contributing to improved social work in the local high schools. In April 1934 the Federation noted that 33 students had returned to school as a result of its intervention.[8]

An important person who helped the Federation unite with local social agencies was Eugene C. Foster, a deacon at First Baptist Church. Foster moved to Indianapolis in 1916 to lead the Charity Organization Society, established in 1880 to provide relief to the poor and reduce the causes of dependency. In 1924 he became director of the Indianapolis Foundation, a local philanthropic institution dedicated to promoting the welfare of local residents. During his twenty-three years at the Foundation, Foster also chaired the Federation's Social Service Committee and served as Federation president (1938-1940).

Women in the Church Federation

Women have played different roles in the church. But, in 1898, local church women gathered at First Presbyterian Church and formed the Missionary Social Union of Indianapolis. This interdenominational association was intended to coordinate the philanthropic and missionary activities of women's church groups.

By the late 1920s, the organization, known as the Indianapolis Council of Federated Church Women, had developed a broad program to involve women of the city's churches. Conversely, the Church Federation, founded in 1912, established a Women's Department in 1925, which encouraged local women to work within their own churches but left interdenominational efforts to the Council of Federated Church Women. Natalie Coffin, a graduate of DePauw and member of Central Avenue Methodist Church, served as executive secretary of the department from 1927 to 1935. Her successor was Dorothy Eller.

Despite the great financial needs in Indianapolis, Jessie (Mrs. Charles) Mueller, first chair of the Federation's Women's Department and President of the Women's Missionary Social Union, embarked upon several programs to help children abroad. The Department sponsored a "Treasure Chest" campaign for children in the Philippines. Participants filled 1,200 attractive tin boxes, costing two dollars each, with items needed by those children; Mrs. Mueller insisted that each box include a children's book. They worked with the Missionary Social Union to prepare school bags for Mexican school children and later sponsored an exhibit of art sent by the Mexican children who had received those bags. Ironically, at the end of the year, the Federation's report cited all the good that was accomplished with these projects, but failed to mention the Women's Department or its members by name.[9]

The Church Federation also endorsed the annual meeting of the National Council of Federated Church Women, which met in Indianapolis, 9-12 June 1931. One of the key efforts of the meeting was to educate church women about social service work. Jessie Mueller proposed cooperating with the National Council of Federated Women (now Church Women United) to enroll women in the wider work of the church.

By the end of the decade, however, the Federation dissolved its Women's Department. Instead, it recognized the Indianapolis Council of Church Women as an affiliated organization and its president became a member of the Federation's Executive Committee.

Advocating for Racial Equality

Relations with the city's growing African American population continued to challenge Indianapolis's churches, particularly over issues of education, businesses, and access to medical care and restaurants. In the mid-1920s the Federation began to invite African Americans to attend its annual meeting and encouraged pulpit exchanges "between colored and white pastors."[10] In January 1930 Executive Secretary Evans addressed a newly formed "colored ministers association." Throughout the remainder of the decade, the Federation took bolder steps and made stronger pronouncements about the need to "demonstrate that Christian Ideals are sufficient to solve difficult problems of race relations in America."[11]

In December 1931 the Race Relations Committee suggested ways to keep the race issue before the public. Chaired by Leila (Mrs. William F.) Rothenburger, the committee recommended that the Federation's section in the newspapers be used during the last two weeks of January and first two weeks of February to reprint articles on race published by the Federal Council of Churches and other inter-racial committees. They called for the use of letters of commendation or criticism, distribution of a new pamphlet entitled "The Negro in Indianapolis," and annual meetings of denominational groups of ministers to discuss race relations.

Clearly, the Church Federation saw the need to bridge the city's white and growing African American communities. Continuing a practice begun in the mid-1920s, the Federation organized Race Relations Sundays, which featured special speakers and choir exchanges. On 4 February 1932, for example, a meeting at First Baptist Church featured Dr. Mordecai Johnson, first black president of Howard University, as speaker; "white people" were urged to attend.[12] Other Sundays included "colored speakers" at church youth groups, pulpit exchanges, and even special "white-Negro women's exchanges" that brought women together to worship and discuss race relations.

Race remained an issue in Indianapolis and the state of Indiana.

The *Indianapolis Recorder*, an African American newspaper founded in 1895, warned of continued "legal Jim Crow-ism" on 4 March 1933, though announced "Job Discrimination Abolished in Indiana" one week later.[13] During the mid-1930s, Henry J. Richardson, one of the first African Americans elected to the Indiana General Assembly, served as a key advocate for civil rights. A member of Witherspoon Presbyterian Church in Indianapolis, Richardson proposed bills to prohibit discrimination in state public works projects and end segregation in public schools.[14] This all came at a time of growing migration of blacks from the South to northern urban areas, including Indianapolis, which resulted in larger populations and the expansion of black churches, including the African Methodist Episcopal, African Methodist Episcopal Zion, the Colored Methodist Episcopal, and a variety of black Baptists. Even though there was an "explosive expansion" among black churches, Indianapolis's African American congregations remained on the margins of the Protestant mainstream of the Federation for many years. These developments led the Federation to realize that it needed to face and address the growing black population in the city.

Among the many concerns voiced by the Race Relations Committee over the decade was about housing conditions for minorities in Indianapolis. At the committee's request, local architect Merritt Harrison gave a presentation on 8 May 1934 about a proposed "slum-clearance" project planned by the federal government. The plan called for an area six blocks by two-and-one-half blocks to be cleared and the construction of model apartments that would rent for $5.00 per room. A special housing committee of the Church Federation drafted a letter of endorsement, which was met with "marked difference" among committee members. Three weeks later, on 5 June 1934, the Federation adopted a recommendation that seemed to question the expenditure of federal funds yet approve the concept of slum clearance:

The Church Federation feels that it is not an agency that should attempt to pass upon the economic, financial or structural plans

involved in the proposed Federal Housing Project in Indianapolis.
But it does approve heartily the idea of removing slum conditions
and in their place erecting modern hygienic homes that may be
rented at moderate rates within the reach of the low wage earner.[15]

A few years later, the Federation petitioned Mayor Walter C. Boetcher (1937-1939) about the displacement of residents resulting from the condemnation and razing of houses, specifically along Indiana Avenue where the Lockefield Garden Apartments, one of the nation's first public housing projects, was being built. The Race Relations Committee discussed the feasibility of identifying $1,000 houses "to take care of colored and white people who will be homeless when condemned houses are torn down." The committee also encouraged the mayor to create a Housing Authority that would oversee the housing needs of the city – and then proceeded to offer advice on particular appointments to that board.[16]

Concerned about this issue, the committee approached the Reverend Cleo Blackburn to "study low cost housing from [the] viewpoint of [the] Negro." Blackburn, a native of Mississippi, came to Indianapolis in 1932 to attend Butler University. After graduating from its School of Religion, he became an ordained minister in the Christian Church (Disciples of Christ) and then worked at Tuskegee Institute. In 1936 Blackburn returned to Indianapolis to lead Flanner House, a social service center established for the black community. By the late 1930s, he had developed numerous programs to provide jobs and housing for the city's poor. As a result of his work, housing continued to be a priority of the Federation.

Under wise leadership, the Church Federation made significant contributions towards the advancement of race relations. Led in the early 1930s by Dr. Charles Winders, the Race Relations Committee offered numerous recommendations and resolutions:

- that the Federation oppose any and all discrimination "against the Negro because of color or race;"
- "that we favor schools for the Negro child equal in every respect to those provided for the white child;"

- "that equal opportunities in business and professional improvement be afforded all races;"
- "that restaurants, hotels, and theaters be open to all races..."
- "that all races be treated as men, and be accepted or rejected on the basis of efficiency and character rather than race or color."[17]

As the decade progressed, the Committee on Race Relations increasingly focused on efforts to end segregation and address its impact on society. The committee, chaired by Dwight S. Ritter, a purchasing agent for Nordyke and Marmon Company and member of Broadway Methodist Church, and co-chaired by Marshall A. Talley, pastor of Mt. Zion Baptist Church, included a broad representation from the community – Lionel Artis, manager of Lockefield Gardens; John Benson, superintendent of Methodist Hospital; Faburn E. DeFrantz, executive secretary of the Senate Avenue YMCA; Elmer G. Homrighausen, pastor of Carrollton Evangelical and Reformed Church; T. F. Reavis, Butler University professor; Robert E. Skelton, pastor of Barnes Methodist Church; Judson L. Stark, Marion County prosecuting attorney; Virgil Stinebaugh, superintendent of Indianapolis Public Schools; and Harry White, the executive secretary of the YMCA.

On 3 September 1935 Pastor Henry L. Herod of Second (now Light of the World) Christian Church died. He had served on the Federation's Executive Committee for six years, but had, since 1898, served Second Christian Church and had become an influential leader in the local black community. His loss was lamented. The Federation's Executive Committee presented a memorial to Herod on 5 September 1935, noting that "Brother Herod" was a respected member of the community and "one of the sanest leaders among the Negroes in our community."[18] In 1936 Lionel Artis, manager of Lockefield Gardens, joined the Federation's Executive Committee to "represent the colored constituency of the city."

Through the work of the Race Relations (sometimes known as the Inter-racial) Committee, the Federation remained in the forefront of addressing the changing landscape in Indianapolis. The committee

77

worked to strengthen Christian feelings and remove the causes of "social injustice." It adopted resolutions condemning discrimination against African Americans and supporting equal opportunity; called for the creation of "Young People's inter-racial committees" and special committees to "investigate community conditions (housing, relief, employment, health)"; and formed study groups on the "life of the Negro and his Contributions." Most notable, the committee took stances on issues of the day, including the famous Scottsboro Case (1931) in which nine young African American males were accused of rape in Alabama and sentenced to imprisonment or death. The Federation's Executive Committee adopted a resolution in December 1934, encouraging Dr. George E. Haynes, co-founder and former director of the National Urban League and secretary of the race relations department of the Federal Council of Churches, to do all in his power to "secure for these boys a fair and impartial trial" and "to put forth every effort possible to prevent the execution of the two boys already convicted."[19]

During the 1930s the Race Relations Committee took bold steps and made bold pronouncements. In June 1936 it adopted a series of principles that guided their work to "further the cause of interracial understanding, which is implicit in the Christian faith." The committee sought to "accept the contributions of other races" and "cultivate the spirit of intelligent understanding and friendship." It proposed for the Church Federation to be "a clearing house for all racial injustices and misunderstandings" and "present the church's convictions ... so as to leave the community in no doubt as to where the church stands on these issues." The statement concluded by noting that "interracial problems and tensions...are solved not by a clear-cut principle and policies, but by the power of personalities who know the fine art of understanding and sympathetic love." The committee said that to accomplish its goals, we must "suffer together and make gains as best we can."[20]

By the end of the decade, it was clear that the Church Federation had worked to promote an integrated society. In 1938 the organization established a race relations award to publicize its efforts in the field and acknowledge those individuals who had been leaders in the efforts to break down racial barriers. Leila Avery Rothenburger, wife of Rev. William Rothenburger of Third Christian Church, was the recipient of the first award. She was recognized for participating in the "Monster Meetings" of the YMCA, which showcased black leaders and national issues in Indianapolis. The committee commended her for "her courageous stand for right and justice,...her voice and pen in spreading the gospel of good will and brotherhood," and her convictions of "friendly appreciation for all races."[21] The next year, Miss Anna Stout, social service worker at Crispus Attucks High School and member of Bethel A.M.E. Church, received the recognition. Most notable, however, was the action of committee chair Ritter who wrote the superintendent of Indianapolis Public Schools in May 1938 to express concerns about potential unequal treatment of black teachers and the inferiority of equipment in black schools. Ritter concluded that when the right person could be found, "there might be a negro assistant superintendent" for Indianapolis schools.[22]

Committees Act to Shape the Local Community

During the 1930s the Federation used its many committees to reach into and shape the local community. Standing committees addressed the basic ongoing concerns in the city. Occasional special committees were appointed or standing committees realigned to focus on specific topics.

The Committee on Evangelism reported on a Layman's Retreat held 4 October 1930 at the country estate of Josiah K. Lilly, Jr. Inspired by its initial success, the retreat subcommittee organized regular retreats for the city's men and asked Executive Secretary Evans to encourage each church to send representatives to the annual gatherings. In October 1932 the committee emphasized the "need to increase [membership and church participation among] young and middle-aged men" and encouraged recruiting speakers that capture the "realities of life" to convince men of the necessity of religion in daily life. At a 16 November 1934 planning meeting, the committee suggested that next year's event should include topics applicable to modern life and a strong Biblical background for discussions.[23] Over the years, the committee discussed a Pulpit Exchange sponsored by the Ministers Association beginning the third Sunday in October, arrangements for Thanksgiving services throughout the city, and a Week of Prayer for Christian Unity. They also decided to have pre-Easter services for one week only and scheduled a ministers' retreat for September.

In 1930 the Good Friday Committee met at the Catholic Community Center at 1004 North Pennsylvania Street. The Committee decided to engage the English Opera House for three hours for its Good Friday Services at the cost of $50. They requested that city street cars and buses be stopped for one minute at 2:59 p.m. and called for grocery stores like Standard, Kroger, and A&P to close from 12 noon to 3 p.m. The committee also used the local Boy Scouts to distribute "We Close" signs to stores in order to promote the observance of Good Friday.

The Student Life Committee met on 11 September 1931 and agreed to an "intensive cultivation of student life" at Indiana Central College, Teachers College in Muncie, and Butler University. They determined to acquire "a list of fraternities and institutions the students belong to, with the idea in mind of acquiring churches to make contacts." Clearly, the committee felt it important for college students to attend religious services.[24]

On 23 January 1933 the Federation's Evangelism Committee met and supported a sub-committee's recommendation to allow ministers to preach on street corners. The motion was seconded and the meeting was adjourned, but committee minutes did not record an official vote to approve the initiative. This move indicated that the Federation believed that street preaching might actually improve the quality of life in Indianapolis.

Most significant, however, was the Federation's consideration to host a meeting of the Federal Council of Churches (FCC). After careful study, the Federation, on 7 May 1930, extended an invitation to the FCC to hold its sixth quadrennial meeting in December 1932 at the Severin Hotel in Indianapolis. Executive Secretary Evans noted that this provided an "unusual opportunity" for the city and the Federation to host "the nation's greatest religious leaders" and "give our city the opportunity for consideration of the federation idea as a step in the development of the Protestant churches." The committee recommended that the Federation recruit "a large number of men...to subscribe one dollar a year for three years" to cover the costs of the conference.[25]

At its gathering in December 1932, the FCC presented a revised version of the "Social Creed of 1908," originally adopted by the Methodist Episcopal Church to express outrage over the lives of workers in twentieth century America, which outlined the Council's effort to transform society into a Christian collective. The next month, Dr. Samuel Cavert, General Secretary of the FCC, noted that the Indianapolis meeting was the best in the Council's twenty-four years of existence. Clearly, the Hoosier capital had made its mark in hosting national events.

The Comity Committee, established shortly after the Church Federation's founding in 1912, changed its focus somewhat during the 1930s because of the Depression and the movement of the more affluent away from the city's center. The committee had been charged with regulating the location of new churches and ensuring that people citywide would be served by a Protestant congregation "so that no new churches would be established or old ones relocated without careful investigation." But, with the growth of the city, committee chair Rev. Rothenburger recommended that the Federation take steps to establish a clearinghouse for information regarding the foreign population of the city. Following contact with Greek and Romanian leaders in early 1930, Rothenburger asked the committee to study the foreign population with specific attention given to their religious life and influences.[26] Compliance with committee recommendations was voluntary, but the policy generally worked. In 1935 the committee tried to prevent groups from organizing new churches where too many churches already existed.

The Federation also became actively involved in politics. In March 1938 the Public Relations Committee, formed by combining Social Service and Public Morals committees in 1936, interviewed two men, one Republican and one Democrat, for Judges of the Juvenile Court. The executive committee encouraged discussion in preparation for the 1939 session of the legislature and urged citizens to write letters to the editors of local and community papers across the state to express their opinions on issues of the day. The Federation clearly felt that the voices of the Protestant faithful needed to be heard in the halls of government.

The Federation's Radio Committee also sought to capitalize on the growing popularity of the medium. It developed new broadcasts over station WKBF, which became known as the "Temple of the Air." Station WIRE asked the Federation to resume a devotional hour each morning. Ministers offered religious messages and the stations furnished religious music. The Federation also established a broadcast hour for the Federated Church Women over WFBM. By 1938 the Reverend Henry E. Chace, chair of the Radio Committee, reported that the Federation had approximately three and one-half hours of religious programming on the radio each day in five separate programs. Programming expanded further when Eugene C. Pulliam, president of Central Newspapers Inc., acquired WIRE radio. He suggested that the station could render a better service to the community by putting six of the ablest ministers on the air for two months each, picking them up by remote broadcasts from their churches for a thirty-minute service on Sunday mornings. By 1939 the committee sponsored eight programs on WFBM, WIBC, and WIRE.

Restoring Public Morality

In the early days of the Depression, the Federation's Public Morals Committee emphasized the importance of enforcing the Eighteenth Amendment to the Constitution. Ratified in 1919 and implemented in January 1920, the amendment prohibited the "manufacture, sale or transportation of intoxicating liquors." The committee believed enforcement was essential, particularly in clubs, social groups, and other settings where liquor might touch children and youth. Executive Secretary Evans urged church people to write to local newspapers to voice their beliefs.

In 1932 the Ministers Association and the Laymen's Committee encouraged discussion of the Prohibition issue as part of upcoming elections, citing that the church "has been lax in education regarding the liquor question." The Federation received support from the Anti-Saloon League, which advocated temperance among students in the public schools, and the Methodist Church, a key proponent of temperance. The Federation supported "dry" candidates in the election and called for the retention of the Eighteenth Amendment. However, Congress passed the Twenty-first Amendment on 20 February 1933, which repealed the Eighteenth Amendment. The Twenty-first Amendment was ratified on 5 December 1933 and became effective ten days later.

A variety of other issues captured the attention of the Federation and its Public Morals Committee during the decade. Pari-mutuel betting, dog racing, open grocery stores on Sunday, lynchings, pornography, massage parlors, and obedience to traffic regulations all garnered attention. A student pastor from the University of Pennsylvania attending a convention in Indianapolis reported that "The places of prostitution in Indianapolis – terrible!" The Reverend Dr. Jean S. Milner of Second Presbyterian Church promised to speak to Mayor John W. Kern Jr. about the immorality found in the city.

Still, Sunday observance remained a concern of the Church Federation. In April 1930 the Public Morals Committee, chaired by Rev. Rothenburger, successfully closed the Indianapolis Home Show on Sunday, an event begun in 1922 to promote home ownership. The committee sent a complaint to the city for allowing a "Mad Marathon," a dance competition, to extend into Sunday. Chairman Rothenburger reported later in the year that he had not received a response to his open letter to auto dealers about conducting business on Sundays. Complicating the matter was the local automobile show, which was open on Sunday; the committee attempted to close the show the following year. The Federation even protested against the Girl Scouts for selling tickets to Sunday horse shows.[27]

Theaters also earned the scorn of the Public Morals Committee. Members were concerned about indecency in local theaters and the "low tones" and "objectionable material" of theater programs and advertising. In January 1930 the committee recommended a study of theater standards with the intent of taking "aggressive action." As a result, it suggested the use of First Baptist Church instead of a downtown theater for its regular Holy Week services. It also agreed that no religious services would be held in the Butler Bowl, the university's football stadium. In April 1931 the Federation even asked the Washington High School Glee Club to cancel its musical performance at the Indiana Theatre in downtown Indianapolis. Ministers in the neighborhood surrounding the school urged parents to object to the concert. The Federation's anti-theater campaign successfully cancelled the concert.

Throughout the 1930s, Social Service Director Linn Tripp reported that he regularly attended sessions of the Indiana General Assembly. He was there when legislators considered bills to legalize gambling at race tracks and slot machines. Since it was the Federation's intent to defeat the pari-mutuel gambling bill, Tripp testified before the legislature, encouraging them to vote against the proposed legislation; his testimony was printed in full in the *Indianapolis Star*. At the Federation's annual meeting in 1936, Dr. Worth M. Tippy of the Federal Council of Churches commended Tripp's work in the social service area, noting that it was the most outstanding in the entire nation. In 1937 all of the gambling bills in the Indiana legislature were defeated. Even though Tripp spent much time following the actions of the Indiana General Assembly and advocating Federation causes, Indiana Attorney General Omer Stokes Jackson in 1938 determined that Tripp need not register as a lobbyist. Regardless, Tripp felt that he should register as a lobbyist and did so.

Continuing Evangelism and Ecumenism

The Church Federation remained committed to evangelism and explored various ways of reaching wider audiences throughout the decade. In January 1930 the *Federated Church News* reported that the Federation had received the names and addresses of 445 new families in the city from the Welcome Wagon. The company,

84

established in Tennessee in 1928, provided new residents in cities with gift baskets representing local businesses. The Welcome Wagon approached the Federation and offered to supply the names of "potential" church members at "approximately 30 cents per family."[28] While the Federation used this as an evangelism tool in reaching new residents of Indianapolis, it strongly encouraged local denominations and congregations to cover their proportionate share of the costs. A one-year report on the Welcome Wagon program indicated that 2,005 names had been forwarded to churches between October 1930 and September 1931; the executive committee subsequently voted to continue the program.[29] An analysis of Welcome Wagon's results revealed, however, that the service proved more successful in "residence communities" than among downtown areas.

While the Church Federation was a Protestant organization, it made efforts to be more ecumenical and inclusive. The executive committee congratulated the Jewish Federation for establishing the Jewish Welfare Fund to support local Jewish programs. The committee also invited Rabbi Morris Feuerlicht of Indianapolis Hebrew Congregation and Monsignor Francis H. Gavisk of the Catholic Diocese of Indianapolis to join in Religious Emphasis Week and International Friendship Week scheduled for 4-7 February 1930.

Much of the inspiration for local evangelism activity resulted from occasional visits of Dr. Jesse M. Bader, the associate executive secretary of the Department of Evangelism of the Federal Council of Churches, a position he held for 22 years. Bader, a minister in the Christian Church (Disciples of Christ), had a passion for the priority of evangelism in the church. He served as Superintendent of Evangelism for the United Christian Missionary Society, developed an interest in the Christian World Communion movement, and ultimately became president of the World Convention of Churches of Christ. In his meetings across the nation, including his visits with the Church Federation, Bader emphasized that the "church is essentially, intentionally, and constitutionally one."[30]

In 1935 the Evangelism Committee met prior to Holy Week at the English Theater — despite an earlier ban on meeting in theaters. The committee discussed plans for Holy Week services that included a mixed choir from all of the churches; the Christian Men Builders Class of Third Christian Church volunteered to usher. The central theme of the services was to be "The Old Gospel for a New Day" or "The Changeless Christ in a Changing World." More than 2,300 worshippers attended the Good Friday service at Keith's Theatre, while 4,780 attended the service at the English Theater. Later that year, a subcommittee on Evangelism for Unified Effort reported, "It is assumed that evangelism is the chief business of the church. Also, there is no disposition to impose a plan on the local church. Each congregation must meet its own needs and shape its program accordingly." Thus, the Federation issued a call for Christian evangelism, but did not require adherence to a specific model.

In the ensuing years, the Evangelism Committee clearly followed the recommendations of Dr. Bader's call for expanded evangelism. They established a Seminar Group in November 1935 where "in various districts of the city two groups of five men each will hold seminars" addressing subjects of attitudes, objectives, methods, and message. At its meeting of 25 January 1937, the Evangelism Committee addressed assorted topics to expand the reach of the church:

- Providing ministers for refugees of the Ohio River flood;
- Encouraging church women to gather clothing for flood victims;
- Increasing evangelistic efforts to commemorate the 100th birthday of American evangelist Dwight L. Moody;
- Encouraging local newspapers to print Fellowship of Prayer devotions each day;
- Promoting evangelistic programming on the radio.[31]

The Federation continued its efforts to promote Christian unity by sponsoring significant meetings in Indianapolis. In January 1936 the Federation hosted the international convention of the Student Volunteer Movement for Foreign Missions. The organization, founded in 1886, recruited U.S. college students for missionary service abroad. Speakers included William Temple, Archbishop of York, and Toyohiko Kagawa, a Japanese Christian pacifist, reformer, and labor activist. From 13-29 May 1937 the Federation hosted the 64th annual meeting of the National Conference of Social Work at the Murat Temple. Evening meetings were held at Cadle Tabernacle, a 10,000-seat revival and convention center at Ohio and New Jersey streets in downtown Indianapolis. Speakers included economist and social worker Edith Abbot of the University of Chicago; U.S. Senator Robert F. Wagner of New York who spoke on "Requirements for Permanent Security;" Charles P. Taft, former chairman of the Community Chest in Cincinnati; and Governor Frank Murphy of Michigan.[32]

By the end of the decade, the Evangelism Committee had increased the number of sub-committees to address its expanded outreach — Students' Sundays, Pentecostal Season, Thanksgiving Union Services, and the usual Good Friday Services, which, in 1939, included three different services over three hours, each including different preachers, musicians, and liturgies. Despite these examples of cooperation, there tended to be hesitation on the part of some churches to join together. Executive Secretary Evans wrote in his 1931-1932 annual report:

There is a general favor throughout the city toward the idea that the churches ought to be getting closer together. But the local church's situation is still a greater factor in preventing this coming together than the common good is in bringing them together. May we think on these things and remember that it is possible for churches and groups of the followers of Christ to come together on the same platform as did the early apostolic church when decisions were sent out, beginning "It seemeth good to the Holy Ghost and us." Human as we are, let us strive with all our imperfections to bring our churches closer and closer together, and to work towards – not great programs that startle in their achievement – but a rich fellowship that makes the city warm and hospitable as the tropical clime.[33]

The Federation Pursues Peace

While the Church Federation expressed concern about the state of religion in Indianapolis, it also voiced its concerns about world issues. In November 1930 local ministers agreed that the Federation should contact the Federal Council of Churches and urge them to encourage President Herbert Hoover to submit the World Court protocol to Congress for approval. They also called for a day of prayer for disarmament on Sunday 31 January 1932. Later in September 1933, the Federation's Good Will Committee presented a letter from the FCC, calling for a revival of public sentiment on disarmament.

By the mid-1930s, it was clear that the world was facing renewed military threats. Japan continued its incursions into Asia. Germany saw the rise of Adolf Hitler and National Socialism, while Italy experienced the rise of Benito Mussolini and Fascism. Meanwhile, the U.S. was determined to maintain its isolationist policies to which it had returned after World War I. Addressing the rising threat of militarism, the Committee on International Good Will sponsored annual Peace Declamation contests to inspire young people to consider alternatives to the militarism. Scholarships for the contests came from church-related colleges such as DePauw, Earlham, and Butler. In 1933 "one of [Social Service Director Linn] Tripp's boys," an Arsenal Technical High School student, won a $700 prize in the Kellogg-Briand Peace Pact essay contest. Earlier in the decade, the committee also started a "Civic Heroes Week," an effort to emphasize non-military heroes. It also encouraged each church to appoint a local Peace Committee. The Federation also received a request from the FCC to become involved in the Japan-China situation by calling for an arms embargo, withholding loans, withdrawing the U.S. ambassador from Japan, and condemning Japanese activities.

Amidst these global tensions, Louis L. Ludlow, a Democratic congressman from Indianapolis, introduced a constitutional amendment in 1935 that would require a national referendum before war could be declared. It stated:

Except in the event of an invasion of the United States or its territorial possessions and attack upon its citizens residing therein, the authority of Congress to declare war and to send military and naval forces to engage in war beyond the confines of the United States shall not become effective until confirmed by a majority of all votes cast thereon in a nation-wide referendum...Shall the United States declare war on _____ ?[34]

At the recommendation of the International Good Will Committee, the Church Federation's Executive Committee officially endorsed the proposed resolution on 4 June 1935.[35] Ludlow continued to introduce his resolution in Congress several times during the late 1930s, but it never passed.

During these years, Indianapolis also began to learn about the plight of Jews in Europe. Following Hitler's rise to power, Germany, in 1935, adopted the Nuremburg Laws, a series of anti-Semitic laws that deprived Jews of German citizenship, prohibited marriage between Jews and Germans, and placed other harsh restrictions on them. Jewish residents in Indianapolis asked the Federation to issue a statement about the alleged persecution of Jews in Germany. In response, the Federation and the National Conference of Christians and Jews sponsored a traveling team of a Jewish rabbi, Catholic priest, and Protestant minister to speak at the Columbia Club in November 1933 on the matter. The Federation also agreed in 1935 to participate in a Brotherhood Day project of the National Association of Christians and Jews.

While world events were brewing, the Church Federation also addressed the issue of a Jewish homeland. Following inquiries from the Indianapolis community, the Federation appointed a special committee to formulate a position on the conflict between Jews and Arabs in Palestine. The committee reported on 28 March 1939 that it was "keenly sensitive to the sufferings of the Jewish people," the overall state of affairs in Palestine, and the "Jews in Europe, [who were] objects of savage and unchristian persecution." The committee noted, however, that there were "deepseated issues" between Jews and Arabs that required a "detailed knowledge of the historical background." Members of the committee concluded that before "giving voice to any opinion worthy to represent the mature mind of the church leadership of the community, the whole problems should be made the subject of much more thorough study."[36] As Edwin Becker noted in his 1987 history of the Church Federation, this "thoughtfully worded" statement left the Federation "on the fence."[37]

As tensions around the world continued to grow, the Federation and its affiliates pursued the path of peace. Mrs. Ernest Piepenbrok, new president of the Federation of Church Women, announced that there would be a peace convention at the YWCA on 18 April 1936 and a peace mass meeting on 4 May. Social Service Director Tripp attended sessions of the Indiana General Assembly to support a bill that proposed an elective high school course focusing on peace. Someone proposed a "Friendship Project" that provided suitcases for refugee children in Spain and a Christmas offering for Spanish, German, and Chinese refugees. With the growing concern about preparations for war worldwide, the Federation's Executive Committee expressed its strong disapproval of war and distributed pamphlets entitled "Churches and the International Crisis" to the city's pastors.

The Federation's 25th Anniversary and Beyond

The Church Federation of Indianapolis celebrated its 25th anniversary on Wednesday 5 May 1937 at Broadway Methodist Church. A crowd of more than 400 heard a tribute to the Federation's six presidents and listened to Dr. Edgar DeWitt Jones, president of the Federal Council of Churches, present the anniversary address entitled, "American Christianity Confronts the Hour." During an open forum on Wednesday, Dr. Samuel McCrea Cavert, executive secretary of the FCC, led discussions on "Christian Unity and the Modern World" where he concluded that "the union of the churches will someday naturally come."[38] That evening, Dr. Jones spoke on the topic, "American Christianity Confronts the Hour." Members also elected Eugene C. Foster, director of the Indianapolis Foundation and deacon at First Baptist, to be Federation president. In assessing the significance of the anniversary celebration, the *Indianapolis Star* noted in an editorial:

..(l)ocal church federations are accepted as the natural agency for co-operative effort. The progress of practical religious leadership is attested by the observance today of the twenty-fifth anniversary of the Church Federation...The movement has succeeded in unifying the various religious groups and...in supplying the nucleus for joint action to further the religious and civic growth of the community...The silver anniversary provides an opportunity for acknowledgement of the service rendered by the federation founders, together with a realization of the greater tasks that await church leadership in the changing social and economic conditions of the time.[39]

In April 1939 the Reverend Dr. Ernest N. Evans, executive secretary of The Church Federation of Indianapolis, died suddenly. Some thought it was because of overwork. Since January 1925, Evans had been leading, preaching, teaching, organizing, and inspiring the committees and members of the Federation. One thing that Evans had accomplished during his tenure was to deal with the Federation's finances, which had always been a struggle. At the Federation's annual meeting held at Meridian Street Methodist Church in May 1939, the Finance Committee announced that revenue for the year was $11,576.64, indebtedness had been reduced, and staff salaries had been restored after having been cut years earlier. The committee also decided that Mrs. Evans would receive her husband's half salary of $187.50 per month until October.

The Federation called a special meeting in the fall of 1939 to select a successor to Dr. Evans. On 27 October 1939 the Federation called the Reverend Howard J. Baumgartel, a native of Pittsburgh and pastor of the First Presbyterian Church of Ebensburg, Pennsylvania, to be its fourth executive secretary. Forty-nine year old Baumgartel was a graduate of Muskingum College in Ohio, received a Master's in Religious Education from the University of Pittsburgh, and obtained his seminary training at the Western Theological Seminary in Pittsburgh. The *Indianapolis Star* called him "athletic and genial." In an early address to the Federation, Baumgartel outlined his key goals for the Federation:

- assist local congregations in evangelistic efforts;
- increase the public's knowledge of the Bible;
- develop Christian personality;
- promote the practice of moral values of social Christianity;
- understand and appreciate other religious faiths;
- cooperate with all "agencies of health" and those "raising the economic and cultural standards of the people."[40]

When Baumgartel arrived in 1939, the Federation had 52 member congregations. At his retirement in 1954, the Federation had 149 member congregations – a nearly 200 percent increase in growth.

Conclusion

The 1930s presented new challenges for the Church Federation and the city's religious leaders. Unemployment, poverty, and homelessness intensified as a result of the Great Depression. Issues of expansionism and militarism in Europe and Asia, the treatment of Jews and war refugees, and the threat to world peace also drew attention. Race relations, however, greatly concerned Federation leaders who actively addressed issues pertaining to social justice for all. Likewise, they expressed concern for cooperative ecumenical action in addressing evangelism, Sabbath observance, alcohol sales, school desegregation, politics, and public morals in general.

Executive Secretary Ernest Evans clearly stated the importance of the Federation in his annual report of 1937:

The Church Federation of Indianapolis is the federation of the Indianapolis Churches. It is not one among the other organizations engaged in Christian work in the city. It is and ought to be the Christian Church struggling with the problems, and enlarging and enriching the life of a great city...This institution is most vital. It is the symbol for the Church to travel on.[41]

A key challenge to the pursuit of Christian unity would come quickly for the Church Federation leaders and members on 7 December 1941 when Japan attacked U.S. military and naval bases at Pearl Harbor in Hawaii. Church leaders and the faithful then had to confront the question of how they would deal with a nation at war yet *again* and fulfill the Christian call for peace, unity, and co-existence with one's brothers and sisters for which they had strived throughout the 1930s.

Endnotes

1 Winthrop S. Hudson, *Religion in America* (New York: Charles Scribner's, 1973), 378.

2 Minutes of the Executive Committee, January 1930, Church Federation of Greater Indianapolis Records (hereafter CF), Indiana Historical Society, Indianapolis, Indiana.

3 Executive Secretary's Report 1931-1932, CF.

4 Deborah B. Markisohn, "Great Depression," *The Encyclopedia of Indianapolis*, eds. David J. Bodenhamer and Robert G. Barrows (Bloomington and Indianapolis: Indiana University Press, 1994), 636-639.

5 "Statistics Compiled from Unemployment Survey Blank," November 1931 and "The Church and Unemployment," November 1931, CF.

6 Executive Committee Minutes, January 1932, CF.

7 "Depressionvilles to Go," *Indianapolis Star*, 27 May 1935, 4.

8 Executive Committee Minutes, January, March, April, and October 1934, CF.

9 Federated Church Women's Yearbook 1933-1934, Church Women United Collection, Indiana Historical Society.

10 Edwin Becker, *From Sovereign to Servant: The Church Federation of Greater Indianapolis, 1912-1987* (Indianapolis: Church Federation of Greater Indianapolis, 1987), 20.

11 "Race Relations and the Housing Problem," Race Relations Committee, 4 December 1931, CF.

12 Executive Committee Minutes, January 1932, CF.

13 *Indianapolis Recorder*, 4 March 1933, 4, and March 11, 1931, 1.

14 Wilma Moore, "A Heart for Service: Inside the Roselyn Richardson Collection," *Traces* (Winter 2011): 26.

15 Executive Committee Minutes, 5 June 1934, CF.

16 Race Relations Committee report, 1937, CF.

17 "Statement and Resolutions Presented by Dr. Charles H. Winders, Chairman of the Race Relations Committee," n.d., CF.

18 Race Relations Committee, September 1935, CF.

19 Resolution presented by Dr. Charles H. Winders, Chairman of the Committee on Race Relations, adopted 4 December 1934, CF.

20 "Principles," Interracial Committee, June 1936, CF.

21 Race Relations Committee, 1938, CF.

22 Race Relations Committee, 13 June 1938, CF.

23 Layman's Retreat Committee, 1932 and 1934, CF.

24 Student Life Committee, September 1931, CF.

25 Executive Committee, May 1930, CF.

26 Executive Committee, January 1930, CF.

27 Public Morals Committee, misc. files, CF.

28 Executive Committee, 9 September 1930, CF.

29 Executive Committee, 14 September 1931, CF.

30 "Jesse Moren Bader," http://en.wikipedia.org/wiki/Jesse_Moren_Bader

31 Evangelism Committee, January 1935, CF.

32 National Conference on Social Welfare, *Official Proceedings of the Annual Meeting, 1937.* (New York: National Conference on Social Welfare, 1937). See: http://name.umdl.umich.edu/ACH8650.1937.001

33 Executive Secretary's Report, 1931-1932, CF.

34 Ludlow Amendment, http://en.wikipedia.org/wiki/Ludlow_Amendment

35 Executive Committee, 4 June 1935, CF.

36 Special Committee Report to Executive Committee, 28 March 1939, CF.

37 Becker, 32.

38 Becker, 36.

39 *Indianapolis Star*, 5 May 1937, 8.

40 Becker, 39.

41 Becker, 36.

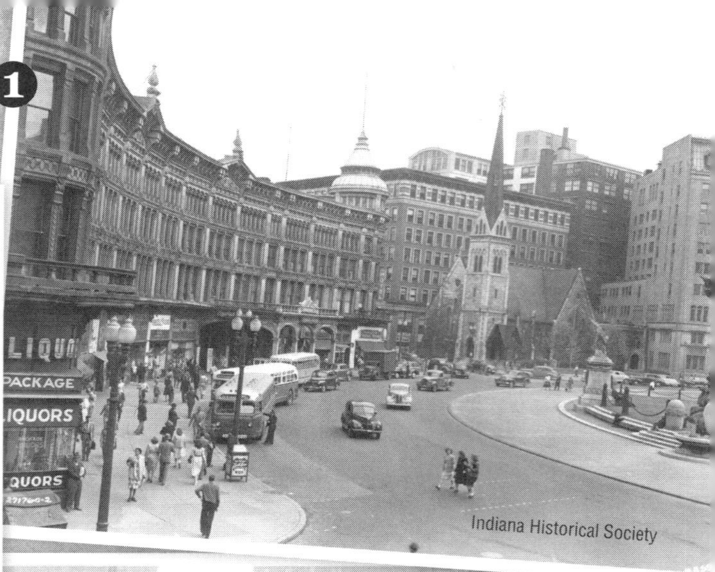

Indiana Historical Society

The Church Federation of
Greater Indianapolis Collection,
Indiana Historical Society

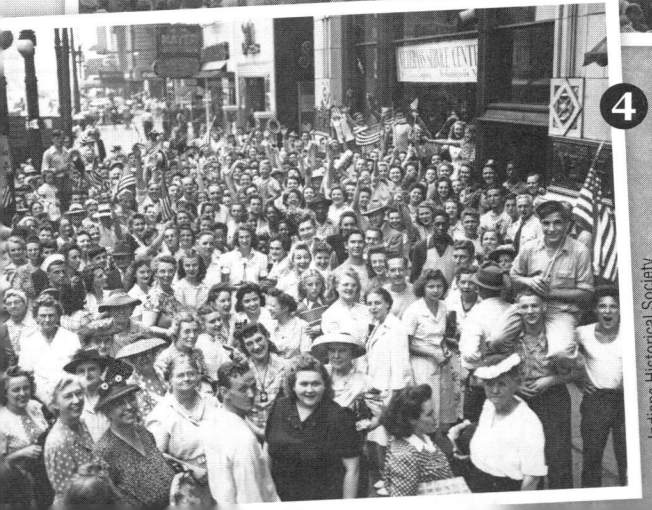

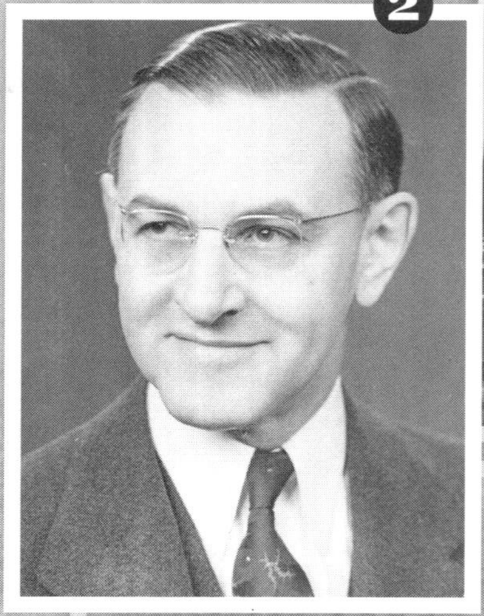

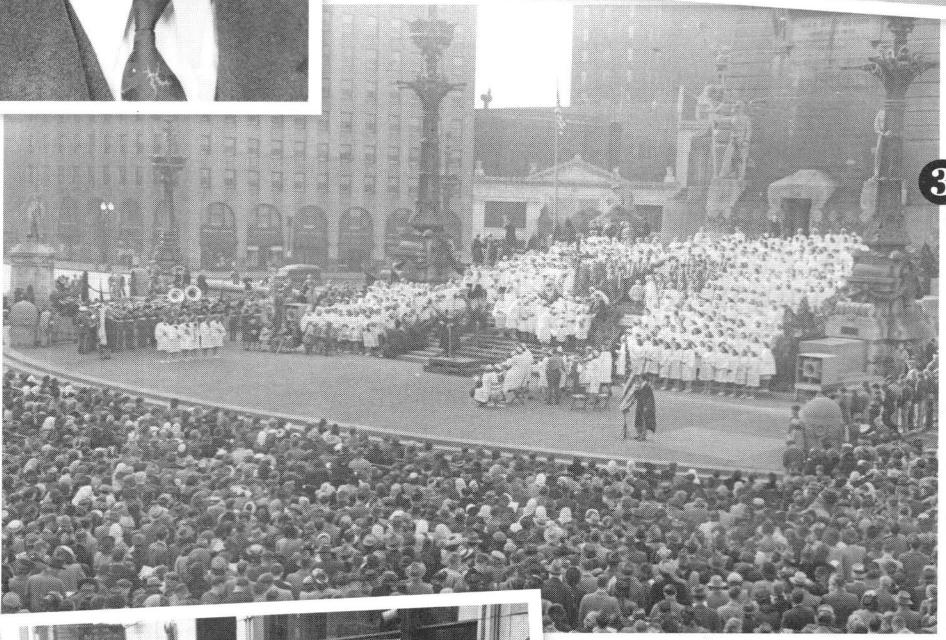

Bass Photo Co. Collection, Indiana Historical Society

Indiana Historical Society

1. Christ Church, on Monument Circle, offered a social hour to service men and women during the war.
2. Executive Director Howard J. Baumgartel
3. Easter sunrise service on Monument Circle
4. Hoosiers celebrating the end of the war, August 14, 1945

1940s

War and Work

Scott D. Seay

T HE 1940S WAS A WATERSHED DECADE FOR AMERICAN Christianity. The nation's entry into World War II lifted the United States out of the Great Depression and ushered in an unprecedented period of economic prosperity for many Americans. The ecumenical movement reached maturity in 1948 with the formation of the World Council of Churches, convincing many that a united church could be an indispensable resource in constructing a post-war "new world order." Catholics and Jews were taking their place in the mainstream, challenging the notion that Protestantism was *the* American religion. The Church lagged behind as efforts toward racial justice accelerated desegregation efforts by the federal government. Each of these trends impacted the city of Indianapolis, and shaped the mission of the Church Federation.

The Leadership of Howard J. Baumgartel

Leading the Church Federation during this watershed decade was the Reverend Dr. Howard J. Baumgartel. Born in Pittsburgh, he graduated from Muskingum College in 1911 and Western Theological Seminary in 1913. Three years later, he completed his M.A. in Christian Education at the University of Pittsburgh and was ordained by the Presbyterian Church in the United States of America. For more than two decades, he served churches in Pennsylvania and New Jersey. In 1939 he closed a successful pastorate at the Ebensburg (PA) Presbyterian Church and began serving as executive director of the Church Federation. Carrying heavy administrative responsibilities, he nonetheless completed a Doctor of Divinity degree at Western Theological Seminary in 1947. He and his wife, Naomi, married in 1915 and raised two children: Howard and Elizabeth. They retired from their work with the Church Federation in 1954 and moved to California; a year later, however, both were killed when a car struck them as they crossed the street in front of their Los Angeles home.[1]

Throughout his fifteen years as executive director of the Church Federation, Baumgartel consistently spoke of the importance of "United Protestantism" for the spiritual and moral health of Indianapolis, the nation, and the world. "Protestantism in its very essence of faith and practice," he wrote in his 1944 annual report, "is dedicated ever to seek to become a reconciling medium among groups through the very spirit of Christ's suffering love." Themes of the Social Gospel resounded through his description of the Federation's mission: furthering the cause of the Kingdom of God on earth, cultivating the "universal brotherhood" of all humanity, and safeguarding the health, security, and happiness of all persons through an application of the "universal truths" of the Gospel. Such a unified Protestant witness, he believed, was indispensable to the "new world order" that he saw emerging, especially after World War II.[2]

What did Baumgartel believe the Church Federation should *do* to reach these goals? In one of his earliest reports to the Executive Committee, he identified at least three major priorities: (1) aid local churches in evangelistic work and Christian education, especially "knowledge of the Bible;" (2) encourage among church people the practice of social Christianity and an appreciation for other religious faiths; and (3) cooperate with all agencies aimed at "raising the economic and cultural standards of all people."[3] These basic goals were later articulated in a more detailed way in the 1941 revision to the Church Federation's articles of incorporation. In many ways, his goals reflect a continuation of the Federation's commitment to robust, triumphalistic evangelicalism on the one hand, and liberal, social Christianity on the other. Virtually everything that the Federation did under Baumgartel's leadership was defined by these goals.

In addition to his administrative responsibilities at the Church Federation, Baumgartel wrote the weekly Saturday morning Bible studies published on the church page of the *Indianapolis Star,* represented the Federation at national and international ecumenical gatherings, and taught occasionally at the Butler University School of Religion.

Responding to War

The thought of their nation's involvement in World War II surely made most mainline Protestants in the U.S. uneasy. Their experience in the Great War (1914-1918) had dashed their "liberal" confidence in human nature and taught them how easily their faith could be recast into idolatrous patriotism. Throughout the 1920s and 1930s, mainline Protestant leaders, especially *Christian Century* editor Charles Clayton Morrison, had urged support for "outlawry of war" movement. Others had found compelling Reinhold Niebuhr's "Christian realism," with its pacifist commitments founded on the ethical teachings of Jesus. At the grassroots level mainline Protestants had participated with great enthusiasm in national and international peace movements. Thus, for more than a generation, pacifism had been a cardinal principle of mainline Protestant piety in the U.S.

Although technically the nation remained neutral in the early years of World War II, President Franklin D. Roosevelt signed into law the Selective Training and Service Act in September 1940, the first peacetime draft in U.S. history. In less than a year, the number of people serving in the nation's armed services swelled from 175,000 to more than 1.4 million, the vast majority of whom were drafted. Later that year, the president called upon the nation to become an "arsenal of democracy," mobilizing its industries to produce planes, tanks, ships, weapons, and ammunition necessary to aid the Allies, especially Great Britain. The president's sense of urgency was clear:

"We must apply ourselves to our task with the same resolution, the same sense of urgency, the same spirit of patriotism and sacrifice as we would show were we at war."[4] Initially very unpopular, these war preparations gained widespread acceptance following the Japanese attack on Pearl Harbor on 7 December 1941 and the mutual declarations of war.[5] The majority of mainline Protestants left their pacifism behind and joined the effort to defeat European fascism and Japanese imperialism.

Less than a month after the nation's entry into the war, Executive Secretary Baumgartel expressed the "conflicted mind" of mainline Protestantism in the nation.[6] He wrote in the Federation's newsletter: "Again our country is at war. In peace time the responsibilities of the church are relatively clear. When war comes the task becomes increasingly difficult." Recalling the problematic role that the church and its leadership had played in the nation's war ideology twenty-five years before, Baumgartel resolutely claimed that "during this emergency... the church must be the *church*. We cannot and dare not play a role that is out of our true character." By focusing on "spiritual service" only, the churches and the Federation could remain sensitive to the pacifist commitments of their members while also patriotically supporting the nation's war effort.[7] The fact is, the Church Federation already had begun rendering this spiritual service by coordinating relief efforts for European refugees, distributing pacifist literature in the churches, and petitioning Congress to help formulate "a just and constructive peace" at the earliest opportunity.[8]

In early 1942 Indianapolis church leaders organized a new committee, the War Emergency Committee for Religious Service, jointly representing the Church Federation of Indianapolis and the Indianapolis Ministerial Association. C. A. McPheeters, pastor of North Methodist Episcopal Church, served as the committee's first chairperson, followed by George T. King, pastor of First Baptist Church. Baumgartel explained that "the single motive of this committee is to render spiritual service" during the war emergency. More specifically, the committee was charged with finding ways to look after "the spiritual welfare of our fellow Americans, who by reason of the necessities of the war are facing a dislocation and interruption of their usual patterns of life." Moreover, the committee was to provide services to the soldiers, sailors, defense workers, and others who come to Indianapolis for war-related activities. "We stand ready to cooperate in any way consistent with that purpose," the executive secretary explained. "We stand ready to render our ministry either within our church buildings, or wherever our services may meet the needs of people."⁹

By the time the War Emergency Committee was established, military personnel were already moving through Indianapolis. The initial World War II draftees arrived at Fort Benjamin Harrison in late 1940, transforming it from a "sleepy facility" into a major military installation. In four years the Induction and Reception Center at the fort had processed hundreds of thousands of draftees and volunteers, making it the largest in nation. The fort also became the home of the U.S. Army Finance Center, a chaplains' school, a school for cooks and bakers, and Billings General Hospital, a 2,000-bed facility specializing in rehabilitation services.¹⁰ Opportunities abounded for the Church Federation to provide spiritual service to the men and women of the armed forces.

On behalf of the Federation, the War Emergency Committee enlisted the support of its member congregations to provide hospitality and wholesome entertainment for service personnel while they were stationed in Indianapolis. Christ Church Cathedral and Roberts Park Methodist Church — both large and strategically located congregations — responded by serving thousands of meals each week and by adding Saturday and Sunday evening worship services to accommodate the demanding schedules of service personnel.¹¹ Churches continued offering these services through the end of the war, although participation sharply dropped after 1944, when most of the induction, reception, and training operations were moved to Camp Atterbury in Edinburgh, thirty-five miles south of Indianapolis.

In 1943 a portion of Fort Benjamin Harrison was fenced off to create a POW compound, and, for the next two years, small numbers of Italian and German soldiers were interred there. They performed maintenance, clean-up duties, and made other improvements to the compound in order to free U.S. soldiers for active duty. Aside from one major riot in 1945, the POW camp was relatively calm. "One story tells of the Germans assigned to put a new roof on the canteen. They carefully divided two shades of shingles and placed them to form a large swastika on the roof. The staff did not discover their handiwork for several days, after which time the job had to be re-done."[12] The Church Federation's spiritual service to these POWs was quite modest; it collected German- and Italian-language books for them to read. This contribution aimed at helping maintain "the comfort and orderly conduct of prisoners of war in the custody of the United States," and conformed to the "Golden Rule."[13]

During World War II, Indianapolis firms were awarded more than $2 billion in defense contracts with the federal government. Allison Engine Company built more than 70,000 aircraft engines during the war, and the Indianapolis plant of the Curtiss-Wright Company became the largest maker of propellers in the nation. Many other city firms were awarded smaller contracts to provide other needed supplies.[14] To keep up with the demand of these contracts, factories operated on long hours, sometimes twenty-four hours a day, seven days a week. Moreover, women and African Americans began to take skilled factory positions formerly held by white men then serving in the military. Long hours and shifts in the composition of the workforce sometimes created tension, although in Indianapolis, such tension was relatively mild.

As early as 1942, the War Emergency Committee expressed concern about the impact these conditions might have on the spiritual and moral health of the city's workforce. Church Federation leaders encouraged its member churches to offer additional worship services at different times, and even to offer meetings in the industrial plants for workers.[15] Congregations were left to decide for themselves how best to offer these additional services.

By far, the Federation's most visible war-related work was its program of peace education. In early November 1942 the Federation co-sponsored the Central Indiana Institute for the Study of the Churches and a Just and Durable Peace.[16] Frances Streighthoff and Naomi Baumgartel served as co-chairpersons for the two-day event. Held at the First Congregational Church, the institute aimed at suggesting "courses of action in which Christian churches could unite to forward a righteous faith for a just and durable peace and to work toward a new world order in which the principles of brotherhood and goodwill might be established." The institute reminded the churches of their "supreme obligation" to influence political leaders and to work with them toward the "peaceful ordering of human life;" encouraged them to support an immediate end to U.S. isolationism and full participation in developing world organizations; urged them to embrace economic policies based on the principles of self-sacrifice, mutual aid, and Christian brotherhood;" and challenged them to dismantle prejudice, discrimination and intolerance against religious and racial/ethnic minorities.[17] The U.S. had been involved in the war less than a year, and the Church Federation was helping Indianapolis Christians consider their post-war responsibilities.

By early 1945 the armies of the western Allies were overtaking Nazi-occupied territories France and advancing into western Germany itself. The armies of the Soviet Union were marching across Poland from the east and liberating Vienna. Allied leaders met at Yalta to plan for the post-war reorganization of Europe. In the Pacific, a joint Filipino and U.S. force had liberated Manila, marking significant turning point in the war against Japan. To most it was clear that the war was ending, and making preparations for peace were even more urgent. Moreover, from 25 April to 26 June 1945, more than fifty Allied representatives met in San Francisco for the United Nations Conference on International Organization. By the end of the conference, a charter had been drafted and the U.N. had committed itself to cooperating in international law, fostering world peace, safeguarding human rights, and stimulating the social and economic development of nations.

Because of these developments, the Church Federation sponsored a number of events to raise awareness and express a "united

Protestant" approval of these developments. On 9-10 April 1945, the Federation convened a second and larger conference on a just and durable peace at First Baptist Church. Co-sponsored with the Butler University School of Religion and the United Christian Missionary Society (UCMS),[18] this conference urged the church in a similar direction as the conference three years before. Dr. Joseph Hunter and Dr. Harold Fey, both leading voices in the Christian Churches (Disciples of Christ), were keynote speakers at this conference. On 23 April Baumgartel and Rabbi Israel Chodos of Congregation Beth-el Zedek led an interfaith prayer service for world peace at the Indiana War Memorial. From 24-26 April the Federation sponsored a three-day prayer vigil at Second Presbyterian Church, inspired both by the untimely death of President Franklin Roosevelt on 12 April 1945 and by the opening of the United Nations Conference.[19] Hopes ran high that a "new world order" was finally emerging from the experience of war.

Baumgartel spoke for most mainline Protestants in Indianapolis when the war finally ended on 14 August 1945: "We are all grateful to Almighty God for the cessation of hostilities at this moment in history." But the Federation's executive secretary continued to emphasize the new responsibilities that people of faith had, namely, "charting the course that will finally bring about a just and lasting peace...This should be a time for prayer, for humility, and for our complete dedication to the principles which will never again permit a recurrence of war."[20] Despite its "patriotic" service during the war, the Church Federation maintained the historic mainline Protestant commitment to peace.

Race Relations and Civil Rights

The decade of the 1940s witnessed significant advances in the civil rights movement in the U.S., motivated partly by the nation's involvement in World War II. As early as 1941, black leaders, most notably A. Philip Randolph, protested the racial discrimination in defense industries and called for the desegregation of the armed forces. To avoid a march on Washington, that same year, President

Roosevelt issued Executive Order 8802, which prohibited such discrimination and established the Fair Employment Practices Commission to monitor compliance with the order. The NAACP continued its legal campaign against segregation, winning significant victories in the Supreme Court on voting rights, interstate transportation, and housing. Two significant race riots in 1943 – in Detroit and Harlem – demonstrated that racial animosities had the potential to become violent. In both cases, tensions over war-related issues sparked the riots. Jackie Robinson played his first game with the Brooklyn Dodgers in 1947 and became an important symbol of desegregation efforts. Under renewed pressure from civil rights activists in 1948, President Harry Truman issued Executive Order 9981 that began the long process of desegregating the U.S. military.[21]

In Indianapolis during the 1940s, race relations were generally cordial as the city's black leaders continued their "polite protest" for civil rights. Unwilling to jeopardize the gains that the well-established community had made, black leaders developed interracial coalitions, circulated petitions, and pursued remedies in the courts. Similarly, white city leaders found it more advantageous for themselves to preserve the status quo through subtly segregationist policies and legislation than to encourage extremist groups like the Ku Klux Klan to manage race relations in the city. Additionally, the slow growth of the black population in Indianapolis in the 1940s was less a cause for white alarm than it was in other northern cities.[22] Thus, for differing reasons, black and white Indianapolis leaders engaged in protracted negotiations where civil rights were concerned in order to avoid the racial upheaval that characterized some American cities in the 1940s.[23]

The Church Federation of Indianapolis emerged as one of the interracial coalitions in which these negotiations took place. Formed in 1927, the Federation's Interracial Committee re-defined its mission in 1936 to be more active in its work. The committee "aims to study and further the cause of interracial understanding, which is implicit in the Christian faith." While it considered Christian love the primary resource for fostering such understanding, the committee recognized the need to apply the "best intelligence" to solve concrete problems. The committee was to be a "clearinghouse" for adjudicating racial misunderstandings and injustices, and aimed at "suffer[ing] together and mak[ing] gains as best we can, solidly and over longer periods of time."[24] Throughout the 1940s, it was a large and active committee; it usually had co-chairpersons, included thirty-five members, and met monthly to handle its business. Those most active in leading the Interracial Committee in the 1940s were Faburn E. DeFrantz and Lionel Artis, leaders of the Senate Avenue YMCA; George Walker Buckner, denominational executive with the Christian Churches (Disciples of Christ); and Freeman B. Ransom, business manager and general counsel for Madame C. J. Walker Enterprises, Inc.

In response to President Roosevelt's 1941 executive order, the Interracial Committee appointed a fact-finding sub-committee chaired by Butler School of Religion ethics professor Dr. Ross Griffeth. Concluding its work in early 1942, the sub-committee found that Indianapolis lagged far behind other northern cities in the employment of blacks in the defense industries. Of approximately 49,000 defense industry employees, fewer than 2,000 were black. The largest firm, Allison Engine Company, employed only 500 blacks, none in "skilled positions." Curtiss-Wright, another firm greatly benefitting from defense contracts, employed only 85 blacks out of more than 2,000 employees.[25] Alarmed by these statistics, the Interracial Committee convened a meeting of representatives from "Negro groups who are interested in this problem" to share ideas with Federation leaders. It quickly became clear that there were no easy solutions to this problem: Indianapolis lacked adequate training programs to equip blacks for skilled industrial positions; those who are qualified for skilled positions often do not interview well; and, most significantly, employers remained obstinate in their refusal to hire black workers. The Church Federation continued to monitor these problems for the next several years until 1945 when the Indianapolis Fair Employment Practices Commission was formed.[26]

At times, the work of the Race Relations Committee became tense.

In a meeting in early 1942, Freeman Ransom raised a concern that Indianapolis newspapers did not publish photos of black soldiers when they ran stories about the war, and moved that letters be written to the editors to address the issue. A lengthy discussion followed, sharply divided along lines of race. When white members of the committee offered possible reasons for the editors' decision, black members pushed even harder by demanding that phone calls to the editors be made instead. Ransom's motion eventually failed.[27] A month later, C. A. McPheeters, chair of the War Emergency Committee, sent letters to the three editors of the Indianapolis papers; of course, they all denied discriminatory practices, and one editor even asked for the name and address of the person making the complaint.[28] Afterward, it appears that the matter was dropped.

In response to a 1944 request from the Federal Council of Churches, the Church Federation appointed a special study commission on local church attitudes and practice regarding "minority peoples," especially blacks. The resulting report, written by Crispus Attucks faculty member Dr. Joseph Carroll, was a forthright statement of the current state of race relations in Indianapolis. "Segregated schools, segregated churches, jimcrowism in public parks, antipathies manifested among peoples of different racial groups in street cars and other public places," he decried, "are all crying shames against Christian civilization about which the church should take the lead in doing something." Unless Christians in Indianapolis are willing to find ways to solve race problems in the city, then "let us stack up our Bibles, close up our churches, and join the Atheistic Society of America." While Carroll applauded the modest efforts that he found some congregations making toward improved race relations, he clearly believed that there was much work to be done. But resistance on all side of the race question appeared nearly insurmountable.[29]

Certainly the high point of its work in the 1940s came when the committee worked with the Federal Council of Churches to hold a two-day Race Relations Clinic on 5-6 June 1945. Headed by the new pastor of Second Christian Church (Disciples), Robert Hayes Peoples, the clinic drew 280 participants equally represented by black and white churches, employers, and civic groups. The purpose of the clinic was to analyze the problems of race relations in Indianapolis, bring together those who are effectively addressing these problems for collaboration, and express a common commitment to racial justice. DeHart Hubbard, Race Relations Advisor for the Federal Housing Authority, led a clinic in an especially important consideration of race and housing in Indianapolis. As a result, participants in the clinic expressed their approval – in principle – of the new Indiana Redevelopment Act of 1945, an urban renewal program; denounced the continued use of restrictive covenants that made it impossible for blacks and other minority groups to purchase or rent homes in certain neighborhoods; and called for state and federal assistance to provide adequate housing for those who could not afford it.[30] As at least two other 1940s housing studies had concluded, the clinic affirmed that racism was the primary contributing factor to the problem of housing for blacks in Indianapolis.[31]

Perhaps just as intractable was the problem of racial segregation in Indianapolis schools. Since 1877, Indiana state law permitted local school boards to assign black and white students to separate schools, as long as facilities and instruction were equal. The Indianapolis school board did not exercise this discretionary power until the 1920s when the Ku Klux Klan influenced school officials to do so. Even after the Klan's influence in Indiana politics waned in the 1930s, Indianapolis maintained segregated schools through carefully orchestrated elections to the school board. By that time it appeared that black leaders in Indianapolis, rather than challenging school segregation, appeared to prefer developing black schools – especially Crispus Attucks High School – into premier educational institutions. After World War II, some civic leaders in Indianapolis began calling for the abolition of segregated schools. After several years of effort, in 1949 the Indiana legislature finally passed a law against segregated schools.[32]

The Church Federation's Race Relations Committee played an important role in the post-war efforts leading to the 1949 desegregation law. As early as 1943, the committee began collecting data about the segregation of Indianapolis schools and providing a forum in which to discuss strategies for political action. Leaders of the Church Federation helped two Republican state representatives from Marion County –William Fortune (white) and Wilbur Grant (black) – write a desegregation bill in 1947 and lobbied to support it.[33] The bill was defeated, largely because of the influence of Virgil Steinbaugh, superintendent of Indianapolis Public Schools. Steinbaugh argued that, "if segregation is widely practiced throughout the city, why...should schools be forced to desegregate?" He also attacked the Church Federation whose member churches appeared hypocritical for supporting the Fortune-Grant bill while remaining segregated themselves.[34]

Indianapolis leaders made a second attempt to pass a bill to desegregate the city's schools in 1949, and the Federation made an important contribution. Willard Ransom, the son of Freeman Ransom and recent graduate of Harvard University Law School, worked through the Race Relations Committee to build a much broader base of support for his bill, which included the NAACP, the newly elected Democratic Governor Henry Schricker, Indianapolis newspaper editors, and many civic and religious organizations.[35] Under dramatically changed political circumstances, Ransom's bill passed the Indiana legislature and became law. *De facto* school segregation continued and the battle to integrate the public schools lasted well into the 1970s.

Revival and Unprecedented Growth

After a long period of decline during the Great Depression, American churches, especially mainline Protestant congregations, experienced a twenty-year revival beginning in the early 1940s. Adult church membership surged from 49 percent of the population in 1940 to just over 55 percent by 1950; this trend accelerated over the next decade until 69 percent of the U.S. population claimed to belong to the nation's churches in 1960. The return of the nation's economic prosperity led churches to begin construction projects that had been delayed during the Depression. Churches remodeled, expanded, and in some cases relocated to meet the demands of an expanding membership. Partly because of their experience during World War II, leaders of American Christianity began forging a clear religious and civic identity based upon the grand themes of the Bible and a romantic vision of the nation's past. Commitment to a church quickly became a civic responsibility, understood to be the antithesis first to idolatrous fascism and then to "godless" communism. This identity resonated with millions of patriotic working class families who aspired to join the middle-class; in fact, belonging to a thriving church became something of a status symbol. Numerical growth, institutional expansion, and renewed identity each contributed to this revival of American Christianity.[36]

The churches of Indianapolis were no exception to these national trends, and thus the Church Federation also experienced unprecedented growth. In 1940 the Federation claimed 52 member churches, six committees carrying out its work, and an annual budget of $11,000. By 1950 the Federation had experienced threefold growth: member churches numbered 153, twenty standing committees carried out the Federation's work, and the annual budget had grown to more than $32,000.[37] Compared to the modest growth of the Indianapolis population during the decade – from roughly 387,000 to 427,000, or 15 percent – the exponential growth of the Federation appears all the more remarkable. Moreover, the Federation anticipated that, with the close of World War II, Indianapolis churches would begin renovation, expansion, and relocation efforts that would cost between $2.5 and $3.0 million. In fact, expenditures on post-war building programs far exceeded expectations.[38]

The Church Federation responded to the needs of the city's growing churches mainly through the work of the Comity Committee. In 1946 the committee commissioned Dr. Frederick A. Shippey, a nationally known church consultant, to assist the Federation in planning for the future. For more than a year, he compiled data, conducted interviews, and analyzed the dynamics of church growth in Indianapolis. His report, released in 1947, provided a "factual background for dealing with church problem of relocation, merger, extension, and program adjustment in Indianapolis." Although he recognized that 93 percent of Marion County residents lived in the Indianapolis metropolitan district, he noted that the churches needed to develop a plan to address the population growth on the periphery of the city. These areas, he concluded, offered the most promising opportunities for new church work.[39]

Shippey urged the Federation and its member churches to cooperate within the framework of comity and utilize a clearly defined Protestant plan. "Intensive competition among the denominations for suburban residential areas usually results in misunderstandings, feuding, and inferior church work."[40] Such a clearly defined Protestant plan apparently never materialized. The minutes of the Comity Committee through the late 1940s include regular complaints that even member churches purchased real estate, developed building plans, and discussed mergers without ever consulting with or informing the Church Federation.

Transitions in the Work of the Church Federation

In addition to its activities inspired by the war, changing race relations, and the revival of mainline Protestantism, the Church Federation continued through the 1940s much of the work that had characterized it from the beginning. This work, however, underwent significant transition.

Since 1926, Linn A Tripp had chaired the Social Service Committee and functioned as a liaison between the criminal courts and the churches. Particularly important was his work in assigning at-risk youth and their families to Indianapolis churches to provide social services. His work was at times controversial, and some, especially the leaders of the Community Fund that underwrote his work, became increasingly dissatisfied. In November 1941 the Community Fund informed the Federation that its funding would be withheld until the work of the Social Service Department was clearly separated into "social" and "religious," so that the Federation services did not overlap with those provided by other agencies. Moreover, Community Fund leaders demanded clarification about

111

the director's specific responsibilities and a greater sense of his accountability to them. By the end of the year, a new agreement between the Federation and the Community Fund apparently had solved these problems. By 1945 similar difficulties arose, and Tripp eventually resigned his position.[41]

Methodist lay minister Grover Hartman assumed his responsibilities as the Federation's director of social service program in 1946 and served until 1954. During his eight years of service, he established a "network of relationships with the social services community" and rehabilitated the reputation of the program in the eyes of the Indianapolis community. Moving easily in a variety of circles, he also was an effective fund-raiser for the Federation's social service program, and gained a national reputation for his innovative programs that brought social service, religious, and civic resources together.[42]

Baumgartel continued throughout the 1940s to speak of "United Protestantism" by which he usually meant *mainline* Protestantism. To the extent that other Christian groups and Jews participated in the work of the Federation, they relied on the good will and acceptance of its mainline Protestant leaders. After World War II, however, the Federation's base of support became increasingly diverse. By the late 1940s, Holiness-Pentecostal congregations, including Nazarene and Assemblies of God congregations, began supporting the Federation's work. Even the Church of Jesus Christ of Latter Day Saints became supporters.[43] This base of support continued to diversify in the following decades, transforming both the identity and mission of the Federation.

Conclusion

Under Baumgartel's able leadership and with the support of countless dedicated volunteers, The Church Federation of Indianapolis continued its faithful witness through the watershed decade of the 1940s. While continuing the effective programs that had characterized its work from the beginning, the Federation also responded effectively to the unique challenges of the time: the

112

nation's participation in World War II, the increasing momentum of the civil rights movement, and the early stages of the revival of mainline Protestantism. The Church Federation also worked to guarantee the continued strength of Christianity in the modern city by pursuing the use of the new medium of television, examining the needs of an emerging suburban population, and addressing the challenges of an increasingly diverse society.

Endnotes

1   C. A. McPheeters, "Introducing Our New Executive," *Federated Church News* (January, 1940), 1, Church Federation of Greater Indianapolis Records (hereafter CF), M0755, Box 139, Folder 2, William Henry Smith Memorial Library, Indiana Historical Society, Indianapolis, Indiana; "Pastor Dies of Injuries in Car Accident," *Los Angeles Times*, 27 September 1955.

2   These generalizations are drawn from Baumgartel's reports to the annual meetings of the Church Federation in the 1940s. See the programs of these annual meetings in CF, Box 184, Folders 6-12.

3   Howard Baumgartel, Report of the Executive Secretary, 4 March 1940, CF, Box 8, Folder 1.

4   Franklin Delano Roosevelt, "The Great Arsenal of Democracy," available at http:www.americanrhetoric.com/speeches/fdrarsenalofdemocracy.html, accessed 20 March 2012.

5   "Induction Statistics," Selective Service System, available at http://www.sss.gov/ Default.htm, accessed 17 March 2012.

6   Edwin L. Becker, *From Sovereign to Servant: The Church Federation of Greater Indianapolis, 1912-1987* (Indianapolis: The Church Federation of Greater Indianapolis, 1987), 39.

7   *Federated Church News* (January 1942), 1, CF, Box 139, Folder 2.

8   Becker, 40; Minutes of the Executive Committee, 3 June 1940, and Minutes of the Executive Committee, 3 February 1941, CF, Box 2 Folder 3.

9   Minutes of the War Emergency Committee for Religious Service, 19 January 1942, CF, Box 24, Folder 4.

10 Timothy Crumrin, "World War II," *The Encyclopedia of Indianapolis*, eds. David J. Bodenhamer and Robert G. Barrows (Bloomington and Indianapolis: Indiana University Press, 1994), 1463.

11 Becker, 40-41; Crumrin, "World War II," 1463-1464; and William Dalton, "Christ Church Cathedral," *Encyclopedia of Indianapolis*, 414.

12 "Italian and German Prisoners of War at Ft. Harrison," Fort Benjamin Harrison, available at http://www.indianamilitary.org/FtHarrison/SoThinkMenu/FtHarrisonSTART.htm, accessed 17 March 2012.

13 "News of the Church Federation of Indianapolis," 12 June 1944, CF, Box 139, Folder

14 Crumrin, "World War II," *Encyclopedia of Indianapolis*, 1464.

15 Becker, 40; "Minutes of the War Emergency Service Committee, 9 January 1942, CF, Box 24, Folder 4.

16 Several months before, the Federal Council of Churches convened a similar conference at Ohio Wesleyan University, featuring Protestant lay leaders John Foster Dulles, Charles Clayton Morrison, Harvey Firestone, and John Mott.

17 "Findings of the Central Indiana Institute for the Study on the Churches and a Just and Durable Peace," CF, Box 27, Folder 7.

18 The UCMS was the comprehensive missionary society of the Christian Churches (Disciples of Christ), headquartered in Indianapolis. The society coordinated the denomination's domestic and international evangelistic work and social justice efforts.

19 Becker, 41, 43.

20 *Indianapolis Times*, 15 August 1945, quoted in Becker, 41.

21 Cornelius Bynum, *A. Philip Randolph and the Struggle for Civil Rights* (Champaign: University of Illinois Press, 2010), 157-184; Michael Klarman, *From Jim Crow to Civil Rights: The Supreme Court and the Struggle for Racial Equality* (New York: Oxford, 2006), chs. 4 and 5; Thomas Sugrue, *The Origins of the Urban Crisis: Race and Inequality in Postwar Detriot* (Princeton: Princeton University Press, 2005), 15-88.

22 Federal census data reveals that the black population in Indianapolis grew from just over 51,000 in 1940 (13.2%) to just under 64,000 (14.9%) in 1950.

23 Richard Pierce, *Polite Protest: The Political Economy of Race in Indianapolis, 1920-1970* (Bloomington: Indiana University Press, 2005), 4-8.

24 "Interracial Committee: Principles," CF, Box 89, Folder 1. .

25 Becker, 59; Minutes of the Interracial Committee, 28 May 1942, CF, Box 89, Folder 2.

26 Minutes of the Special Committee, 9 June 1942, CF, Box 89, Folder 2; Pierce, 94-99.

27 "Minutes of the Race Relations Committee, February 12, 1942," CF, Box 24, Folder 4.

28 James Stuart, Managing Editor of *The Indianapolis Star*, letter to Dr. C. A. McPheeters, Pastor of North Methodist Episcopal Church, 26 March 1942, CF, Box 24, Folder 4.

29 Joseph C. Carroll, "Report of the Study Commission of the Local Church and Minority

Peoples," CF, Box 89, Folder 3.

30 "Statistical Report of Race Relations Clinic," CF, Box 89, Folder 4.

31 Pierce, 62-63.

32 Pierce, 26-55; Emma Lou Thornbrough, *Indiana Blacks in the Twentieth Century* (Bloomington: Indiana University Press, 2000), 145-147.

33 Minutes of the Race Relations Committee, 24 January 1947 and 24 October 1948, CF, Box 89.

34 Pierce, 37.

35 Minutes of the Sub-Committee on Education, Race Relations Committee, 24 January 1947, CF, Box 89, Folder 6.

36 Robert Wuthnow, *The Restructuring of American Religion: Society and Faith Since World War II* (Princeton: Princeton University Press, 1988), 14-34.

37 "Church Federation of Indianapolis: Uniting Church and Community," CF, Box 141, Folder 9.

38 Minutes of the Comity Committee, 19 February 1945, CF, Box 25, Folder 4.

39 Frederick Shippey, "Protestantism in Indianapolis" (Indianapolis: Church Federation of Indianapolis, 1946), v.

40 Shippey, 31.

41 Becker, 52-53; Report of the Study Committee on the Role of the Church in Court and Probation Work, CF, Box 2, Folder 6.

42 Becker, 54-55.

43 "Honor Role of Churches," *The Thirty-Fifth Annual Meeting of the Church Federation of Indianapolis, Inc.* (Indianapolis: Church Federation, 1948), 12-13, CF, Box 184, Folder 12.

Christian Theological Seminary

The Church Federation of Greater Indianapolis Collection, Indiana Historical Society

The Church Federation of Greater Indianapolis Collection, Indiana Historical Society

Bass Photo Co. Collection, Indiana Historical Society

1. Dr. Alfred Edyvean conducting television workshop.

2. Timothy Church Mouse

3. Executive Director Laurence T. Hosie

4. Indianapolis 1950s cityscape.

1950s

Evangelism:
Telling the Story

Jeffery A. Duvall

OR THE CHURCH FEDERATION OF GREATER
Indianapolis, the 1950s was a decade of unprecedented
growth and success, marked by occasional controversy.
Between 1950 and 1960, the Federation's membership rose
to 189 churches; programming expanded to include multiple weekly
broadcasts on local television stations; chaplaincy services were
established in the police and sheriff's departments; and the organization
significantly expanded its involvement with the city's troubled youth.
The Church Federation continued to provide year-round training and
workshops on topics ranging from marriage to race relations. The
decade ended on a triumphant note, denoted both by the Federation's
involvement in bringing Billy Graham, then at the height of his fame as
the nation's foremost evangelist, to Indianapolis and with preparations
being made to move from its offices in the downtown YMCA into new
and significantly larger space on North Meridian Street.

At times, however, the Federation found itself embroiled in
controversy over matters as varied as the enforcement of Sunday
observance by local stores and Cold War politics. Moreover, in
its efforts to promote the notion of a "united Protestant witness,"

perhaps most visibly manifest in the decade-long effort to establish "Reformation Day" as a permanent fixture in the calendar of the city's social and religious life, the Federation periodically found itself at odds with members of Indianapolis's other faith traditions.[1] This proved especially true of the Federation's relationship with the city's Catholic population, which was all too frequently characterized by a subtle (and at times not so subtle) prejudice against Catholicism.

Indeed, even within the city's Protestant community, the Church Federation discovered that agreement was neither always possible, nor perhaps altogether desirable. Federation-sponsored surveys indicated that the group's laudable efforts in support of integration were far from universally accepted, even within the congregations that comprised its own membership. By the end of the 1950s, it was also clear that for all of its efforts Reformation Day was a failure, and as successful as the Billy Graham Crusade proved to be, not all members of the Federation supported the effort and, in turn, were anxious to express publically that they were not associated with it. Even so, the Church Federation concluded the decade stronger than it ever been before and ready, if not entirely prepared, to face the controversies and upheavals of the 1960s.

Proven Leadership

In 1950 the Church Federation observed the tenth anniversary of the appointment of Dr. Howard J. Baumgartel as Executive Secretary. Local newspapers celebrated the occasion by noting the Federation's remarkable growth during Baumgartel's tenure. Membership had risen from 52 to 133 congregations over the preceding decade; the annual budget had grown from $11,000 to a barely adequate $40,000; the staff had more than doubled in size; and the Federation's headquarters had expanded from a single room to an entire suite of offices in the downtown YMCA. Much was made of the Federation's successful efforts as a "clearing house for religious activities for both government and the churches" during World War II, and its leadership role in both the city's Sunday School Program and the Weekday Religious Education Program.[2]

The Federation also made significant progress in advancing ecumenism and establishing the role of the Church in addressing urban issues. It cooperated with Butler University's School of Religion in offering a three-day seminar on urban church strategy led by Dr. Albert T. Rasmussen of Colgate-Rochester Theological Seminary. In Cleveland, Ohio, the Federation helped to establish the National Council of Churches of Christ in the USA, a consortium of several ecumenical bodies including the Federal Council of Churches. The Federation also drew positive attention from local newspapers for its continued efforts in support of improved race relations, work with displaced persons, focus on family life, and its liaison work between "the churches and the social welfare agencies of the county."[3]

Besides the work of the Church in the city, the Federation found itself addressing key political issues of the day. The Federation's Executive Committee sought to liberalize the 1948 Displaced Persons Act, adopted by Congress to admit certain European persons displaced by the war and Nazi persecution. The committee recommended an amendment that would provide "adequate quotas of Protestants."

The Federation also fell victim to the rabid anti-Communism of the day. In May 1950 it planned a celebration of United Nations Day at the Columbia Club in downtown Indianapolis. The Club refused to allow the Federation use of its facilities following the discovery that a scheduled speaker, Louis Dolivet, a French left wing activist and editor of *United Nations World* magazine, had been accused by a Congressional committee of being a Communist. The Federation was not only forced to cancel the event, but also to make amends through a very public display of appeasement toward the increasingly strident anti-Communist sentiment engulfing the nation. First, the Federation issued a news release "affirming the Federation's thirty-nine year service" to the city's churches. It then released a second statement, asserting that the Federation was both "autonomous from outside organizations" and "unalterably opposed to communism, its materialism, its atheism, its denial of Christian ethics, its totalitarianism, and its

119

fallacious economics." Indeed as a result of the embarrassment caused by this incident, the Federation's Executive Committee adopted a policy that from henceforth "any member could suggest that [a] matter being considered [was] a controversial issue," which would trigger a vote by the committee to determine whether or not a majority of the members agreed. If the vote determined that the matter under consideration fell into that category, then it was agreed that no position "shall be taken unless approved by a two-third vote of the members..."[4]

The New Media

Early in the decade, the Church Federation spearheaded the local religious community's efforts to embrace the emerging new medium of television as a means of "carrying their message where the voice from the pulpit [had] never reached" before. Having added "TV" to the Radio Committee's name in 1951, the Federation entered the television age by sponsoring two programs in cooperation with WBFM-TV – a monthly half-hour commentary program hosted by local ministers called *This is Your Community*, airing Tuesday evenings; and an hour-long program called *Hymn Time*, airing daily at 11:45 a.m. Several months later, the Federation, in cooperation with the Indiana Council of Churches, began a third television program, the *Hoosier Pulpit*, broadcast each Sunday on WIBC-TV. This was followed shortly thereafter by an agreement to sponsor the broadcast of a series of half-hour programs hosted by Dr. Norman Vincent Peale and his wife Ruth Stafford Peale titled *What's Your Trouble* on WBFM-TV on Monday evenings. The Federation explained that the program was designed to "dramatize the idea that ministers in Indianapolis, and everywhere, stand ready to hear about the troubles of human beings and to offer what help they can." Even so, local church leaders voiced their concern over what they viewed as the local religious community's tardiness in venturing into the new media as a means of reaching the city's large un-churched population.[5]

Race Relations

As part of its on-going effort to promote better relations and understanding between the city's races, the Federation launched in 1951 an in-depth, city-wide survey on the "racial practices of individual churches" in Indianapolis and Marion County. Sponsored by the Race Relations Committee, the survey was conducted by the Reverend Thomas Allen, Ph.D., director of the Department of Interracial and Intercultural Relations of the National Council of Churches, with the stated purpose of gathering "factual material on which to build a program that will serve as a guide to the Church Federation in its efforts to serve Protestant Churches in the area of racial and cultural relations."[6] Covering a total of 118 congregations (98 white and 20 African American), participants in the survey represented 31 percent of the city's churches and 22 percent of the county's. Altogether, 53 percent of those churches who submitted information were members of the Federation and represented 27 of the 39 denominations listed in the city directory.[7]

Considered a major success in the organization's long-standing efforts to promote improved race relations that same year the Federation's Inter-Racial Merit Award was presented to the Indiana High School Athletic Association in recognition of its decision to award the annual Trester Medal for Sportsmanship to Robert Jewell, center for the Crispus Attucks High School basketball team. This occurred just a few years after the Federation's censure of the IHSAA for their failure to admit African American high schools to their membership. By the mid-1950s at least fifteen local African American congregations were contributing members of the Church Federation and the Inter-Racial Merit Award would be bestowed on a range of local firms, including L.S. Ayres Company, Morris Plan, Vonnegut Hardware Company, and the *Indianapolis News*, thereby citing each business for their "fairness in employing capable persons regardless of their race or creed."[8]

Spirit of Ecumenism?

While the Federation's relationship with the city's African American congregations appeared to be improving by the early 1950s, its relationship with the city's Catholic community proved to be somewhat more problematic. First, the Executive Committee lent its endorsement to a short-lived, anti-Catholic national Protestant newspaper, *The Protestant World*, published with Butler, Indiana and New York City on its masthead. Then, the Federation chose to weigh in on President Harry Truman's controversial appointment of General Mark W. Clark as U.S. Ambassador to the Vatican. Taking the lead in speaking for the city's Protestant community, and endorsing the views expressed earlier by the National Council of Churches of Christ, USA, the Executive Committee unanimously adopted a resolution condemning the appointment. Stating that the appointment of an ambassador to the Vatican would be "provocative of religious tensions and destructive of those activities and relationship which have helped to foster the religious and spiritual life of our community," the resolution began with an affirmation of the Federation's continued support of those "principles" guiding the work of the ecumenical National Conference of Christians and Jews, which included Roman Catholics as well as Protestants, and which had assisted church membership in the United States to grow "to the largest percentage of the population in our history."[9]

Following this nod to the spirit of ecumenism, however, the Executive Committee laid out its objections to the appointment on the grounds of the "separation of church and state," citing its belief that Truman's decision would result in preference to "another... large religious group among us," and "religious liberty," noting that "this action" would "violate" the concept of "equal status" for all religious groups, large and small. Arguing that the appointment of an ambassador would "open the door" to a host of "dangerous possibilities," the Federation concluded its resolution by declaring its "intention to resist this proposal in the spirit of Christian love with all the means we may enlist among 50,083,000 Protestants...for the sake of democracy and religious liberty – the priceless heritage [that] we cherish and must maintain."[10]

Survey on Race Issues

In January 1952 the Race Relations Committee presented findings of the Federation's survey on racial practices to the Executive Committee. The next month, the Federation sponsored a workshop at First Presbyterian Church in order to present its recommendations about how best to address the issues that emerged in the final report. Having questioned whether or not the "smaller number" of African American churches participating in the survey "indicated a problem with the relationship between 'Negro' churches and the Church Federation," the Race Relations Committee noted that "reports of the churches indicated discrepancies between the views expressed in response to the reports they submitted and their known, actual, practices in terms of welcoming members of other races to their services and or membership."[11] At the same time, however, most of the surveyed congregations also "indicated an awareness of existing problems in the city or the neighborhoods, particularly the latter." Among the problems pointed out by respondents were "housing, employment, health, use of hotels, restaurants, theaters, hospitals, public facilities, recreation facilities, and public school." The "migration" of African Americans into "white communities" was particularly noted as a matter of concern.[12]

Out of the 118 churches participating in the survey, only 14 indicated that they had "no [racial] problem" while 82 recognized at least one problem. The most frequent problems listed were "unfriendly racial attitudes in the congregation," the "changing racial composition of the neighborhood," and the "use of church facilities for interracial meetings."[13] Having initially been tasked by the Executive Committee with gathering "factual material on which to build a program that [would] serve as a guide to the Church Federation in its efforts to serve Protestant Churches in the area of racial and cultural relations," the Race Relations Committee responded to

123

the survey by suggesting that the Federation strive to educate local churches to work on problems that "stem from attitudes within the congregations," and that it work to "re-orient church's programs" in order to deal with problems that "stem from them." Additionally, the need for a "study of changes going on in the racial composition of areas in the city and their meaning for the churches in those areas" was acknowledged by the committee. Indeed, the Executive Committee recommended that the Race Relations Committee work in cooperation with the Comity Committee in seeking solutions to the later issue. The report concluded by suggesting that "aid may also be had from those organizations in the city which are seeking to eliminate racial discrimination in housing.[14]

Another notable achievement of the Church Federation in the 1950s was its continued work with the city's juvenile court services. Between 1952 and 1953 alone, the Social Service Department reported that the court had referred 1,242 juveniles who were, in turn, referred to 177 different churches for assistance. At the same time, the Juvenile Aid Division of the Indianapolis Police Department was referring up to 300 boys and girls a year to local ministers who would then work to keep them out of trouble. Noting that "many of these children – all under the age of 18 years – are not [in fact] delinquent," the Federation's Social Service Department reported that "only one-third [of the latter group of children] are held for Juvenile Court action, but that all need the help of constructive community forces."[15]

The 1950s was the decade during which the Church Federation severed its ties to the city's Weekday Religion Education program and instead focused its energies upon improving and expanding programming for Sunday School and Vacation Church (or Bible) School programs. The Federation's Division of Christian Education also joined forces with the Social Service Department to develop a series of programs in family life education whose purpose was "to bring churches and social agencies together to address issues affecting the family in the city." Seminars and study groups developed as part of the resulting series of Family Life Clinics would go on to address issues ranging from "preparing for Christian Marriage," to "what does the Christian faith have to offer toward the basic issues families face?[16]

Perhaps one of the more unique activities sponsored by the Church Federation during this decade was a 1952 rally to celebrate the publication of the new Revised Standard Version of the Bible. Held at Cadle Tabernacle, the mass meeting included an address by Dr. Ralph Stockman, pastor of New York City's Christ Methodist Church, and music provided by a large choir organized by the Indianapolis Choir Directors Association. Among the many events were a community-wide service of "thanksgiving and dedication" held at Bridgeport Methodist Church; a lecture entitled "The Word of Life in Living Language" delivered by Dr. Robert Montgomery, associate professor of Bible at DePauw University; a special exhibit of Bibles in "various languages, versions, translations and parchment;" one lecture series on the "Living Bible in a Living Language" followed by another on "The Bible and Americanism;" and a pageant performed by members of Northwood Christian Church on WFBM-TV.[17]

Religious Census of the City

In 1953 the Church Federation reported the results of the Greater Indianapolis Religious Census, Evangelistic Visitations and Evangelistic Mission. Launched on 7 December 1952, a day called "Religious Census Sunday," the census was conducted by over 9,000 volunteers recruited from 290 congregations. By the time the summary report was presented to the Executive Committee in March 1953, over 129,000 home visits had been completed. Of those people who completed the survey, the Federation discovered that 234,547 men, women, and children residing in Indianapolis identified themselves as being members of, attending, or preferring, "Protestant, Catholic, or Jewish places of worship in Indianapolis or Marion County." Additionally, the report identified another 22,269 respondents expressing "no preference" of any kind. After noting that Indianapolis was the largest city in the nation where Protestants, Catholics, and Jews had successfully cooperated in conducting such a city-wide census, local papers reported that the Federation, acting through its Comity Committee, was using the results of the survey to approve the location of sixteen new churches.[18]

Sunday Observance

Encouraged, perhaps, by the success of the census, the Church Federation reached out that same year to the local "authorities of the Catholic Church" in order to renew the effort to enforce Sunday observance. Noting that "many civic-minded citizens, business men and housewives" had requested an investigation as to whether "these conditions [could] be remedied without bringing undue hardship on the business firms," the Committee on Moral Welfare reported that local "business organizations now open[ly] wanted to discuss this matter, and on their own initiative, work out a solution."[19] After much deliberation, the Federation concluded that drafting a statement explaining the reasons for closing stores on Sunday and "providing an opportunity for all the stores to indicate their desire to cooperate in [the] movement" would be more than sufficient to bring the community around to their way of thinking. The list included six reasons for Sunday closings ranging from the purely religious – the "moral law of God that one day of the week should be set aside for rest and worship" – to the purely economic – "closing stores on Sunday will in the long run be more economical and profitable because of the higher cost of operation and overhead expenses involved in Sunday operation."[20]

The Federation set Sunday 4 February 1954 as "C-Day" (Closing Day). Hoping for "100 percent participation," the group called upon local merchants voluntarily to support their campaign to "rededicate" Sunday as a day of rest and worship" by signing agreements to close their stores on Sundays, "provided their major competitors also [agreed to] close." Before "C-Day," however, H.C. Hegelskamp, secretary of the Indiana Retail Grocers and Meat Dealers, warned the Federation that for the closing plan to succeed over the long haul, it would need to have "solid" support throughout the entire city.[21]

Working with the Indianapolis Council of Church Women, the

Church Federation also sponsored a public forum on the subject of public morality and the Church's role in combating urban vice. Attendees called for "50 good men of high Christian principles who [could] take an active interest in law enforcement and good government." They also heard from Albert E. Huber, former chair of the Marion County Crime Commission, who reported that Indianapolis was rife with rackets ranging from "baseball pool tickets, lotteries, pic 'n' win tickets, tip books, dice games, and poker and horse-books." Shortly afterward, the Layman's Committee of the Federation launched a new Sunday night radio program called *The Church Layman's Roundtable*. Broadcast over WISH radio, the program sought to enlist concerned layman to do something "constructive through the churches, to overcome juvenile delinquency; secure better housing; endeavor to open public schools and church buildings for study, fellowship and recreation and stimulate laymen generally to help make [the] community a better place to raise their sons and daughters."[22]

New Leadership

The retirement of Executive Secretary Baumgartel in December 1954 inaugurated a period of major transition in the history of the Church Federation. His final year in office was not entirely a pleasant one since Baumgartel and Federation president Dr. Ozie D. Pruett, pastor of First Baptist Church, encountered criticism from board members and others over the Federation's continued membership in the National Council of Churches—clearly illustrating a conservative bent among certain board members.[23] Nevertheless, Baumgartel's year ended on a relatively high note with a record number of churches providing support for the Federation's work, and a commemorative dinner that brought together representatives from various racial and religious groups in order to celebrate Baumgartel's years of service and the Federation's accomplishments during his tenure in office.[24]

A new chapter in the history of the Church Federation began in 1955. The organization adopted a new name that represented the growing city – "The Church Federation of Greater Indianapolis" –

and installed the Reverend Laurence T. Hosie as the new Executive Secretary in March 1955.[25] An ordained Presbyterian minister, Hosie had served five years as head of the Presbyterian Labor Temple of New York City and nine years as director of the Council of Churches of Syracuse and Onondaga County, New York, prior to taking up his appointment in Indianapolis. Stressing a "church centered program," Hosie called for an examination of "all activities to see if they meet requirements; namely to serve members churches, provide [the] necessary supplement to denominational programs, carry out essential and desired cooperative enterprises, and contribute to the spirit of Christian unity and service."[26]

Under the new executive secretary, the Church Federation launched several new programs. It created an institutional chaplaincy service, overseen by the Ministry to Institutions division, which provided chaplains to both the police and the sheriff's departments, and supervised the implementation of a similar chaplaincy service for the Marion County Juvenile Court. Before the end of the decade, these services would also be extended to additional local institutions and groups such as the Suemma Coleman Home, nurses at General Hospital, LaRue D. Carter Hospital, Riley Hospital, and Sunnyside Sanatorium.[27]

The Federation expanded the work of the Community Education Committee, the Court and Probation Committee, and the Family Life Committee to address the changing needs in the city. For example, the Court and Probation Committee's work increasingly focused upon both the American Baptists' Camp Okalona project, which was designed specifically to work with delinquent children, and the on-going policy of the Juvenile Aid Division's referral of boys and girls, who came to the their attention, to pastors in their local neighborhoods.[28] During this same time period the Federation also began enrolling community agencies, such as the Indianapolis Social Hygiene Association, Crossroads Rehabilitation, the Adult Education Division of the Indianapolis Public Schools, and the Girl Scouts, to participate in "clinics" designed to "relate the Christian faith to family problems, to guide churches in improving family programs, to increase co-operation between churches and community agencies serving families and to assist churches in developing family leaders."[29]

Strengthening Protestantism

The Church Federation strived to balance its support for its member churches in their individual denominational work while working toward greater unity across denominations as well as across boundaries of race and faith. Still, the organization maintained a self-conscious awareness of itself as a uniquely Protestant entity. In late 1955 the *Federation Forecast* examined the reason for the Church Federation's continued support for the observance of Reformation Day by explaining that "so long as men are free, new groups with no insight will spring into being challenging the older churches." And though "we do not visualize the time when all Protestant churches will belong to a great monolithic church...we do see the day when we shall work side by side, serving our Lord, honoring one another, rejoicing in one another's victories, and stimulated to new efforts by them."[30]

It was also in the mid-1950s that the Church Federation first began discussions about the possibility of hosting the Billy Graham Crusade in Indianapolis. Initial discussions centered on the financial aspects of the project, both in terms of the cost of planning, organizing, and hosting such an event, as well as the issue of how Billy Graham and his staff were compensated, and where and how the money raised by the crusade would be spent. Efforts to bring the Crusade to the city continued for several years while issues and scheduling conflicts were hammered out.[31]

Dealing with the Modern City

In the spring of 1956 the Federation issued a "call to prayer" in response to events unfolding in Montgomery, Alabama. Noting that the "crucial and far-reaching issues that center in race relations have put the church in the spotlight," the Federation acknowledged that the "church was being judged as much by what it does not do as what it does do," and accepted the fact that it was being both criticized and

129

praised for what it had "not done." Even so, the Federation remained reluctant to make a "forthright public statement about Montgomery and the conviction of a Christian minister there." Perhaps not coincidentally, 1957 would be the last year the Church Federation would award its Inter-Racial Merit Award.[32]

It was during this period when the Federation began seriously to question the meaning of Reformation Day. The editor of the *Federation Forecast* noted in the October 1957 issue that "our Protestant heritage is a great one" and that it was a "tragic fact that many of our laity still think of the Reformation as essentially a negative attack condemning the Roman Church." After acknowledging that there were indeed "profound differences" between themselves and the Catholic Church, the editor laid out the reasons for the continued celebration of Reformation Day in Indianapolis:

to proclaim the richness of our faith, the place the Bible has for us as the word of God, the place the laity have in the life and direction of the church [and] the reality of the Living God as he comes through his Holy Spirit to inspire our heart and direct our work.[33]

By November, however, low attendance of the Reformation Day observances forced the leaders of the Federation to confront the question of whether or not the city's Protestants actually even desired a "single service in the year honoring their Reformation forebears and publicly witnessing to their common heritage and spiritual unity?"[34] Although the Federation concluded that it was their duty to continue supporting Reformation Day, arguing that it was necessary in light of the "sobering fact" that a consequence of the "ecumenical life" was that it provided "no basic center for the average church member," lack of public interest eventually led to the end of the annual event by 1960.[35]

The issue of Sunday observance arose again in 1957. Recognizing that the Federation needed to provide direction to its member congregations and convince the city as a whole, the Executive Committee issued the following principles for Sunday closings:

Sunday is a special day in Christian teaching and tradition and should be set aside for worship, rest, and family life; It is desirable that a climate should be cultivated in the Indianapolis community that would encourage all citizens to observe Sunday as a special day for worship, rest, and family life [and] therefore the Church Federation of Greater Indianapolis encourages church people to refrain from doing business not of necessity on Sunday and to encourage only such business activities on Sunday as will further objectives set forth in the above.[36]

Feeling optimistic, Federation leaders went so far as to claim that local "business and commercial leaders" actually felt that the "commercialization of Sunday is ultimately bad for the community and for all concerned" and that it "would not be difficult to remain closed on Sunday if responsible citizens of the community did their business on other days."[37] Shortly thereafter, however, the Federation acknowledged that the "effort to get voluntary compliance on Sunday closing…has not been successful," prompting a discussion about whether the organization ought to seek assistance from public authorities to "enforce existing closing Sunday legislation or possibly bring the law up-to-date." [38] The issue remained unresolved at the end of the decade.

Between 1958 and 1960 the Federation continued to find its relationship with the city's Catholic community to be a complicated, if not troubled, one. In 1958, for example, Federation leader expressed concern over a full page advertisement placed by the local diocese in the *Indianapolis Recorder*, the city's black newspaper. Claiming that the "Roman Catholic leadership" believed that "Protestantism [had] lost the Negro," the Federation argued that the "political implications of this [were] tremendous," and that now was the time, late as it was, for "a Protestant strategy." In fact, the Federation concluded that the real issue was white Protestantism's "inability to grasp the world implications of…race relations in this country and its meaning for the church [which] must be faced on the ecumenical level."[39]

This was followed shortly by the decision of the Federation's

Board of Directors to make a public statement against Indiana House Bill 53, which provided for state payments to school districts for supplementary transportation expenses because of its failure to include the word "public" in its provisions for school children. Speaking on behalf of the "Protestant community," the Church Federation argued that "this was an attempt to lay the basis for further transportation of parochial school children at public expense," and that this would open the door to the "alarming prospect of extend[ing] the use of public funds for parochial uses." Placing the issue in a broader context, however, the Federation concluded that "Protestant differences in philosophy have made it impossible for us to have a consistent position on the parochial school issue and [as a result] local communities become engaged in these skirmishes which do little other than to create uncertainty and ill feeling. This is a national matter upon which as yet we have very little national leadership."[40]

In 1957 the Church Federation successfully launched a new television program, on WLW-I, called *Timothy Church Mouse*. The half-hour program, which aired Sundays at 10:30 A.M., was "developed and directed" by Muriel Lee under the guidance of Dr. Alfred Edyvean, professor of communications at Butler University's School of Religion, and was the Federation's first effort in children's programming. That same year, Executive Secretary Hosie announced at the November meeting of the Board of Directors that two more television programs, *Insight* and *Five Minutes to Live*, would soon begin airing. By February 1958 the *Federation Forecast* proudly reported that both *Timothy Church Mouse* and *Insight* were delivering ratings that placed both programs in the "highest bracket for public service telecasting." Indeed, *Timothy Church Mouse* proved so popular that it was moved to Saturday mornings by the fall of 1958 and picked up by other stations outside the Indianapolis market.[41] Finances for television programs, however, remained problematic and, in 1958, the Gemmer Family Christian Foundation donated $1,000 to the Federation to support its television work. In 1960 Hosie and Edyvean secured an additional $5,000 from local denominational leaders and, in conjunction with the Indiana Council of Churches and Christian Theological Seminary, began to produce a series of documentaries on such controversial subjects as "narcotics, Black unemployment, restrictive covenants, the correctional system and funerals."[42]

Even as the Race Relations Committee opted to quit presenting its annual award in 1958, it took up the challenge of marshaling support for Dr. Martin Luther King's rally at Cadle Tabernacle in December. Noting that "few things would demonstrate more effectively to the Negro Community our genuine concern for improved interracial relations than strong support of the King meeting by white leaders," the committee maintained that it would "indicate to them [that] we are open-minded to the message and challenge of a responsible Negro Christian leaders, and have a real interest in the progress of the Senate YMCA." Reporting back to the board in December, the committee concluded that supporting King's appearance would offer "a kind of bridge by which the gap between racial interests [would] be partially closed."[43] Several weeks later, following Dr. King's appearance in Indianapolis, the board opined that "while not a project of the Federation...with approximately 4,000 in attendance [the meeting was] strongly indicative of the growing concern of Negro Christian leaders for a church program that will implement the pronouncements of all major denominations on race relations [while] the large number of white people attending indicated a similar concern among white church leaders."[44]

Billy Graham Crusade

By the end of the decade, following years of intense preparation, local Protestants and Federation leaders were focused on the Billy Graham Crusade, which was scheduled to take place 6 October through 1 November 1959.[45] As early as January, the *Federation Forecast* predicted that the issue facing local religious leaders for much of the year would be "whether or not people will be so absorbed in Crusade activities [that all other matters] will take a minor position." Indeed the Board of Directors indicated that there was already "considerable feeling [being voiced in the community] that the Reformation Day Service should be abandoned one year [since] the Crusade only holds Sunday afternoon but no Sunday evening meetings."[46] Calling upon all ministers in the state, the committee issued a statewide request for prayer meetings in support of the Crusade and proceeded to book several venues in Indianapolis, including the State Fairgrounds and Monument Circle, for its services. By May the *Federation Forecast* reported that the "Graham Crusade [was] gaining momentum and... taking more of the Executive Secretary's time and much church leadership."[47] The following month, the Federation reported that the "energies of the Protestant community [would] be absorbed from now on in preparation for the Graham Crusade," making note of the fact that there were now "400 churches of central Indiana [which] have become cooperative members with the Crusade and [that] it [was] estimated that nearly 2,000 volunteers are available for the mass choir." This same report, however, also noted that the Graham Committee was making a "determined effort...to prevent any kind of embarrassment to the Federation or to any church in the Federation which [did] not cooperate with the Crusade."[48]

Reporting to the Board one day prior to the opening of the Crusade, Executive Secretary Hosie acknowledged that his "liaison function [between the Federation and the Graham Committee] has involved your secretary in far more time than he anticipated, probably more than the board anticipated at the time they agreed to the arrangement," proving the prescience of the Board's prediction in January that the successful launch of the Billy Graham Crusade would become the organization's primary accomplishment in 1959. After Graham left the city, however, the devotion of so much of the Federation's time and energy to the Crusade seemed, by most calculations, more than justified. At a total cost of $254,000 with $30,000 being raised in the last evening's offering, the Crusade drew over 350,000 people spread over 25 different services. The final night's service at the Indiana State Fairgrounds attracted a crowd of 35,500 and an open air service held on the Circle the week before attracted between 12,000 and 20,000 people. By the time the Crusade concluded, over 9,300 people had been converted.[49]

Still, not all members of the Federation seemed enthusiastic about the organization's involvement with the Graham Crusade. Addressing this issue following the final service, Executive Secretary Hosie acknowledged that "as is the case in all Crusades, reports vary greatly and attitudes vary from bitter denunciation to blind hero worship." Hosie went on to confirm his continued faith in the integrity of Billy Graham and concluded by noting that although a "few member churches feel [that] they have been compromised by his activities...others have expressed satisfaction that he...worked on the [Billy Graham Crusade's] Executive Committee.[50]

New Headquarters

While the Billy Graham Crusade took center stage on the Church Federation's agenda as the decade drew to a close, the organization continued, with far less fanfare, to increase in size and expand its programming. By the end of 1959 an additional 31 congregations had joined the Church Federation, bringing total membership to 189 churches. Additionally, having outgrown its space at the downtown YMCA, the Federation launched a search for a new location for its headquarters. Bankrolled by a gift of $90,000 from the Lilly Endowment, the Federation purchased property at 1622 North Meridian Street in February 1960 and relocated its headquarters there in September. In an effort to plan for the future, the Church Federation created a Research and Planning Division tasked with the job of seeing "what is happening to the population [of Indianapolis and Marion County] and the implications of population change for the churches." As one of only "seven or eight" such programs in the nation, the Division of Research and Planning ended the 1950s by projecting the Federation's continued involvement in the inner city as well as the developing suburbs of Indianapolis and laying the foundation for a plan for Protestant churches in those areas. As the decade concluded, the Reverend Fred Michel, director of Research and Planning, predicted continued growth and prosperity for the

Federation's members in the suburbs, but acknowledged concern for congregations located within the inner city, arguing that while "a new development in the suburbs will be relatively stable for 40 years...the inner city changes a little at a time from month to month."[51]

Conclusion

As the calendar changed from 1959 to 1960, the Church Federation of Greater Indianapolis could reflect with great pride regarding its accomplishments over the past decade. Federation membership grew from 133 to 189 members. It purchased a new and larger headquarters on North Meridian Street, which would house a larger, more professional staff and accommodate the work of expanded programming and outreach. The Federation was lauded by the local community for its work on behalf of troubled youth and minorities and for establishing chaplaincy services for local law enforcement agencies. It embarked upon new ministries via radio and the rapidly expanding television broadcasting. The Federation emerged from the 1950s as a respected participant in not only the city's religious life, but its political and social lives as well. While the Federation's choices had not all been equally inspired, or perhaps in retrospect, praiseworthy, by decade's end, there seemed to be little reason to quibble with its overall success. Following in the wake of the enormous success of the Billy Graham Crusade, interpreted by many as another indication of the continued triumph of American Protestantism, there seemed to be little reason for concern over what the 1960s might bring for The Church Federation of Greater Indianapolis. Even with the foreknowledge of the continued decline of Protestant churches in the inner city, there seemed to be every reason to expect the coming decade to be one of continued stability, growth, and success.

Endnotes

1 Edwin L. Becker, *From Sovereign to Servant: The Church Federation of Greater Indianapolis, 1912-1987* (Indianapolis: The Church Federation of Greater Indianapolis, 1987), 45. Although Reformation Day was launched in 1948, it was the 1950s with which it would be most closely associated, in terms of the life of the city.

2 "Dr. Baumgartel's 10 Years of Church Service Pay Rich Results to Him and to Indianapolis, *Indianapolis Times*, 14 May 1950.

3 "Church Federation Triples in Decade," *Indianapolis News*, 28 October 1950.

4 Becker, 45-46.

5 Ibid., 64. See: "Mass Media Carry Church Message," *Indianapolis News*, 3 November 1951. One local minister put it this way, "I definitely feel that on the local level we are far behind on how to produce and use the materials of the whole field of audio-visuals." For Peale's program see "Church Federation to Sponsor TV Series," *Indianapolis Times*, 8 November 1952.

6 Executive Committee Minutes, 1913-1986, Church Federation of Greater Indianapolis Records (hereafter CF), M0755, Series 1, William Henry Smith Memorial Library, Indiana Historical Society, Indianapolis, Indiana.

7 Ibid.

8 "Three Firms Win Church Federation Interracial Award," *Indianapolis Times*, 29 April 1953. The *Indianapolis News* was praised for its "frank and straightforward news articles dealing with problems of human relations and racial tensions." See "News Is Cited for Racial Articles, *Indianapolis News*, 28 April 1954.

9 See both "Vatican Envoy is Protested," *Indianapolis Times*, 6 November 1951 and "City Church Federation Protests Vatican Envoy," *Indianapolis Star*, 6 November 1951. Also see Catholic File, 1950-1955, CF, Series 5, which is devoted to this issue. The views of the Federation reflected those of the larger, national Protestant community and in January 1952 General Clark withdrew his nomination and Truman let the matter drop. It was not until 1984 that the United States would appoint its first ambassador to the Holy See.

10 Ibid.

11 Board of Directors Minutes, 1948-1991, CF, Series 1. The Race Relations Committee questioned whether or not the smaller number of African American churches participating in the survey might be due to an "assumed threat to the existence to Negro churches," posed by the Federation itself. The committee also noted instances where respondents were apparently unaware of the fact that their own denomination's had already publically "adopted statements in favor of open door policies."

12 Ibid.

137

13   Ibid.

14   Ibid.

15   Becker, 55-56; Minutes of the Social Service Committee, 1954-1959, CF, Series 2.

16   Becker argues that the Church Federation and the Board of Weekday Religious Education eventually parted ways over budgetary issues combined with a lack of clear delineation of their respective responsibilities. He also speculates that part of the reason for the split between the two groups may have been related to the fact that while the Lilly Endowment was a major contributor to the Weekday Religious Education program during these years, it was not equally generous to the Church Federation. Becker, 51-52, 91; "Family Life Clinic Sets Workshops," *Indianapolis Times*, 13 July 1957; "Families Fight Most Over TV, Discipline, Survey Shows, *Indianapolis Times*, 16 January 1958, and "3-Day Family Life Seminar to Open," *Indianapolis News*, 18 January 1958.

17   Becker, 55-56; "Mass Meetings to Herald Modern Version of Bible," *Indianapolis Star*, 28 September 1952; "Strike Curb Aim of Church Group," *Indianapolis News*, 10 October 1952.

18   Executive Committee Minutes, 1913-1986, Board of Directors Minutes, 1948-1991, and Race Relations, 1927-1969, CF, Series 1 and Series 5; "Life Begins at 40 for Federation," *Indianapolis News*, 25 April 1953, "Needy," *Indianapolis News*, 5 May 1953; Becker, 49.

19   Minutes of the Executive Committee, 9 November 1953.

20   "Church Group Asks Stores be Closed Sundays," *Indianapolis Star*, 17 November 1953 and "Church Federation Sets C-Day," *Indianapolis Star*, 4 December 1953.

21   Ibid.

22   Executive Meeting Minutes, CF, "News Release," 3 February 1954. Over the year topics of the weekly program included such disparate topics as "How should religious bodies view current legislative investigations practices and McCarthyism?" and "Is Sunday shopping good for America?" to "Is the Church responsible for our present widespread juvenile delinquency?" to "The Church and the United States Supreme Court decision to outlaw racial segregation?"

23   Becker notes that Baumgartel's announcement of his pending retirement, eighteen months in advance, left him as something of a "lame duck," and that his "problems with the Federation Board stemmed [also] in part from the desire of some to separate from...the National Council of Churches." The reason for this desire is not explicitly spelled out, but the rift was serious enough that the Personnel Committee reported that he "may wish to seek other employment to take effect before that date." Becker, 66.

24   Becker, 66-67. At the time Baumgartel retired there were 168 churches providing financial support to the Federation. Among the attendees of the Dr. Howard J.

138

Baumgartel Appreciation Dinner, held at the auditorium of the Central YMCA on 14 December 1954, were Rabbi Maurice Goldblatt of Indianapolis Hebrew Congregation and Father Raymond T. Bosler, representing the city's Catholic community. Moreover, the event was chaired by prominent local African-American attorney Henry J. Richardson, Jr. The overall sense of the event was that it summed up the Baumgartel years as ones during which the Church Federation had strived to break down "racial and religious barriers."

25 Ibid., 67. The name change actually occurred several months prior to Hosie's arrival.

26 Ibid., 69-70; "Church Federation to Seat New Secretary," *Indianapolis Star*, 5 May 1955.

27 Executive Committee Report, 43rd Annual Business Meeting, 26 April 1955, CF.

28 Ibid.; Becker, 89-90, 92; "Federation Cited for Work with Juveniles, *Indianapolis News*, 10 August 1957.

29 "Family Life Clinic Sets Workshops," *Indianapolis Times*, 13 July 1957 and Board of Directors Meeting Minutes, 7 October 1957, 1, CF.

30 *Federation Forecast*, November 1955.

31 In a report made to the Board of Directors, it was explained that according to Billy Graham's manager (a Mr. Haymaker) although it was impossible to give an "actual figure of cost in any location until studies can be made... these costs could run anywhere from $75,000 to $150,000, depending upon such matters as supplementary equipment for seating, auditorium rentals and the costs of campaign headquarters." Graham's manager went on to explain that the "general procedure for raising funds begins when a Graham Committee comes to a city three to six months in advance of the meetings to work with the local committee on raising funds in the community." The Board of Directors was assured that "the Graham Committee provides all the plans and organizational know-how," and that "no assessment is made against any church," and that "churches, as churches, do not assume any financial obligation." Rather, the "community as a whole, individuals, industrial and business groups will be asked to give." The Board was then assured that "Graham is on a salary, as are his associates," and that "there is no love offering... all books are audited and published in local papers." Finally it was noted that "the bulk of the money raised is spent locally." Report of the Executive Secretary, 7 November – 5 December 1955, 2, Board of Director's Minutes, CF.

32 By 1960, however, the Church Federation was more willing to take a public stand in support of civil rights endeavors. At the annual meeting that year the delegates resolved to "support those in the South expressing their hopes through lunch-counter sit-ins." "Church Group Here Backs South Sit-ins," *Indianapolis Times*, 4 May 1960.

33 *Federation Forecast*, October 1957, 1.

34 *Federation Forecast*, November 1957, 1.

35 Ibid.; Becker,45.

36 *Federation Forecast*, October 1957, 3.

37 Ibid.

38 Executive Committee Minutes, 1957, CF.

39 *Federation Forecast*, January 1958, 2.

40 *Federation Forecast*, 2 March 1959.

41 Becker, 86; *Federation Forecast*, February 1958, 2. Becker indicates that by 1966 *Timothy Church Mouse* was being aired outside Indiana and was being watched in 33,000 homes "according to ARB ratings." At times the Church Federation sponsored as many as ten television programs, in addition to up to five different radio programs, per week as well as special produced for religious holidays.

42 Becker, 86-87. Becker reports that Edyvean indicated that the first local TV stations had small news departments and were unable or unwilling to "tackle" such controversial topics and therefore welcomed the efforts of the Federation in this area. This did not mean, however, that the Federation was entirely supportive of the TV Committee's efforts in this area. In 1962, for example, concerns were raised over the possibility that a program satirizing Protestant funeral practices might alienate the owners of the Flanner and Buchanan Mortuary, but the board eventually opted not to pull their sponsorship of the program.

43 *Federation Forecast*, 1 December 1958, 1.

44 *Federation Forecast*, 5 January 1959, 1.

45 Among the members of the 12-member Indiana Graham Crusade committee were Dr. Laurence Hosie, executive secretary of the Church Federation, and the Reverend Robert Koenig, pastor of the University Evangelical United Brethren Church and chair of the Federation's Evangelism Committee. See "Graham's Crusade Open October 6," *Indianapolis Times*, 12 November 1958.

46 *Federation Forecast*, 5 January 1959, 2.

47 *Federation Forecast*, 4 May 1959, 1.

48 *Federation Forecast*, 1 June 1959, 1.

49 Becker, 73; Edward L. Queen II, "Revivalism," *The Encyclopedia of Indianapolis*, eds. David J. Bodenhamer and Robert G. Barrows (Bloomington & Indianapolis: Indiana University Press, 1994), 1192-1193.

50 *Federation Forecast*, 2 November 1959, 1.

140

51 "Churches Unite in Plans for Growth in '60s," *Indianapolis Times*, 5 January 1960. Rev. Michel indicated that the Federation was engaged in a "problem study" covering just one small area of Indianapolis's inner city during the pilot phase, in an effort to find solutions to the problems facing Protestant churches, many of which were, in his words, "dying." Much of the Federation's efforts in the coming decade would be devoted to helping inner-city congregations adapt to their new circumstances.

1. Minister-led memorial service on Monument Circle in commemoration of death of Rev. Martin Luther King, Jr.

2. People marching in CORE Ten Mile March for Freedom.

3. Robert F. Kennedy breaking news of Rev. Martin Luther King, Jr.'s assassination.

4. Church of God congregation with Elder Eli Lewis.

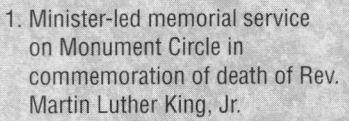

Indianapolis Recorder Collection, Indiana Historical Society

Indianapolis Recorder Collection, Indiana Historical Society

Indiana Historical Society

Indianapolis Recorder Collection, Indiana Historical Society

1960s

Growing Up and Out

Raymond R. Sommerville, Jr.

ULLY EMBRACING ITS NEW NAME ADOPTED IN 1954, The Church Federation of Greater Indianapolis entered the new decade with a sense of confidence and optimism about the future. For, at the close of the 1950s, the Protestant establishment in Indianapolis, which the Federation largely represented, was still going strong. Church attendance was higher than ever. Weekday religious instruction was reaching thousands of children in public schools. The Federation continued to sponsor the annual Holy Week services at downtown and neighborhood churches, although attendance had dropped sharply in the previous decade. It also supported religious services and staffed chaplains for the Juvenile Center and other healthcare and social agencies in Marion County. New ventures in ecumenical and interfaith cooperation were developing as Protestants, Jews, and Catholics reached out to each other. This period of the Federation's history can be thus characterized as an era of consensus for Protestant mainline churches.

Building on the religious and social capital of white mainline churches, the Federation's Executive Secretary Reverend Laurence T. Hosie initiated a "church centered program" designed to "serve member churches, provide necessary supplement to denominational programs, carry out essential and desired cooperative enterprises, [and] contribute to the spirit of Christian unity and service."[1] He ambitiously expanded the staff during his tenure to include seven professionals to meet these goals. In 1960 Carl Hatfield, a former army and hospital chaplain, replaced Gilbert T. Hunter as Director of the Social Service Division. In 1958 Dr. H. Otho Blackburn succeeded H.B. Holloway for a critical two-year stint as business manager, which included overseeing the move to a new Federation home at 1622 North Meridian Street in 1960, before Warren G. Davis assumed the position of associate executive secretary. In 1956 Catherine Carter, a Disciple of Christ minister, became director of the Christian Education Division. Christian Theological Seminary professors Alfred R. Edyvean and Franklin T. Rector filled part-time positions as directors of TV and Religious programming and research and planning for the Comity Committee, respectively. Other than Carter, women on the staff held the predominant roles of secretaries and bookkeepers, including Grace Walker, Fannie Mae Geisler, Dolores G. Burch, Loretta Brown, Viola Ziebell, Mrs. Johnnie Vorhis, Betsy Sluder, and Donna Smith. African American Christians and other racial-ethnic minorities had only token representation among the staff and constituency of the Federation at the beginning of the 1960s.

Still, there were signs of change on the horizon for the Church Federation and the Greater Indianapolis community. For the first time in its history the Federation had to face the decline of mainline Protestantism in Indianapolis and across the nation. The demographic center of the city had shifted both geographically and culturally. These changes would have profound implications for the white mainline leadership of the Federation and the churches that comprised its ranks. The 1960s thus marked the decline of the Protestant consensus and gave rise to an era of confrontation and decline. The earlier name change reflected the Federation's realization that suburbanization and other trends had transposed the city into a sprawling metropolitan area of distinct communities, sharply segregated by race, economic status, and even religion. In

1959, for instance, Second Presbyterian Church moved from the corner of Vermont and Pennsylvania streets to its present location at 7700 North Meridian Street. One year later First Baptist Church moved from its downtown corner of Vermont and Meridian streets to 8600 North College Avenue, partly to make way for the completion of the Indiana World War Memorial Plaza. As more of the big steeple churches moved further from Center Township to the outlying suburbs, the Church Federation turned its sociological and mission focus on the problems of the "Inner City." Perhaps no one was more prescient about the looming crisis of the "inner city" than Executive Secretary Hosie, a seasoned veteran of ecumenical urban ministry in the state of New York before joining the Federation in 1955. But not even Hosie could fully anticipate the cataclysmic challenges the Federation would encounter during the 1960s.

When Hosie arrived to lead the Federation in 1955, mainline churches in Indianapolis dominated the city's religious and cultural landscape. For example, the Director of the Division of Research and Planning reported the following demographics on 606,000 white citizens of Marion County:[2]

Religious Grouping	Constituency	% of Population
Cooperating Protestants	175,011	28.9
Independent Protestants	52,864	8.7
Orthodox	3,000	.5
Roman Catholic	86,106	14.2
Jewish	7,000	1.1
Other (e.g. Unitarian and Mormons)	1,717	.3

The Methodist Episcopal Church led all Protestant constituencies with 8.6 percent of the white population, followed by the Christian Church (5.1 percent), Presbyterians (4.4 percent), American Baptists (3.4 percent), and Episcopalian (1.2 percent). Together these mainline denominations constituted a Protestant establishment in Indianapolis, providing religious, social, economic and cultural leadership for the city from its earliest settlement.

Not surprisingly, these demographics on the white population of Marion County ignored the spectacular growth of the African American population, which grew five times faster than the general population between 1950 and 1960, and was mostly confined to congested neighborhoods south of Crown Hill Cemetery, near Crispus Attucks High School and Indiana Avenue, and the Martindale neighborhood on the east side.[3] At its Executive Board meeting of 3 October 1960, the Federation moved to address this oversight of African American churches by launching a study of these churches, jointly funded by the Lilly Endowment and Christian Theological Seminary. The Reverend William K. Fox Sr., an African American student at Butler, was hired to conduct the study under the auspices of the Federation's Division of Research and Planning. Fox, a minister in the Christian Church (Disciples) and graduate of the University of Chicago, became the first black employee of the Federation.[4]

Also encapsulated in the Division of Research and Planning's report was the nebulous category of "independent Protestant Churches." This group represented the expanding presence of non-mainline churches whose beliefs and practices marginalized them from the Protestant establishment represented by the Federation. Their numbers included such churches as Holiness, Pentecostals, Seventh Day Adventists, Jehovah's Witnesses, and a segment of conservative Christians who self-identified as "evangelical" or "fundamentalists." It was the latter – the evangelical and fundamentalist constituencies – that would challenge the hegemony of the Federation and the mainline Protestant establishment to speak for all Christians in Greater Indianapolis on matters of faith and morality.

One early sign of this growing tension had surfaced in the 1950s with the Federation's support and sponsorship of Billy Graham crusades in Indianapolis in 1955 and 1959. In each instance, Graham, by now the most famous evangelist in the U.S., stipulated that he would not conduct a crusade without the full support of the Church Federation, both an indication of Graham's widespread appeal to mainline Christians and the religious influence of the Federation. But there were constituent members of the Federation who vigorously opposed the Federation's endorsement of the crusade and found it embarrassing. Objecting to Graham's approach to mass evangelism and fundraising methods, a group of Federation members petitioned the board in 1955 to drop its endorsement of the crusade, but the Board instead voted to extend the invitation. By the time of the next Billy Graham came to Indianapolis in 1959, there was less direct criticism and résistance within the ranks of the Federation, as many mainline leaders readily joined Graham on the platform and about 35,000 residents attended the 5 October to 1 November crusade at the Indiana State Fairgrounds.

Graham's appeal went beyond his dramatic preaching of the gospel and literalistic interpretation of the Scriptures, but extended to his diatribes against the threats of godless communism and immorality in the U.S. Fear of communism during the country's entrenched Cold War with Russia helped to create a greater cooperation among mainline, evangelical, and fundamentalist Protestants alike. In many ways Graham marked a turning point from the older style Protestant fundamentalism of the early twentieth century often caricatured in the 1925 Scope's trial in Dayton, Tennessee. The older style was dogmatically combative, proudly anti-modernist, and politically apathetic. Graham fully embraced the label "evangelical" to refer to a more dynamic, progressive, and non-defensive expression of true Christianity. Led by Graham, other luminaries and para-church organizations like the American Council of Christian Churches (ACCC) and the National Association of Evangelicals (NAE), this growing movement was poised to challenge the consensus of the Protestant establishment by the early 1960s. In their view, the new style Evangelicalism represented a stark alternative to the diluted orthodoxy and social gospel liberalism of the National Council of Churches of Christ (NCC) and The Church Federation of Greater Indianapolis.

Throughout the 1960s the Church Federation's executive secretaries and board responded periodically to criticisms from evangelicals and fundamentalists who yoked these two mainline, ecumenical bodies as anti-Christian and anti-American. Many of these highly publicized clashes between the Federation and its detractors occurred in the local press. In March 1960 the *Indianapolis Star* printed a story concerning the publication of an Air Force training manual that warned officers about religious leaders influenced by Communism, especially leaders affiliated with the NCC. A *Star* editorial on 4 March 1960 directly quoted from the manual:

A lot of prominent members of the National Council of Churches have sponsored and supported – and continue to sponsor and support – open Communist political groups and drives, and so called Communist "front" organizations.[5]

The *Star* concluded that the manual "should be read by all Americans." The Federation's leadership responded to the charges with a statement in the local press, "A Statement on the Indianapolis School Board Decision on Scripture Reading and Prayer by the Church Federation of Indianapolis."

In a board of directors meeting on 7 March 1960, Hosie referred to the recent editorial in the *Star*, which accused the NCC of supporting Communism and chided religious leaders for joining and remaining in a subversive organization. A combative Hosie strongly defended the ecumenical cause:

In a day when men desperately need the security from colleagues united in a divine and holy purpose, a perverse twist can turn that need into a holy war, sanctifying the hate and prejudices being directed at our movement.[6]

He conjectured that the real motive behind the writer's attack on the NCC was the organization's witness to unity and work in race relations. Furthermore, Hosie directly addressed the accusation of Communist affiliation by denying it as being untrue and reiterating "our unity against Communism," while acknowledging that "in recent years we have failed to adequately recognize the utterly ruthless nature of the Communist conspiracy."[7] The board responded to Hosie's statement with a motion to circulate a statement to Indianapolis churches that would "accurately and intelligently combat this unfavorable and uninformed movement to discredit leaders in Protestantism and Christianity."[8]

In 1961 J. Irwin Miller, a prominent industrialist and philanthropist from Columbus, Indiana, and Disciples of Christ lay leader, was elected president of the NCC. The Federation saw this as an opportunity to re-introduce the NCC to Christians in Indiana, some of whom were growing uneasy with the NCC's escalating social activism in response to the civil rights movement and the escalation of the Vietnam War. On 15 May Miller addressed an audience of 700 persons at Second Presbyterian Church in an effort to defuse local tensions about the mission and activities of the NCC. After his address, 162 attendees volunteered to continue the dialogue in a "constructive discussion group."[9] This proposed dialogue with grassroots constituents— lay and clergy—was crucial as the Federation sought to filter and interpret future NCC statements and policies. Hosie warned that the Federation had to counteract opposition to the ecumenical movement from two sources: "by friends who are sincerely troubled by some actions of both denominational and interdenominational bodies, and those who see the church as threatening their own privileges and interests and who would destroy the church's united mission."[10]

As the traditional guardian of public morality in Indianapolis, the Federation also faced mounting pressure from constituent members and vocal opponents to address legal and public policy decisions that negatively affected religion. One example was the Indianapolis Schools Board's decision in 1962 to uphold the Supreme Court's ruling to rescind policies permitting public and Bible reading as proscribed school activities. The Federation's board and membership debated the implications of the decision before instructing its Social Action Committee to issue a cautiously worded statement that seemingly played both sides of the fence. On the one hand, the statement defended the First Amendment prohibition of state-established religious practices, while on the other hand, asserted the Christian roots and identity of the U.S. The Federation's support of the school board's decision further opened it to vilification from its local and outside detractors, who derided their acceptance of the school board's decision as yet another example of the apostasy of the mainline establishment.

In 1965 the Federation board again responded to public reactions to the NCC's prophetic stance against the escalation of the Vietnam War. This time it was a syndicated "news article" by Fulton Lewis Jr., which negatively interpreted a NCC resolution and letter sent to President Lyndon B. Johnson from Bishop Reuben H. Mueller, president of the NCC and an Evangelical United Brethren (EUB) bishop from Indiana. The Federation's board of directors voted in its April meeting to send copies of the NCC's "Resolution on Vietnam" (adopted 25 February 25 1965) and Bishop Mueller's letter to its constituent members. This mailing was followed up with the creation of a phone-in service for local residents to voice their views on the NCC controversy and a meeting with Hosie and 104 ministers on 17 September to discuss the "hate messages" received. Bishop Mueller wrote a memo to Hosie earlier on 10 May, which characterized Lewis' article as "full of falsehoods" and announced that the NCC staff was writing a reply on the issues raised in the article about the NCC's tax exemption status and lobbying activities.[11]

These reactionary efforts had two primary effects: to temporarily stanch criticism of the NCC's anti-war rhetoric and activism and to neutrally elicit local reactions to the NCC and the Vietnam War. The Church Federation itself, though internally divided on support and opposition of the war, issued no statements to either effect and thus maintained a semblance of neutrality.

If the Federation's official response to the Vietnam War in the mid-1960s was neutral, its response to the insurgency of the civil rights movement was much more decisive and constructive, at least from the perception of the white mainline establishment. The Church Federation could boast that its Committee on Race Relations, organized in the 1920s during the Ku Klux Klan's ascendency in Indiana, had a significant role in promoting interracial understanding and racial equality for more than forty years.

150

The Church Federation could further boast that it had included some of the most influential leaders in the African American communities on this committee, beginning with Faburn E. DeFrantz, executive director of the Senate Avenue YMCA; Freeman B. Ransom, prominent attorney and business manager of the Madame C. J. Walker Enterprises; and Reverend H. L. Herod, pastor of Second (now Light of the World) Christian Church. Through the intervening years the Federation, influenced by a new succession of African American leaders, promoted such activities as the annual observance of Race Relations Sunday, hosted a Race Relations Clinic in 1945, and instituted the annual Inter-Racial Merit award.

As an ongoing expression of its race relations ministry, the Church Federation targeted the "Inner City" as the focus of its work in the 1960s, with the Research and Planning Unit directly confronting this challenge with a variety of new initiatives. In his Executive Secretary Report to the Federation board on 25 April 1961, Hosie described Indianapolis as a rapidly growing metropolitan area with fourteen regional groups of churches. He defined its inner city as "an area of rapid social change, usually with aggravated situations such as family breakdown, delinquency, etc." He also noted that denominational leaders and constituent churches within the inner city were looking to the Federation to give leadership in this perplexing area. Hosie further pointed to the rapid population growth of the African American community and their restlessness for change. "One hundred thousand Negroes are becoming more aware of their origins," wrote Hosie. "They are taking new pride in their history and are confident in their future." Although he characterized most of their churches as being "local in character" and not "ecumenically minded," Hosie said the Federation is "expecting strong support and new vision from these churches and their leadership."[12]

In 1962 the Reverend Andrew J. Brown, pastor of St. John's Baptist Church and president of the local chapter of the Southern Christian Leadership Conference (SCLC), officially requested membership into the Federation. He was joined by the Reverend

H.L. Burton, pastor of Phillips Temple CME Church and president of the local chapter of the National Association for the Advancement of Colored People (NAACP); the Reverend R.H. Peoples, pastor of Second Christian Church; Dr. F. Benjamin Davis, pastor of New Bethel Missionary Baptist Church and president of the Indianapolis Ministerial Alliance; and the Reverend Frank Carlson, also from New Bethel. From 1967 to 1970 Davis served as the president of the Church Federation's Board of Directors, presiding during turbulent era in the city and the Federation's history and becoming the first president from a non-founding denomination.

These leaders introduced the Federation leadership and board to the civil rights activism sweeping the country through national organizations like the NAACP, the National Urban League (NUL), Congress of Racial Equality (CORE), SCLC, and Operation Breadbasket, which had local branches in Indianapolis. In a 1964 invitation to member churches, the Church Federation praised the NAACP for demonstrating "responsible leadership in the struggle for civil rights" and encouraged "all Christians who are working for the achievement of brotherhood to consider membership in the NAACP as an important means of achieving brotherhood."[13] However, when the Federation, the Indiana Council of Churches, the Catholic Archdiocese of Indianapolis, and the Jewish community issued a joint statement a few months later supporting federal civil rights legislation, Hosie reported that the Federation was "roundly criticized for an innocuous statement, the feeling being that it should have been taken a stronger stand." Stung by this criticism from unnamed sources, he expressed a desire for the Federation to develop a consensus on its leadership role in the struggle, and reiterated that his primary concern throughout his tenure had been to keep Christians addressing issues in a spirit of love and unity.[14] Once again the Federation's consensus as the voice of the mainline establishment was being challenged internally and externally.

Closely related to civil rights and inner city problems, the next urban challenge the Church Federation confronted during the 1960s was that of open housing. The post-World War II suburban boom that hit

Indianapolis in the 1950s brought almost 52,000 new housing units to the city, mostly in the northern townships of Lawrence, Washington, and Perry. This housing boom was largely fueled by federal mortgage support for veterans and funds for new highway construction. With few exceptions, African American residents were locked out of this suburban development by opposition from white neighborhood associations and restrictive realty policies. Consequently, in 1960, 90 percent of all African Americans were crammed into overcrowded and substandard housing in Center Township. Compounding the plight of these inner city residents was the adamant refusal of city leaders to accept federal funding for urban renewal projects, despite the dissent of newly elected Democratic Mayor John J. Barton (1964-1967) and others who argued it was foolish for the city not to do so. During his tenure, Barton reactivated the Indianapolis Housing Authority, organized during the Depression and disbanded in 1958, and secured federal funds to create 3,000 low-income housing units for families displaced by the interstate highway project and slum clearance projects.

In May 1964 the Federation's Human Relations Committee, chaired by the Reverend Richard Hamilton of North Methodist Church, presented to the board of directors its own solution to the housing crisis in Center Township. "A Proposed Open Occupancy Ordinance" forthrightly defined open occupancy as the "right of any individual, regardless of race, creed, or color, to purchase, rent, or lease a residence wherever his interests make it seem desirable."[15] The proposal outlined the advantages and disadvantages of passing such an ordinance, particularly its implications for racial integration. The ordinance, for example, could create "new and dangerous tensions." "Prejudice and violence would be delayed rather than expedited. Whites would concentrate even more strongly in the suburbs, where the ordinance would not apply," warned the proposal. The committee soundly rejected this argument and grounded their support for the ordinance on the bases of "the Christian faith, democratic principles, and the human dignity of all mankind."[16]

In a follow-up report by the Division of Mission and Service at the

153

June 1964 board of directors meeting, chairwoman Letta I. Shonle further identified two major problems brewing in Indianapolis. The first was "sub-decent living standards of a large segment of the population, both white and non-white, with special reference to education, jobs, housing, and race relations." The second problem was the unwillingness of a "segment of leadership" to address these problems." Appearing before the Church Federation's Conference on Urban Renewal in 1961, Bruce Savage, an Indianapolis realtor and a U.S. Public Housing Administration Commissioner, delivered a speech "Federal Aid for Urban Renewal and Public Housing in which offered scathing criticism of obstructionists to public housing:

Unfortunately, not enough is known about public housing in Indianapolis, for it has been the victim of an extremely bigoted and antagonistic press, revolting demagoguery, and a small, hard core of citizens, who, in large degree, control the decisions of our civic, political and economic life-men, who have for years been saying, 'We can do all the housing needed for our lowest income families locally through free enterprise, but in twenty years, since the creation of the public housing program by Congress, have yet to lay the first brick of housing construction...[17]

While some members of the board thought the Church Federation should address the plight of the inner city separately from civil rights activism, the board conceded that its inner city thrust "will, without doubt, aid the Civil Rights Movement in Indianapolis but neither is that its main focus."[18] That distinction became increasingly blurred as the Federation implemented a range of new inner city initiatives during Hosie's tenure. Among them were creating an interracial and interdenominational Task Force on the Inner City, establishing a Task Force on Race Relations to evaluate the contemporary situation, launching an independent study of law enforcement to examine police attitudes and actions toward citizens, and actively recruiting African American pastors, churches, and denominations to the Church Federation.

As it began to take firmer stances on civil rights legislation and anti-poverty measures, the Church Federation also engaged in internal debate and soul-searching about its mission in the public realm. Apparently, some board members were worried about how public perceptions of the Federation's advocacy role could negatively impact constituency support, especially as the Federation was in the midst of seeking funds to build a new Interchurch Center. The total cost for the Center was estimated at $840,000, of which $650,000 was expected to come from church bodies and $190,000 through capital gifts. The Indiana Interchurch Center opened 5 July 1967 at the corner of Michigan Road and 42nd Street, on land donated by Christian Theological Seminary. In addition to the Federation, the original owners and tenants of the Indiana Interchurch Center Corporation included the Indiana Council of Churches, the Catholic Diocese of Indianapolis, the United Church of Christ, the Methodist Church, Indiana Area, The Christian Church, (Disciples of Christ), the United Presbyterian Church, Synod of Lincoln Trails and the Episcopal Church, Diocese of Indianapolis.

At the first board meeting of 1965, Hosie read a letter of resignation from the board from the pastor of South Irvington Church of the Nazarene. Although the letter did not specify any reasons for the resignation, the board's subsequent actions that year suggest that it was becoming more concerned about public perceptions of its mission. In response to a report from its Social Education and Action Committee on the Church's role in legislation, the board reviewed its policies of recent years. The Church Federation board then affirmed three primary goals in relation to legislative advocacy:

- The Federation has stressed to Christians that "all legislation has moral and spiritual significance."
- The Federation has highlighted those issues for which the "religious person has a special responsibility."
- The Federation has presented the pros and cons "of matters in which there will be difference of judgment as to where the weight of Christian responsibility lies."[19]

155

The board debated the merits and weaknesses of these approaches in light of new challenges.

During this period of self-review in the mid-1960s, the Church Federation also engaged in a fifteen month review and revision of its constitution, focusing on the questions, "Who are we?" and "What kind of program should result from our concept of what we are?" Reflecting the language and consensus of the wider ecumenical movement, the Church Federation identified its objective as "to provide opportunity for the expression of unity we already recognize as existing and through discussion seek further comprehension of our faith as it relates to our common life." Specific revisions called for expanding the role of the General Assembly in the election of new members and as an advisory body to the board of directors and additional denominational representatives; electing the officers of the Federation; assigning the board responsibility for establishing policy and "initiating, approving, and overseeing all program acidities of the Federation."[20] Furthermore, the revised constitution renewed commitments to and relationships with city, state, and national councils of churches, particularly the Indiana Council of Churches, the NCC, and the WCC. With a newly revised constitution and restructured Federation in place, Hosie was now ready to retire and pass the torch to his successor and new executive secretary, Dr. Robert W. Koenig, who was unanimously elected in 1965.

Koenig, a native Hoosier from Freelandville in Knox County, had most recently served as the Superintendent of the Western District of the Indiana Southern Conference of the Evangelical United Brethren Church (EUB). He had served previously as a pastor at University Heights Christian Church and as a missionary in Japan, Hong Kong, and the Philippines. Not a stranger to the Federation, Koenig had served on the Church Federation's Board of Directors and chaired its Evangelism Committee in the 1950s. He was elected to lead the Federation that now consisted of 151 constituent churches and denominations, which had contributed more than $40,000 (40 percent) to the Federation's 1964-1965 annual budget.

In 1968 Koenig's EUB denomination merged with several other denominations to form the United Methodist Church.

Executive Secretary Koenig spent his first eight months on the job honing the foundational structure of Federation and consolidating administrative staff positions. He restructured the Federation from a divisional operation to major programs units administered by staff members: Inner City, Leadership Development (Koenig); Community Concerns, Communications (Thomas Stratton); Research and Planning (Richard Myers); Social Service, Christian Education and Special Ministries (Paul McClure).

Myers, appointed director of research and development in 1963, replaced Fred Michel, who was the Federation's first research director, appointed in 1958. Myers was a Methodist minister and former executive director of the Bureau of Research with the Greater Chicago Federation of Churches for eleven years. From 1956 to 1958 The Lilly Endowment funded the Church Federation's research projects, but, by the mid-1960s, the Federation's member denominations were contributing the majority share of the research and planning budget, as denominational leaders and planners looked to this unit for advice and resources. In a pamphlet entitled "The Church Federation of Greater Indianapolis: What it is, What it Does," the following tasks were listed for the Research and Planning Unit:

- Studies the factors that make up a complex society;
- Provides information for ministers and denominational leaders concerning the community;
- Gives guidance in placement of new churches or relocation of churches….;
- Is completing an updated Master for suburban church placement in the eight county metropolitan Indianapolis area;
- Is making a detailed study of Center Township to help in urban planning.[21]

In 1968 the Federation published the first of Myers' three-volume study on Center Township. Entitled "Center Township Study: Vol. 1

157

Historical Perspective," the work provided a "historical background of the religious organizational development as well as a more detailed analysis of the present day population and living conditions of Center Township."[22] At the June 1969 meeting of the board of directors, Myers presented a progress report on research on the Master Plan for suburban churches. This long-awaited study was published in the early 1970s under the title "Church Planning Strategy in Marion County, Indiana, Vol. I: The Master Paper and Vol. II: The Master Map." Ironically, both of these studies were completed around the same time as the 1970 unification of city and county governments (known as Unigov) under Republican Mayor Richard Lugar's administration. Neither of Myers' studies foresaw this surprising political development and thus provided little analysis or insight on the implications of this development for church planning strategy.

While these studies by the Church Federation did not foresee political developments like the creation of Unigov, they did accurately predict other religious trends; namely, the increase in the number of non-Protestant residents, especially Catholics and Jews, and the spread of African Americans and lower-income whites to outlining areas of the county. Not all neighborhoods and churches would welcome these new residents, the report concluded. The study also included a chapter entitled "Integration in Churches and Synagogues," co-written by Myers and the Reverend William E. Fox, the Federation's former Director of Special Studies. Based upon their research, these men expressed their skepticism that "integration will become a great overwhelming movement in either the Protestant or Roman Catholic church" and observed that "[t]he factors within the Negro community that run counter to such a trend are too strong in this generation."[23]

The Church Federation's recognition of the growth of the Catholic and Jewish communities in Marion County paved the way for new ecumenical and interfaith partnerships with these faith communities during the 1960s. The Federation had taken note of interfaith concerns raised by Jews and Catholics in 1960. "Many members of the Jewish community appear to be restless at the increasing expression of

Christian ideas and practices in public life," observed Hosie. "Many Catholics are disturbed at the possibility of the injection of religious issues in the coming [U.S. presidential] election." In November of that year, Senator John F. Kennedy of Massachusetts was elected as the nation's first Catholic president.

In 1964 local Catholics and Jews joined the Federation and the Indiana Council of Churches in issuing a "Statement of Religious Leaders on Civil Rights." This statement pledged their mutual support for the passage of a new civil rights bill by the U.S. Senate. Three years later, the Federation joined Project Equality, a national and interdenominational program sponsored by the National Catholic Conference for Interracial Justice. The program was designed to ensure that church hiring and purchasing practices promoted racial equity. The Federation's Board approved the Social Service Unit's recommendation that the Federation work with the Indiana Council of Churches, the Indiana Catholic Conference, the Jewish Community Relations, and member judicatories to implement this concept statewide.[24] The Federation's survey of hiring policies and practices of the businesses with which it contracted yielded limited and mixed results.

Catholic and Jewish representatives also joined the Federation that year in starting H.O.M.E., Inc. (Housing Opportunities Multiplied Ecumenically, Inc.), a faith-based housing initiative. Launched on 13 November 1967 at North Methodist Church, the organization, by the end of its first year, had applied for a Federal Housing Authority (FHA) application for 39 housing units and 85 groups had joined the organization as supporting members.

In response to the wave of riots erupting across the nation after the assassination of Dr. Martin Luther King Jr. on 4 April 1968, this multi-faith coalition of Catholics, Protestants, and Jews hosted a four-day "Community Roundtable for Human Discussion" at the Interchurch Center. The official letter of invitation to selected community leaders included the names of Rabbi Sidney Steiman, Beth-El Zedeck Congregation; Beauford A. Norris, president of Christian Theological Seminary; James P. Galvin, Superintendent,

Catholic Schools; and Robert E. Koenig, Executive Secretary, Church Federation. The city of Indianapolis breathed a sigh of relief that a massive outbreak of violence had been avoided in the city, thanks in great part to the calming intervention of Democratic presidential candidate Robert F. Kennedy. On a campaign visit to Indiana on 4 April, it was Kennedy who announced to an audience of mostly African Americans gathered in a park at 17th and Broadway streets that King had been shot and who proceeded to deliver a moving speech on the need to maintain peace. Just two months later, Kennedy himself was assassinated in California.

There were, however, sporadic clashes between African American protestors and the Indianapolis police. The protestors not only expressed their grief over King's death, but also their simmering frustration with the failure of white society and government to address adequately the problems facing the African American community. This mounting frustration led African American residents to turn to more militant organizations like the Nation of Islam (Black Muslims), the Black Panthers, and the local Black Radical Action Project (BRAP), whose grassroots strategies included self-defense, direct action and confrontation, all of which garnered heightened public concern and police surveillance.

A younger cohort of African American religious leaders also expressed discontent with the perceived moderation and political irrelevancy of the Federation in the Black Freedom Struggle. Leaders like the Reverend James C. Cummings, pastor of Trinity CME Church and a city councilman; Father Boniface Hardin, pastor of Holy Angels Catholic Church; and the Reverend T. Garrott Benjamin, pastor of Second (now Light of the World) Christian Church were just as likely to be influenced by the non-violent philosophy of Martin Luther King Jr. as they were the Black Power rhetoric and theology of Malcolm X, Albert Cleage, and James H. Cone. Their searing analysis of the entrenched racism of white power structure presaged a rupture in the Federation's already tenuous relationship with African American churches. That relationship was further tested in 1969 when African American representatives

160

interrupted local church and synagogue services to deliver copies of the "Black Manifesto," a document castigating white churches and synagogues for their complicity in the enslavement and oppression of African Americans and demanding $500 million in reparations. The "Manifesto," written by James Forman, the former executive secretary of the Student Nonviolent Coordinating Committee (SNCC) in the early 1960s, was first introduced at the 1969 National Black Economic Development Conference in Detroit. On Sunday 4 May 1969 Forman took the "Manifesto" to Riverside Church in New York, across the street from the National Council of Churches' Interchurch Center and Union Theological Seminary, all bastions of mainline Protestant ecumenism. Throughout the summer of 1969 these "visits" took place at churches and synagogues throughout the country, including Indianapolis.

The Church Federation of Greater Indianapolis held a full discussion of the "Manifesto" at its quarterly board meeting that June. After considerable discussion, the Federation adopted an ambiguous statement to be sent to churches in the metropolitan area. It encouraged "churches to receive the visitors in an orderly fashion and in Christian patience." The Federation explained that the "Manifesto" is a "symbol of remaining unmet needs of minority groups in Indianapolis and in the country" and encouraged churches to "give their people opportunity to discuss the problems and needs which it highlights." The statement concluded with various responses from other denominations and church councils. The Federation stressed in its statement that it clearly did not endorse the "Manifesto" or its ideology.[25] While this statement certainly did not bolster the Federation's support among African American churches, it did not deter the Federation from its mission to the inner city.

Executive Secretary Koenig's direct oversight of the Inner City Affairs Unit on the restructured administrative staff assured high visibility and focused attention to this area throughout his tenure. It became the touchstone of the Federation's witness to both to the emerging "secular city" (Harvey Cox) and the "suburban captivity of church" (Winter Gibson). It also was the living matrix through

161

which all of the Federation's units and programs converged. Even the relocation of the Federation's office to the Interchurch Center, located in the Butler-Tarkington neighborhood of the city's northside, was symbolic of this matrix. As more mainline churches moved further away from Center Township, they remained connected to the inner city either through the inner city ministries of the Church Federation or their denominations. The Butler-Tarkington neighborhood, located close to the boundary between inner city and the transitional suburban community, was a neighborhood that had embraced racial integration in housing and education prior to other exclusively white neighborhoods in Marion County. It, along with the Mapleton-Fall Creek neighborhood located south of 38th Street and east of Meridian Street, was the site of several mainline churches that resisted the flight to the suburbs. North Methodist Church, Broadway Methodist, Tabernacle Presbyterian Church, Trinity Episcopal Church, Our Redeemer Lutheran Church, and University Christian Church were among the religious bodies in these transitional neighborhoods committed to urban ministry.

The relocation also placed the Federation closer to Christian Theological Seminary (CTS), a major ecumenical partner and educational and research resource for the Federation. As a mainline, ecumenical seminary affiliated with the Christian Church/Disciples of Christ, the school had been strongly connected with the Federation from the school's establishment in 1958, and even before then when it was a part of the Butler School of Religion. Many of the school's faculty served as Federation board members, associate staff members, and research consultants. Beginning in the mid-1950s, two CTS professors worked as part-time staff for the Federation: Alfred R. Edyvean oversaw the TV and Religious programming, and Franklin E. Rector directed the new research and planning section for the Comity Committee. J. Irwin Miller, the school's prime benefactor and chair of its Board of Trustees, was actively involved in the Federation during the 1960s while serving as president of the NCC and member of the Executive Committee of the WCC.

162

Conclusion

In retrospect, the Church Federation was deeply affected by the whirlwinds of change – social, cultural, political and religious – that the 1960s ushered in. The confidence and consensus it assumed as the religious and moral guardians of Greater Indianapolis were challenged by both secular and religious voices in the public square – Evangelicals, Fundamentalists, Pentecostals, Catholics, Jews, civil rights and Black Power activists, anti-war demonstrators, counter-cultural youth and others – who questioned the authority and relevance of consensus organizations like the Federation. Ensconced in its new offices at the Interchurch Center, an embattled Church Federation revamped its structure and engaged in serious reflection about its role and mission to a metropolitan area undergoing rapid demographic, political, and social change. These changes rendered obsolete many of their ambitious projections for Protestant churches envisioned in their latest Master Plan for the Suburbs and Center Township. Recognizing that the ground was shifting, the Church Federation did not dare to abdicate it mission to Greater Indianapolis, but braced itself to do so more from the margins than from the center.

Endnotes

1   Edwin L. Becker, *From Sovereign to Servant: The Church Federation of Greater Indianapolis, 1912-1987* (Indianapolis: Church Federation of Greater Indianapolis, 1987), 69; 1956 Annual Report of the Church Federation of Greater Indianapolis, Church Federation of Greater Indianapolis Records (henceforth CF), William Henry Smith Memorial Library, Indiana Historical Society.

2   Division of Research and Planning Report, 23 November 1960-24 January 1961, CF, Box 10, Folder 13.

3   David J. Bodenhamer and Robert G. Barrows, eds., *The Encyclopedia of Indianapolis* (Bloomington & Indianapolis: Indiana University Press, 1994), 57.

4   Minutes of the Board of Directors, 3 October 1960 and 5 December 1960, CF, Box 10, File 13.

5   *Indianapolis Star,* 4 March 1960; Becker, 75-76.

6   Executive Secretary's Report, 7 March 1960, CF, Box 10, File 14.

7   Ibid.

8   Minutes of the Board of Directors, 7 March 1960, CF, Box 10, File 14.

9   Minutes of the Board of Directors, 5 June 1961, CF, Box 10, File 14.

10 Ibid.

11 Minutes of the Board of Directors, 20 September 1965, CF.

12 Executive Secretary's Report, 25 April 1961, CF.

13 "Tentative Statement," 23 January 1964, CF.

14 Minutes of the Board of Directors, 4 May 1964, CF.

15 "Study Memoranda," Minutes of the Board of Directors, 4 May 1964, CF.

16 Ibid.

17 "Federal Aid for Urban Renewal and Public Housing," 1961 [?] in Board of Directors Minutes, September-October 1961, Box 10, File 14, CF.

18 Minutes of the Board of Directors, 17 September 1965, CF.

19 "Report from the Social Education and Action Committee" and Minutes of the Executive Board, 1 February 1965, CF.

20 Minutes of the Board of Directors, 1 March 1965, and "Proposed Revised Constitution," 2 March 1965, CF.

21 Minutes of the Board of Directors, 11 December 1967, CF.

22 Richard Myers, "Center Township Study: Vol. ! Historical Perspective," The Church Federation of Greater Indianapolis, 1968, iii.

23 "Church Planning Strategy in Marion County, Indiana, Vol. I: The Master Plan and Vol. II: The Master Map," Church Federation of Greater Indianapolis, 1970s[?], 48-49.

24 Minutes of the Board of Directors, 11 September 1967; "Memo from the Social Service Unit to the Board of Directors of the Church Federation on Equal Opportunities," 6 September 1967.

25 Minutes of the Board of Directors, 9 June 1969, CF; "Memo on the 'Black Manifesto' to the Churches of Metropolitan Indianapolis from the Church Federation Board of Directors," [1969], CF.

1. Marion County Sheriff Chaplain speaking to an inmate

2. Indiana Interchurch Center

3. Executive Director Paul E. McClure

4. Executive Director Robert W. Koenig

1970s

Expanding Christian Unity

Thomas F. Best

THE CHURCH FEDERATION OF GREATER Indianapolis entered the 1970s as one of the oldest church federations in the United States. It enjoyed a generally stable staff structure and was widely recognized as the body best enabling Indianapolis churches to act together on issues of common concern.

But the decade proved to be one of the most tumultuous in the Federation's history. This must be seen against the sense of crisis which swept the nation in 1970. The United States had just landed a man on the moon in 1969, yet the Vietnam War and opposition to it were at fever pitch. Apartheid in South Africa generated violence and international opposition. President Richard M. Nixon proved to be increasingly polarizing. Despite the Civil Rights Act of 1964, progress toward desegregation and better economic opportunity for African Americans was agonizingly slow. Furthermore, a decade of civil unrest in communities around the nation had led to increased despair and tensions with civil authorities, particularly the police.

At the same time, the ecumenical movement was gathering force. Inter-church dialogues advanced. The Consultation on Church Union (COCU) offered hope for a visible and effective church union among the major denominations. The Second Vatican Council transitioned the Catholic Church, which had been insular up to that time, to greater involvement with the wider Church. "Mainline" churches spoke out against racism and injustice. But, there were growing signs of disquiet. The white middle-class base of these churches was giving way to challenging diversity. The churches' stands against racism and the war in Vietnam proved highly divisive, and fundamentalist Christianity was increasingly prominent in the media and public mind.

Indianapolis, the nation's eleventh largest city, along with its churches, exhibited these tensions. The city hosted a major U.S. Army post and defense finance center and, while hardly a center of opposition to the Vietnam War, it had a vocal anti-war movement. Nearly 20 percent of the city's population consisted of minorities, predominantly African Americans, who faced increasing poverty. The city's public school system stood under indictment in a federal court on grounds of racial segregation. In 1970 Indianapolis and Marion County consolidated city and county government (Unigov) as residents and businesses of the central city moved out to the expanding suburbs. Thus, the 1970s proved to be a decade of change and uncertainty.

The Beginning of the Decade

In 1970 the membership of the Church Federation embodied a wide range of Protestant churches, both white and African American, as well as social service and advocacy organizations. The Catholic Church was not yet a member, although personal links had been established with the diocese, priests, and individual parishes. Orthodox Churches also were not members, though valuable contacts were in place. Evangelical and Independent churches were scarcely involved, thereby demonstrating their opposition to ecumenical initiatives.

There were clear guidelines for membership in the Federation. In correspondence with The Most Reverend George J. Biskup, Catholic Archbishop of Indianapolis, Federation Executive Director

Robert Koenig cited three basic qualifications for participation: "Belief in Jesus Christ as Divine Lord and Saviour; Willingness to work with other Christians in common mission; and Some financial contribution each year, amount designated by the church."[1]

The Membership Development Committee discussed whether membership should require "a signed membership covenant" or financial contribution. It agreed that "'tight signed membership' was not a proper goal," rather churches should be free to "give and participate in [the] program according to their ability and interest without being tagged 'member' or 'non-member' churches."[2] This paved the way for involvement by a wide range of groups, such as the Christian Scientists, which had concluded they could not "actively participate," but wanted to "lend every support possible to the work being done;" they backed this by a contribution of $100.[3]

The Federation's board of directors had a tradition of broad representation. Dr. F. Benjamin Davis, an African-American pastor at New Bethel Baptist Church, concluded his three-year term as president in 1970. Davis was the first president from a non-Federation-founding denomination and the second African American to hold the position. Two years later, Shirley A. (Mrs. Beauford) Norris, a member of Northwood Christian Church (Disciples of Christ), was elected the first woman president of the Church Federation.

The board met at least annually, with an executive committee meeting at least monthly to make substantive decisions. The Denominational Concerns Commission (DCC), which met monthly, kept the Church Federation in direct contact with its member denominations.

These also were the days within the new programmatic structure introduced in 1969 when the cumbersome eight Program Units had been collapsed into four. The goals of the Units, each assigned to a senior Federation staff member, were sharply focused as Urban Affairs (social witness issues), Special Ministries (chaplaincies and social service programs), Research and Planning (mission strategy and church planting), and Communication (witness, especially through broadcast media). The Federation presented its life and

169

work widely through such events as the "Get Acquainted with Your Church Federation" breakfast and information session on 30 September 1970.[4]

At the start of the decade, the Reverend Robert W. Koenig, a United Methodist minister, was two-thirds of the way through what was to be a six-year term (1966-1972) as Executive Director. Committed to reconciliation, he made clear his intention to continue the Federation's engagement in social issues. He noted, "I can see no other approach than to be concerned with these 'sticky affairs'"[5] and personally assumed management of the Urban Affairs unit. Other senior staff included layperson Paul E. McClure, responsible for Special Ministries; Richard A. Myers, Research and Planning; and the Reverend Thomas Stratton, Communication. Cassius Fenton handled the Federation's finances, soon to be replaced by Donald Trout in 1971. Many office staff provided long and faithful service to the Church Federation, including Marilyn Wilkes as office manager. Students from nearby Christian Theological Seminary were assigned part-time programmatic work.

The Research and Planning Unit was dissolved in June 1970 in a spirit of growing denominationalism. This ended a long collaboration with denominations in "comity" agreements that avoided competition in planting new congregations. The following year, however, saw the establishment of the Congregational Concerns Unit (CCU), which renewed efforts to address needs among Federation members. The Church Federation also emphasized its grassroots and lay base, noting "The Federation is people — people, lay and clergy, who make up the life of the churches in Indianapolis." This led to calls for nominations to two groups: an "Advisory Council" of 52 persons, reflecting the "day by day activity of the local church"; and a "President's Council" of 42 "laypersons giving strong leadership at Community level."[6] Both were official groups of the Federation. The first sought to increase lay activity in the Church Federation at both the congregational and denominational levels; the second sought to involve Christian "community leaders" in its work. The goal of both groups was to promote the Federation's work in congregations and the community, and to help the Church Federation listen to congregational and community concerns.

The Federation experienced a significant increase in membership in 1972. Catholic parishes were allowed and indeed encouraged by Father Richard F. Terrill, ecumenical liaison for the Archdiocese of Indianapolis, to join the Church Federation. As a result, the Federation invited the Archbishop to nominate a representative to the Denominational Concerns Committee, this being "not a legislative body."[7] The first parish to join the Federation was St. Thomas Aquinas on the city's northside. The improved relationship with the Catholic Church also was recognized by the election of Father Joseph Dooley to the Federation's board of directors.[8]

At the end of 1972 the board of directors adopted a long-range planning committee report. It foresaw "a process of reformation and risk which is designed to bring new life to the federation." Principal goals included increasing participation by "blacks, increasing Roman Catholic involvement and insuring the growing working relationship with the Jewish community." Executive Director Koenig expressed his hope to include "some of the more evangelical groups in the community." With piercing candor, the report noted:

The federation is viewed with mixed feelings. It is a good thing when it can help us, a problem when it competes in program areas, a difficulty when it needs money, an embarrassment when it takes a public stand when we would rather it not do so, a time demand that often conflicts with other interests.[9]

Nevertheless the Church Federation continued to seek wider involvement in its life and work. A press release for the Federation's annual meeting dated 9 May 9 1974 noted that the organization's new structure "will mean more involvement from the local church - the man in the pew" and "greater communication between the Federation and the local church."[10]

Engagement Locally, Nationally, and Internationally

The Church Federation was deeply involved in social witness locally. It organized a Consultation on Community Organization on 31 October 1970, and enabled the formation of neighborhood organizations such as the North West Community Organization (NWCO), the United South Side Community Organization (USSCO), and the Near East Side Community Organization (NESCO). It organized a Hunger Project and sponsored a conference on hunger, malnutrition, and poverty in the fall of 1970. Federation representatives also appeared before the Township Trustee, the State Tax Review Board, and the Indiana Tax Commission to advocate on behalf of food stamp programs and better school lunch programs.[11]

The Denominational Concerns Commission (DCC) was active in its own right, addressing several contemporary issues. In 1973 Indianapolis Motor Speedway officials decided to move the world famous Indianapolis 500 race to Sunday. The Federation voiced its opposition to this change, arguing that it made worship attendance impossible for those living near the track. Racetrack authorities countered and the courts later rejected these arguments.[12] Two years later, another controversy arose over church signage, which city officials unexplainably interpreted as "advertising," prohibited them, and issued citations for several congregations. The Federation again voiced its opposition and asked the city "to cease all citation and prosecution of churches for their use of signs."[13] Another significant program ended in 1974 when the Church Federation cut its long-standing support for Weekday Religious Education. The program allowed release time from public schools for religious education and which as late as 1968 had received $84,000 in support from local congregations. But, declining interest, an outdated curriculum, and lack of financial support led to its ultimate demise.[14]

During the 1970s, the Church Federation began to stretch its theological boundaries. On the "evangelical" side, it "served as a conduit" for a Lilly Endowment grant to support the Bill Glass

Crusade in 1970 and endorsed "Key'73," a cooperative evangelism project to unite adherents of many religions, by providing staff assistance.[15] On the "religious tolerance" side, the Church Federation endorsed the "Faith for a City" concert, a "festival of faith" held on the 150th anniversary of the city of Indianapolis on 26 September 1971, to express general human aspirations rather than any Judeo-Christian content. In the emerging and controversial realm of personal ethics, the Federation sponsored a Clergy Workshop in 1972 on the issue of abortion.

Nationally, the Church Federation drew attention to sensitive contemporary issues. For example, it participated in a worship service at Christ Church Cathedral on 4 July 1971, in which Protestants, Catholics, and Jews gathered to pray for an end to the Vietnam War. The Federation earned criticism for its "liberalism" when it invited Cynthia Wedel, President of the National Council of Churches of Christ in the USA (NCCCUSA), to speak on 13 April 1972 at the Federation's 60th anniversary meeting.[16] The Federation demonstrated its support for ecumenism by sending Paul McClure to the National Workshop on Christian Unity (19-22 March 1972)[17] and President Beauford A. Norris and Executive Director Robert W. Koenig to the NCCCUSA meeting in Dallas.[18] The Federation board also approved an Urban Affairs Unit resolution endorsing the Equal Rights Amendment to the U.S. Constitution, another action that brought criticism upon the organization.[19]

The Church Federation also believed in internationalism, or political and economic cooperation among nations. It promoted the World Day of Prayer in March 1970;[20] supported the Halloween "Trick or Treat for UNICEF" campaign, despite some local opposition to the United Nations;[21] supported the Multipurpose International Center for Indianapolis;[22] backed the "Decision 1974 Program on World Affairs" sponsored by the Indianapolis Council on World Affairs;[23] and supported the Church World Service clothing appeal.[24] The Federation promoted an "ecumenical eucharist" on 30 September 1975 in preparation for World-Wide Communion Sunday on 5 October.[25] Its Congregational Concerns

Unit organized the annual Week of Prayer for Christian Unity celebration together with Catholic and Orthodox representatives, using texts produced by the Faith and Order Commission of the World Council of Churches (WCC) and the Catholic Secretariat for Promoting Christian Unity. But, disappointingly, the Federation did not respond publicly to the 1971 *Reader's Digest* attacks upon the World Council of Churches.[26]

This survey of activities demonstrates that the Church Federation's agenda reflected a "Life and Work" understanding of ecumenism. This was typical of many, though not all, church councils at the time. With so much practical cooperative work to be done, they asked why they should spend energy on "divisive" "Faith and Order" issues such as baptismal recognition and the eucharist. The Church Federation was content to leave such matters to the Indiana Council of Churches' Faith and Order Department.[27]

Leadership Changes

February of 1973 witnessed a significant leadership change at the Church Federation. After serving six years as executive director, Robert W. Koenig retired to become minister at the Roberts Park United Methodist Church. Staff member Paul E. McClure, a Methodist layman, assumed the directorate. McClure was the son of a Methodist minister and veteran of World War II and the Korean War. A graduate of Purdue University, he taught Vocational Education for eight years in Gary, Indiana, and then began graduate studies in New Jersey when, in 1959, North Methodist Church called him to serve as the congregation's director of education. In 1966 McClure joined the Federation staff to oversee the Social Service and Education programs.

There were other staff changes that occurred in 1973. The Reverend Fred H. Erickson, a Disciples minister, replaced Thomas Stratton as head of Communications. Erikson served until October 1978 and was then replaced by the Reverend Richard E. Davies, a Methodist. Dr. Alfred R. Edyvean, a leading figure in Christian communications at Christian Theological Seminary, remained a valuable advisor throughout the decade. Further changes saw the Reverend Donald Carpenter hired part-time in 1974 and full-time in 1977, to lead the Urban Affairs and Special Ministries units. In the area of finance, Donald Trout departed in May 1971 and several staff, working from 1975 with Cassius Fenton, ensured continuity.

Finances

The Church Federation struggled continually to balance vision, costs of programs, promised income from member churches, and actual contributions. Entering 1970 the Federation had a deficit of $44,618. During that year 142 congregations representing thirteen denominations contributed $41,854.74.[28] Debt was reduced in 1971 by almost $13,000, with an additional gift of $10,000 from the Lilly Endowment. Knowing that a tough financial road lay ahead, the Executive Committee, upon receiving the news, noted that "Moderately restrained jubilation ensued." Under Treasurer Rickard Blankenbaker, the deficit was reduced through 1972 to some $12,000.[29] Working with Charles Williams of the Lilly Endowment, McClure reduced the Federation's debt to $3,533 at the beginning of 1974. Still, as from the early years, finances remained a pressing concern for the Federation.

A Review of Programs

The Spring 1973 issue of *The Forecast*, the Federation's newsletter, offered a survey of the Church Federation's activities in the early years of the decade. From this list, one can easily see the diverse concerns of the organization:

- "Congregations and the Church Federation" — Alcohol & Drug Problems; Apartment Houses; Celebration [the "Faith for a City" program]; Christian Unity; Church Education; Day Camping; New Families; Financial Records; Fire Alarms; Key 73; Orientation for New Pastors; Public Relations; Religion & Public Education.
- "Community Institutions and the Church Federation" — Abortion; Campus Ministry; Counselling; Courts; Fire

Department: Hospitals; Law Enforcement; Mental Health; Older Adults; Scout Camps; Unwed Mothers.
- "The City, The Region and the Church Federation" — Child Care; Criminal Justice; Community Organization; Employment; Housing; Medical Services, Public Education; Public Transportation; Social Justice; Social Worker and Minister Groups; Welfare.
- "Communications and the Church Federation" — Television; Radio; Inter-church Information Service; Public Service Announcements.
- "Youth and the Church Federation" — Young World Development; Youth Communications Workshop.[30]

This "snapshot" of the Federation in all its diversity offers a context for understanding key developments throughout the decade. While its strength remained in its core local programs, issues of leadership, membership, and finance also proved to be crucial.

Chaplaincy

Under Paul McClure's leadership of Special Ministries, and then as Executive Director, the Church Federation provided a chaplaincy service to public safety institutions. On 7 January 1970 the Reverends Cauthen T. Boyd and Wilbur Harvey were installed as chaplains for the Indianapolis Police Department. Under the headline "Pastors to the Police," the *Forecast* of September 1970 emphasized cooperation with Catholic chaplain Father Laurence Lynch and Reverend Harrison C. Neal, then Chaplain to the Sheriff's Department and County Jail;[31] the Federation's Personnel Committee even asked the Lilly Endowment to divide its program support between the Federation and the Catholic Archdiocese. A Special Task Force noted that "the Indianapolis Police Department and the Church Federation of Greater Indianapolis have embarked on a unique, exciting and rewarding program with the creation of the first full time Police Chaplaincy Program in the United States," stressing both its cooperation with local officials and its support by the Lilly Endowment.

The Reverend Gerald E. Roberts, Sr. replaced Rev. Harvey on his retirement, and Robert Medcalf continued his service as chaplain to the Indianapolis Fire Department. With the support of the Lilly Endowment, Rev. Harrison served as chaplain in the Sheriff's Office; the Reverend Stanley Moneymaker served as County Jail chaplain from 1971, and was later replaced by the Reverend Urias Beverly. The Reverend Benjamin Friend continued as chaplain at the Juvenile Center and was joined part-time by the Reverend Joshua Cutler in 1970; in 1971 the Reverend Frank Carlson took over the work. This was augmented in June, 1976 by a part-time program at Juvenile Court provided by the Reverend Sterling L. Williams, who was succeeded by the Reverend Richard Gray and the Reverend Gloria Tate. From 1970 Stacy Shields became part-time chaplain at General Hospital.[32]

Investigative reporting in the *Indianapolis Star* in 1973 and 1974 impacted the Federation's chaplaincy program. Reporters Richard C. Cady and Harly Bierce reported on corruption within the Indianapolis Police Department, for which they received the Pulitzer Prize in Journalism. The *Star* asked the Federation to provide "moral leadership" in the community so that the investigative findings would not be ignored. Minutes of the Federation's Special Ministries Committee of March 1974 noted the resignation of Police Chief Winston Churchill, Deputy Chief Donald Schadel, and Safety Director William Leak. Police Chaplain Harvey reported bluntly that these resignations would not "clean up the department [and] that as long as the department is controlled by political considerations we will have the kind of situation as exists with the release of these men." Nevertheless, the Federation thanked Chief Winston Churchill for his support of the chaplaincy program, and asked J. Ralph Beatty "to appoint a panel to study the Criminal Justice System in Metro-Indianapolis."[33] During a press conference held by the Denominational Concern Committee, 29 religious leaders issued a "call to action" for a special prosecutor to review the case.

The committee met with James Kelley, Prosecutor-Elect for Marion County, to discuss criminal justice issues, including the "narrow representation" on the grand jury, which was predominantly white. Between 1974 and 1976 the committee interceded between the police and Prosecutor's office, meeting with Police Chief Kenneth Hale and Deputy Prosecutor Leroy New.[34] Committee minutes for 9 December 1976 noted Police Chaplain Cauthen T. Boyd introducing Chief of Police Eugene Gallagher, followed by a "frank discussion" of corruption, the recent probe, and friction between himself and Prosecutor James Kelley. A major goal of the Federation was to increase the African American presence in the police department in hopes of reducing tensions within the community.

These controversies did not deter the Church Federation's work. Executive Director McClure reported in 1976 that it pursued "a very substantial chaplaincy program which includes full time chaplains in the Marion County Jail, Indianapolis Police Department, the Marion County Juvenile Court and Center and 3/4 time chaplain in Wishard Memorial Hospital and a part time chaplain in the Fire Department."

Special Ministries continued to press its concerns over community issues. At a meeting chaired by the Reverend Harry Huxhold of Our Redeemer Lutheran Church, discussions covered the Victim Assistance program, alcoholism among "supervisory personnel," conditions in the Juvenile Center, provisions for a chaplaincy at Wishard Memorial Hospital, and provisions for Bible study in the Marion County Jail. Chief of Police Gene Gallagher "expressed appreciation for the work of the Chaplains and the presence of this [Church Federation] Unit at the Police Department." He addressed the "high divorce rate among police officers," noting that "the chaplains are trying to help deal with this problem." In 1978 Special Ministries sought to reconcile the Victim Assistance Program and the Public Action in Correctional Effort (P.A.C.E.) program, aimed at helping ex-offenders.

On another front, the Denominational Concerns Committee established a campus ministry program in 1971-1972, which involved the Lutheran Church of America, Catholic, Methodist, and Episcopal pastors. Under Federation auspices, the program was supported by the Disciples, Episcopal, Lutheran Church in America, Catholic,

Southern Baptist, United Church of Christ, United Methodist Church, and United Presbyterian judicatories. Incorporated in 1973 and governed by its own board, the Metropolitan Indianapolis Campus Ministry (MICM) was present on a wide range of campuses from state universities to technical schools, and was related to the Indiana Commission on United Ministries in Higher Education (IUMHE). MICM featured the work of the Reverend Dan Motto (Indiana University Purdue University Indianapolis) from 1974 and the Reverend Mike Jacobs (Butler University) from 1976.[35]

Social Service

Social services were another core program area of the Church Federation. In some cases the Federation initiated programs, then transferred them to other agencies. The Housing Opportunities Multiplied Ecumenically, Inc. (H.O.M.E.) program, for example, was established in 1967 with some 35 congregations to coordinate churches' efforts to provide affordable housing. George Mailoy, acting director of H.O.M.E., suggested in December 1971 that the program merge with the existing local group, Community Interfaith Housing. Despite tensions among community groups, the merger was concluded in order to streamline operations and unite the strengths of the two organizations. Community Interfaith Housing program, as it was known, immediately faced financial problems, but overcame them through a grant from the Lilly Endowment.

In other cases, the Church Federation joined with existing organizations in order to promote issues of common concern and avoid duplicating administrative energy and fundraising efforts. One example was the Federation's support of the Coalition for Adequate Transportation (CAT), a local organization promoting public transportation in Indianapolis to ensure that disadvantaged persons had access to work opportunities. McClure testified before the State Board of Tax Commissioners in 1974 on CAT's behalf. In 1970 the Federation had partnered with the Lilly Endowment in setting up a "Contingency Fund" to be used for inter-church project aiding persons in need. The Federation also served as a conduit to bring funds from the Lilly Endowment to institutions such as Happy House, a "half-way house" located near the Juvenile Center.

Other programs remained solely Church Federation ventures. One major undertaking in 1975 was the Emergency Food Project, directed by the Reverend James Bradley and funded initially by an anonymous grant of $100,000. The Denominational Concerns Committee reported in May 1975 that the program had served 16,000 persons, or 3,500 families, with $75,000 worth of food, working through various social service pantries. The Federation made direct cash distributions to purchase food and fuel, and also testified before the Indiana General Assembly in 1977 on behalf of "Poor Relief" reform. Toward the end of the decade, the Federation, through staff member Lois Meyer, serviced the Central Indiana Council on Aging in efforts to coordinate services for the elderly.

But social service ministry, central to the Church Federation's identity during the 1970s, proved to be a perilous undertaking, as exemplified by the acquisition of the Metro Urban Center. In 1977 the Whitewater Valley Presbytery offered to deed the historic former First Presbyterian Church, located at 16th and Delaware streets, to the Church Federation. After the congregation moved and merged with Meridian Heights Presbyterian Church at 4701 Central Avenue, the building became the Metro Urban Center, housing a range of social service agencies and two congregations. The Presbytery offered to deed the Center to the Federation and supply $70,000 a year for five years to operate the facility. Following a tour by its executive committee and the completion of a feasibility study, the Church Federation agreed in 1978 to receive and operate the Center as a "Christian multi-purpose human development agency," concerned mainly with poverty, youth, senior citizens, the handicapped, and those with special needs.[36] The Center opened under the direction of Sister Antoinette Ressino and soon re-absorbed programs such as a food pantry, which had been transferred to the Community Service Council.

Despite support of $70,000 per year for five years promised by the Presbytery, the Church Federation's commitment to cover maintenance and program costs proved to be a heavy burden. This

180

produced tensions between the Center and the Federation, and intensified problems in keeping the Center's finances distinct from those of the Federation. Ominously, the Federation's Annual Meeting of 26 April 1979 cited the need to increase Metro Center funding "outside" the usual church and denominational sources. Much of the burden fell on attorney David Rees, chair of the Metropolitan Center Commission, which had been established to "determine policies, employ and dismiss staff."[37] Within the year, the Center was mortgaged in order to meet financial obligations for operations. The Metro Center continued as the Federation's most challenging issue into the 1980s.

Yet another undertaking by the Church Federation was the Program for Independent Living (PFIL). Led by Carol Roberson and accepted by the Board of Directors on 10 December 1979, PFIL was an "exciting opportunity for expanded ministry to the aging by the churches of Indianapolis." The Federation considered this to be "a major project, and accepting responsibility for it required some restructuring of the Federation's social service and financial organization," which resulted in the creation of a Structure Committee chaired by Father Stephen Wallsteadt of Christ the Savior Orthodox Church. PFIL stood "on an equal status" with the Metro Center and the other units of the Federation.[38]

Desegregation and Race Relations

Throughout the decade, no issue occupied the Church Federation so intensely as that of public school desegregation. Federation historian Edwin L. Becker, writing in his 75th anniversary history, noted that this issue "hung like a cloud over the city for more than a decade."[39] The underlying issue was systemic racism in the city of Indianapolis. The "presenting issue" was the policy of busing in order to give students from disadvantaged areas access to a better education. This brought white and African American communities into unaccustomed contact, which for many whites threatened the character of "their" local schools. As a long-time primary actor in race relations and justice matters, the Church Federation

181

supported busing in its initial stage in 1973, noting that it gave all students "the opportunity to attend school with others of different backgrounds - racial, religious and economic."[40] The practice proved to be highly divisive. As minutes from the Congregational Concerns Unit meeting of 19 November 1973 noted, "Paul McClure reported that some ministers have received very negative reactions from their parishioners, resulting in cut off of funds, and decreased [church] attendance." McClure, along with the Urban Affairs Unit chair Virginia Blankenbaker, bore the brunt of the criticism, though supported the Coalition for Integrated Education, a city-wide pro-equal opportunity organization, and organized meetings between school principals and religious leaders in the affected areas.

Responding to the next wave of busing in 1976, the Church Federation held meetings with pastors and convened a "Concerned Clergy Conference" with Christian leaders and prominent Jewish Rabbi Murray Saltzman who spoke on behalf of integration and tolerance. Under the headline "A Christian Approach to School Transfer is Suggested," the Federation issued an open letter from Larry S. Osmon, Chair of Urban Affairs, to the city's clergy. This is striking in its combination of Christian principles and practical suggestions:

....it is our hope that clergymen will demonstrate leadership in this matter, co-operating and covenanting together to act as "ministers of reconciliation." Your personal position on this controversial ruling is not the issue here. Whether you are for or against bussing to achieve school desegregation, as clergymen let us express our approval or disapproval in peaceful ways and encourage our parishioners to do the same, taking every preventive measure to assure our children that they will receive an education without injury or risk. Peacemaking is our responsibility.[41]

Following the citation of Paul's "love passage" in I Corinthians 13, the letter concluded with some suggestions on what clergymen could do to promote peace in schools and neighborhoods:

- Be present at school on days when tension would seem to be high.
- Ride on buses with the children.
- Open churches for dialogue forums and meetings.
- Ask church school classes, committees, groups and boards to become concerned.
- Find the facts of the situations and help counter rumors.
- Continue to prepare parishioners for living in an integrated society. "How blest are the peacemakers; God shall call him his sons."[42]

Appropriately, the Church Federation published this "call for peace" together with an announcement about a forthcoming talk for clergy by The Very Reverend Samuel Bennett Crocks, Dean of Belfast, on efforts to end violence between Protestants and Catholics in Northern Ireland.

By the end of the decade the Indianapolis Public Schools had not made sufficient progress in desegregation. But, another crisis loomed in spring 1979 when U.S. District Court Judge S. Hugh Dillin ordered desegregation measures for ten other public school districts in the Greater Indianapolis area. Again, the Federation took decisive action, with President Dr. James R. Bradley calling for denominational leaders, together with one clergy and layperson, to meet on 8 May 1979 to form a planning committee, which "will be able to help achieve peaceful school desegregation."[43]

Minutes from the Church Federation's Steering Committee on School Desegregation (SCSD) meetings of 5 and 11 April 1979, cited experiences of other cities, particularly Boston and Louisville, and affirmed "church pairings" in affected areas as an effective Christian response. The committee also noted the need "to add Jewish and Orthodox leaders" to the group. Significantly, Federation president Bradley and director McClure, along with Father Francis Tuohy, administrator of the Catholic Archdiocese of Indianapolis, had "been asked by community leadership to be participants in plans for peaceful desegregation, and to represent churches in this effort."[44]

Over the summer McClure met with pastors in affected communities. A Federation Goals Committee, chaired by Father Larry Voelker, director of Catholic Charities in the Indianapolis Archdiocese and archdiocesan coordinator of the Indiana Catholic Conference, identified six goals for the process:

1. Those promoting peaceful desegregation should receive all the support they need;
2. Information about the situation would be provided continuously;
3. Informational and planning meetings would be held with clergy and congregations;
4. Partnerships among clergy, congregations, and schools would be formed;
5. The committee would host community forums;
6. The committee would ensure the involvement of black parents "in distant schools to which their children are bussed."[45]

On 7 August 1979 Judge Dillin granted a Stay, thus giving school districts the chance to develop their own desegregation plans. In "Churches and School Desegregation: A Personal Report," the Reverend Richard Davies, director of the Federation's Communications Unit, recounted the process, including discussions with the U.S. Justice Department, and noted the sense of loss after investing enormous energy in preparing for a crisis which had not occurred. Casting this as a preparation for the next round of desegregation measures, Davies noted that "without the sometimes routine work the Church Federation does... the churches would not have played the vital role they played in helping the cause of peace and people in our latest desegregation case."[46]

In the midst of this turmoil, Indianapolis Public School teachers held a strike in fall 1979. Once again, the Federation sought reconciliation among the parties involved. A committee of 19 pastors, chaired by the Reverend Dr. Richard Hamilton of North United Methodist Church, called together representatives of the parties involved, including members of the school board and teachers' union officials. Six from the meeting met with the school board, the superintendent, and their negotiators, and then with leaders of the teachers' union and their negotiators.[47] Dr. F. Benjamin Davis, Rev. James Bradley, and Margaret S. Robbins, past and current Federation presidents, met with parents and pastors in the affected areas. This issue of desegregation also remained a preoccupation of the Church Federation well into the next decade.

Communications

Through its quiet competence the Federation's Communications Unit remained a success story with statewide reach. Indeed, it was the "unsung hero" of the decade. The unit sponsored network programs. But, as early as 1973, the Reverend Thomas Stratton, a Disciples minister, sought to harness the newly-developing medium of cable television for the churches' witness. A 1973 review noted no fewer than five Saturday television programs, six on Sundays, four daily and one on Monday; six Sunday radio programs as well as three "news programs." The Church Federation also sponsored three Sunday programs produced by the Communications Commission of the NCCCUSA.[48] The popular program *Time for Timothy* continued through the decade, at which point it had been broadcast continuously for more than twenty years – an extraordinary record in the media world at the time. Sponsored programs included *A Lamp Unto My Feet* on CBS, and the imaginative *Marshall Efron's Illustrated, Simplified and Painless Sunday School*. Other approaches included Youth Communication Workshops in the summers through 1972. But, changes were underway. The 1970 budget was approximately $42,000 and denominational contributions were falling, reaching $35,632 in 1972, and continuing to drop through the decade.

Ongoing Programs

Other programs of the Church Federation continued apace. In 1977 the Congregational Concerns Unit noted its continuing work on problems such as the church signs issue, church bus safety ordinances, hospital clergy liaison, the Week of Prayer program, a training program for church bookkeepers, and the "Indy 500" race issue, as well as a range of community concerns.[49] It fell to the Congregational Concerns Unit to deal with the 1978 demise of the Indianapolis Ministerial Association, the group responsible for the creation of the Church Federation in 1912. In response, the Federation sought to link the various ministers' organizations in the city, including regional groupings of ministers and the predominantly African-American Interdenominational Ministerial Alliance.

Church Unity and Interfaith Concerns

The Church Federation combined local unity efforts with national ecumenical concerns. They invited Cynthia Wedel back to Indianapolis, this time to preach in the service for the Week of Prayer for Christian Unity on 23 January 1977. Wedel was noted as a World Council of Churches President and former first woman president of the NCCCUSA.[50]

Through this period, "interfaith" concerns meant mainly continuing valuable connections with the Jewish community, including involvement of Jewish leaders in some program units. But, two key issues arose. The first, in 1975 and 1977, involved proselytizing at Christmas and the public display of Christmas decorations. The Church Federation's balanced response supported Christmas observances as private expressions of religious belief, but rejected the use of public funds to support them. The second, in 1978, was the proposed publication of the *Christian Yellow Pages*, promoting Christian businesses at the expense of others. Here, the Federation's response was unequivocal. Its statement claimed that the "Buy Christian" campaign was a distortion of the Christian life; that it divided Christians, harmed inter-faith relationships, and destroyed community feeling; and that it haunted "Jewish friends" in particular. It was the latter point where the Federation referred explicitly to Hitler's "buy Christian" campaign of the 1930s. The Federation's suggestions included:

- Churches should not distribute the *Christian Yellow Pages*.
- Christian business and professional people should not buy advertising in the *Christian Yellow Pages*.
- Do not let the *Christian Yellow Pages* dictate where to shop.
- The *Christian Yellow Pages* should not list a church without official approval, "lest such an appearance be considered an endorsement."[51]

More quietly, but equally significantly, the Federation continued to nurture Christian-Jewish relations, for example, by participating in a Seder on 2 April 1978 at the Indianapolis Hebrew Congregation.

The Church Federation also helped spawn the Interfaith Education Conference (IEC). According to a proposal made to the Lilly Endowment this

grew out of informal conversations, and then a meeting 17 March 1977 at the Indianapolis Hebrew Congregation including Paul McClure, Rabbi Murray Saltzmann, then Rabbi of the Indianapolis Hebrew Congregation, and several religious educators who were concerned by an apparent deterioration of Interfaith understanding, cooperation and goodwill in Indianapolis.[52]

Executive Director McClure became a member of the IEC, and the Federation continued to promote its work into the 1980s.

Membership and Participation

Catholic parishes continued to join the Church Federation throughout the decade. Their motives are exemplified by St. Lawrence Catholic Church in 1976, when the Reverend Joseph V. Beechem wrote, "Our hope in joining your organization is to further the interest of the growing ecumenical movement within our great city."[53] Significantly, Catholic Social Services joined the Federation in 1979. This echoed the Catholic pattern throughout the 1970s of not joining as a denomination – the main barriers being questions of proportional representation and fear of being associated with public statements not reflecting its own position – but, allowing individual parishes and programs to join ecumenical bodies.

The Membership Development Committee (MDC) continued to pursue churches which, whether formal members or not, had not made a contribution to the Federation. They specifically mentioned the "Eastern Orthodox Churches in town" and resolved to meet with their representatives.[54] Long contacts bore fruit in 1978 when "all Eastern Orthodox Churches became affiliated with the Church Federation," and Father Stephen Wallsteadt became a member of the Board of Directors.[55]

The Church Federation continued to attract new members, not the least from more conservative, Evangelical, Pentecostal, and Independent churches. The Board of Directors accepted the First Southern Baptist Church of Mooresville into membership in December 1978. Minutes of the Membership Development Committee of February 1979 indicated that Federation membership had been augmented by three National Baptist churches, a Southern Baptist church, Christ the Savior Orthodox Church, and the Faith Church of God in Christ. In the fall, the committee recommended the application of the Church of the Holy Spirit, which was accepted unanimously at the Board meeting in December 1979, noting, "the Committee was impressed with the diversity and vision of the ministry of this congregation."[56]

The most controversial case during the decade, however, was the membership inquiry by the predominantly gay and lesbian Metropolitan Community Church. The Church Federation rejected its membership application in March 1977.[57] Ironically, later in October 1977, the Federation defended the civil rights of the gay and lesbian community by opposing the "Rally for Decency" organized by singer and critic of homosexuality Anita Bryant.[58]

Other, less familiar groups showed interest in joining the Federation but also were not accepted as members. These included the Universal Spiritual Kingdom of God, Inc.; Buggs Temple Church of God in Christ , James C. Buggs, pastor; and the Universal Church of Trust of the First Born, Rev. Ruth Beck, pastor. Minutes of the

Federation's Special Ministries Unit for 14 June 1977 reflect a discussion of Reverend Sun Myung Moon's World Unification Church as well as wider concerns about cults. In fact, the Federation received – and rejected – a formal "Moonies" membership application in 1984. As a result of the rise of these new churches and the expansion of cults in the U.S., the Federation received numerous requests for information regarding these religious groups, particularly following the mass suicide of Peoples Temple members at Jonestown, Guyana, in November 1978.[59]

Beyond congregational and denominational membership, volunteer engagement was an important measure of the Federation's support. A survey of "volunteers and service hours given in the work of the Church Federation in 1978" revealed 844 persons serving the Congregational Concerns, Communications, Special Ministries, and Urban Affairs units, the Metropolitan Center, Healing Community, Contingency Fund and Project on Aging programs, with a total of 21,891 hours volunteer time dedicated. This did not include volunteer contributions from the Interfaith Educational Conference, police-community project and others.[60]

A New Constitution, Renewed Identity, and Membership

In 1979 the Church Federation adopted a new constitution. It restated the Federation's identity, goals, and geographical extent and offered "a basis for a co-operative effort among the churches of Christ of Greater Indianapolis" [to provide] "an organization…to manifest the oneness in Jesus Christ as Divine Lord and Savior, and through it increase the understanding and acceptance of his Lordship." Article II defined the organization's objective:

To provide opportunity for the expression of the unity we already recognize as existing and through discussion seek further comprehension of our faith as it relates to our common life and to work together to further the mission of the church by: 1. Fostering a sense of oneness in advancing the cause of Jesus Christ as the Divine

189

Lord and Savior; and 2. Witnessing to the principle of brotherhood in Jesus Christ.

Member churches were exhorted anew "to carry their proportionate share...of the Federation budget." They "shall be required to contribute annually no less than the "Basic Core" cost of servicing member churches..." In addition, the Federation cast its net wider by defining "Greater Indianapolis" as including the surrounding counties of Boone, Hamilton, Hancock, Hendricks, Johnson, and Shelby. Membership now covered three categories:

- "Any group organized as a local church and located in Greater Indianapolis...";
- "Any denomination...";
- "Individuals from the metropolitan community..."

All members had to accept the Preamble and Objective, as well as commit to annual financial support. Organizational charts used for the board of directors' orientation session in September 1979 revealed the ongoing effort to balance denominational judicatories and congregations. Standing committees included Nominations, Finance, Membership Development, Personnel, and the Metropolitan Urban Center. Program units included Communications, Congregational Concerns, Urban Affairs and Special Ministries.[61] At the end of the 1970s, the Federation's board of directors included 69 members plus 12 *ex officios*, embracing some 34 denominations. Membership included "mainline" Protestant denominations – Presbyterian, Methodist, Lutherans, Christian Church/Disciples of Christ, Episcopalians, various types of Baptists, and Friends—, Catholic parishes, Eastern Orthodox churches, the Salvation Army, affiliates of the Church of God in North America, Church of the Living God, and other Pentecostal and Independent bodies. Organizations such as Church Women United and the Interdenominational Ministers Alliance also were affiliated.

Programs and Commitments

The annual report of 1979 activities, released at the annual meeting on 1 May 1980, with no fewer than 700 persons present, offered a "snapshot" of the Federation's priorities at the end of the decade. One presentation emphasized the "Real need for a Church Federation" as shown by the "two school crises" of fall 1979, namely the impending desegregation orders and the teachers' strike. The Federation had performed a crucial "ministry of reconciliation," laying the issues out clearly for the first time in public forums and the media. Other activities included new chaplaincy services at Marion County Home, pastors' workshops on funerals, a Week of Prayer for Christian Unity, an employment program, a renewed food pantry network, the developing program at the Metro Urban Center, accepting responsibility for the Program for Independent Living, chaplaincy to five major institutions, the production of seven regularly broadcast television programs, providing child care for 113 children, and supporting a thrift shop serving 1,700 clients. All demonstrations of faith in action in the city.

The Executive Director's *Report* to the board in December 1979 also demonstrated the extent of the Church Federation's reach. McClure reported that he had been involved in no less than 73 "working and planning meetings where he had some responsibility" just in the previous month alone. Of those, 41 were programmatic and administrative meetings of the Federation, six were related to campus ministry programs, ten to "problem areas for public education," and 16 to "other common projects."[62] All in all, the Federation had significant impact on the city and its residents.

Another important effort to establish new links to evangelicals came with the Federation's support of the Billy Graham Crusade planned for Indianapolis in 1980. Anchoring this to the Federation's core involvements, the board of directors heard that "There is a growing realization among evangelical people of the need to develop a social consciousness...that more is called for from the evangelical as regards to the needs of the poor and oppressed."[63]

Finance

The Lilly Endowment's support remained crucial throughout the decade. In 1977 the Endowment provided $50,000 to support a Federation development plan.

The Financial Report given at the Annual Meeting of 1 May 1980 stated that actual 1979 giving had amounted to $219,997, a significant increase over the 1978 total amount of $177,723. In 1979 the Church Federation had received $64,202 from churches (down slightly from $66,273 in 1978), and $92,321 from denominations (down noticeably from $97,367 in 1978); the overall improvement was due to increased giving from other sources, particularly foundations. But there were worries: the decrease in giving from both congregations and denominations; the burden of the Church Federation's accumulated deficit, which had required borrowing some $40,000 to pay continuing bills; and long-term concerns about Metro Urban Center finances.

Conclusion

In 1977 the Church Federation reported that its Congregational Concerns Unit "is serving and assisting member congregations by working together on projects that are too big for one congregation to handle alone."[64] Understanding "congregations" to include their parent denominations, this statement exemplified the self-understanding of the Church Federation throughout the 1970s.

Given the work of the Federation during the decade, two critical questions must be posed. First, how far did the Church Federation's breadth of membership and diversity of programs dissipate its focus and energy through the decade? On any objective view, the organization was seriously overextended as it increasingly addressed more and more issues affecting contemporary life. And second, how far would a systematic investment in "Faith and Order" matters, including reflection on church-dividing issues such as sexuality and personal morals, have enriched the life and work of the Church Federation as a whole?

Nevertheless, none can deny that throughout the 1970s the Church Federation offered a courageous Christian witness, did manifold good works, and served as an important agent of reconciliation in Greater Indianapolis. It pursued its vision and mandate faithfully and with zeal. In the process it touched many thousands of persons who, through doing and receiving its work, gained a more prophetic and generous vision of the Christian faith as well as of its churches.

Endnotes

1   Letter of Executive Director Robert W. Koenig to George J. Biskup, 8 September 1972, Church Federation of Greater Indianapolis Records (hereafter CF), William Henry Smith Memorial Library, Indiana Historical Society, Indianapolis, Indiana.

2   Minutes of the Membership Development Committee, 30 March 1971, CF.

3   Letter of Rollyn E. Mayer to Paul McClure, 21 September 1973, CF.

4   *The Forecast*, Vol. VIII, No. 6, September 1970, CF.

5   *Indianapolis News*, 24 June 1966, 9; Edwin L. Becker, *From Sovereign to Servant: The Church Federation of Greater Indianapolis, 1912-1987* (Indianapolis: The Church Federation of Greater Indianapolis, 1987), 100.

6   *The Forecast*, Vol. X, No. 5, December 1972, CF.

7   Letter from Robert W. Koenig to George J. Biskup, 8 September 1972, CF.

8   Becker, 103.

9   *Indianapolis Star,* 13 December 1972.

10 *News of the Church Federation of Greater Indianapolis,* 9 May 1974, CF.

11 Becker, 106-109.

12 Becker, 131.

13 Ibid., 136.

14 Becker, 130.

15 Ibid. 113.

16 *The Forecast,* Vol. X, No. 2, March-April 1972, CF.

17 Letters from Paul E. McClure, 27 March 1972 and 13 April 1972, CF.

18 *The Forecast,* Vol. X, No. 5, December 1972, 4, CF.

19 *The Forecast,* Vol. XII, No. 3, 1974, 3, CF.

20 *The Forecast,* Vol VIII, No. 2, February 1970, CF.

21 *The Forecast,* Vol. VIII, No. 8, December 1970, CF.

22 *The Forecast,* Vol. XI, No. 1, February 1973, CF.

23 *The Forecast,* Vol. XI, No. 4, December 1973, CF.

24 *The Forecast,* Vol. XII, No. 1, Spring 1974, CF.

25 *The Forecast,* Vol. XIII, No. 3, Winter 1975, CF.

26 Becker, 114.

27 Minutes of Board of Directors, 17 November 1971, CF.

28 Minutes of Membership Development Committee, 30 March 1971, CF.

29 Becker, 113.

30 *The Forecast,* Vol. XI, No. 2, Spring 1973, CF.

31 *The Forecast,* Vol. VIII, No. 6, September 1970, CF.

32 Becker, 128-129.

33 Minutes of Board of Directors, 14 March 1974, CF.

34 Becker, 122-123.

35 Becker, 128 ; "Brochure," Metropolitan Indianapolis Campus Ministry [no date], CF;
    The Forecast, Vol. X, No. 3, Summer 1972 and Vol. X, No. 5, December 1972; Minutes,
    Denominational Concerns Committee, 18 April 1974, CF.

36 *The Forecast,* Vol. XVI, No. 2, Spring 1978, CF; Becker, 132.

37 By-Laws, Church Federation of Greater Indianapolis, 12 June 1979, CF.

38 *The Forecast,* Vol. XVIII, No. 1, January-February 1980, CF.

39 Becker, 121.

40 See the Church Federation's "goals for public education" as described in Becker, 121.

41 *The Forecast,* Vol. XIV, No. 2, 1976, 1 — emphasis original.

42 Ibid., 2.

43 Letter from James R. Bradley to Denominational Leaders, 24 April 1979, CF.

44 Minutes of the Steering Committee on School Desegregation, 24 April 1979, CF.

45 *The Forecast,* Vol. XVII, No. 7, 1979, 2, CF.

46 *The Forecast,* Vol. XVII, No. 8, October 1979, 1-2, CF.

47 Report of the Executive Director, 8 October 1979, CF.

48 *The Forecast,* Vol. XI, No. 3, September 1973, CF.

49 *The Forecast,* Vol. XIV, No. 3, Winter 1977, 4, CF.

50 *The Forecast,* Vol. XIV, No. 3, Winter 1977, 1, CF.

51 *The Forecast,* Vol. XVI, No. 3, May 1978, 4, CF.

52 Notes by Paul McClure on the IEC Steering Committee meeting, 1978 ; Minutes, IEC, 28 November 1979, CF.

53 Letter, Rev. Joseph V. Beechem to Paul McClure, 11 March 1976, CF.

54 Minutes of the Membership Development Committee, 24 September 1975, CF.

55 Becker, 118.

56 Minutes of the Membership Development Committee, 10 December 1979, CF.

57 Ibid., 29 April 1975, CF.

58 Minutes of the Board of Directors, 14 March 1977 and 10 October 1977, CF; Becker, 119.

59 For more on the Jonestown event, see: Catherine H. Thrash with Marian K. Towne, *The Onliest One Alive: Surviving Jonestown, Guyana* (Indianapolis: Marian K. Towne, 1995).

60 "McClure's Memo," *The Forecast,* Vol. XVII, No. 5, 1978, 2, CF.

61 Constitution, Church Federation of Greater Indianapolis, Inc., 1 May 1979, superseding that of 11 March 1974.

62 Minutes of the Board of Directors, 10 December 1979, CF.

63 Ibid.

64 *The Forecast,* Vol. XIV, No. 3, Winter 1977, 4, CF.

1. Gleaners Food Bank has made significant strides in reducing the number of residents who go hungry each night.

2. Metropolitan Center of the Church Federation

3. Indianapolis skyline, circa 1980

4. Mayor William Hudnut and new pastors

Indianapolis Star

The Church Federation of Greater Indianapolis Collection, Indiana Historical Society

Indianapolis Star

The Church Federation of Greater Indianapolis Collection, Indiana Historical Society

1980s

Seeking Common Missions

Marian K. Towne and Amanda J. Koch

B Y THE 1980S THE RELIGIOUS LANDSCAPE OF Indianapolis had changed dramatically. Where once mainstream Christian denominations were dominant, the city encountered what historian Jan Shipps called "an evangelical-fundamentalist-pentecostal-holiness coalition, ... a Catholicism more obviously integrated into the life of the city after Vatican II, ... the appearance of organized stakes and wards of the Church of Jesus Christ of Latter-day Saints, and ... the arrival in the city of a surprising number of citizens entirely unconnected to the Judeo-Christian tradition: Buddhists, Hindus, and especially Muslims." The city also witnessed a variety of "unconventional congregations" emerge, including Spiritualists, Unity associations, gay and lesbian fellowships, among many others. Thus, the religious marketplace had become more crowded and certainly more diverse.[1]

It was in this religious marketplace that The Church Federation of Greater Indianapolis continued to be involved with matters affecting the public at large. Poverty, homelessness, and unemployment remained pressing issues, but new concerns over police-community relations, school desegregation, hunger, state-sponsored gambling, jail conditions, and others now vied for the Federation's attention as well.

Ecumenical relations remained at the forefront of the Federation's work, and expanded radio and television programming supported those efforts. But, there were also the persistent financial problems facing Federation leaders that hindered them from aggressively pursuing their goals. Nevertheless, the Church Federation remained true to its mission.

Expanded Ecumenism

Executive Director Paul E. McClure led the Church Federation into the 1980s. A member of the staff since 1966 when he was called to oversee social service and education programs, McClure was responsible for the increased ecumenical focus of the Federation since assuming the directorate in 1973. Throughout the 1970s, Catholic, Eastern Orthodox, Pentecostal, and independent churches joined the ranks of the clearly Protestant majority membership of the Federation in response to McClure's outreach. As a result, the spirit of ecumenism was evident when Monsignor Raymond Bosler, founding editor of the Catholic weekly newspaper *The Criterion*, chaired the Federation's membership committee in 1981-1982 and Jewish rabbis served on the Race Relations Committee. In April 1981 the Federation appointed a task force to sponsor a series of Jewish-Christian inter-faith education conferences that would bring together thousands of church- and synagogue-goers together.

Over the course of the decade, more "non-traditional" churches expressed interest in joining in the work of the Federation. To accommodate that, Federation leaders in 1983 adopted rules for membership. They decided that if the church was not among the denominations already recognized by the Federation, new members should:

- be recommended by two churches in good standing;
- have at least 50 members;
- have been organized for at least three years.[2]

The Federation also concluded that any member church that had not provided financial support for three years would need to reapply for membership in the organization.

Given this expanded ecumenical spirit, the Church Federation welcomed in several new members. In 1984 seven congregations of the Church of God in Christ and a Pentecostal Holiness denomination with a predominantly African American membership, were accepted as members. That same year, the Unification Church, a South Korean-based religious movement led by Sun Myung Moon, approached the membership committee about joining the Federation. But, the National Council of Churches (NCC) had already appointed a commission to determine if the Unification Church met doctrinal criteria to be a member of the NCC. When the NCC determined that the Church did not qualify, the Federation informed the local Unification Church that it would not be admitted. By 1985 twenty-two denominations were represented on the Federation's board of directors – eight from the founding denominations and fourteen who were considered "newcomers."

Another example of the Church Federation's effort at ecumenism was working with a group of Vietnamese Buddhists who were searching for a place to worship. Indianapolis was among the many urban areas in the U.S. that provided assistance to Vietnamese refugees in the mid-1970s when the South Vietnamese government fell to Communist control. Gregory Do, president of the local Vietnamese organization, inquired about membership in the Federation for the nearly 600 Vietnamese in Indianapolis. Executive Director McClure replied that the Federation might consider an affiliate membership as had been done in California.

During this decade, the Federation and mainline Protestants also began to discuss their theological differences with the growing Fundamentalist Christian population of the city. This was evident in a 1980 conversation broadcast over radio station WNTS with Dr. Greg Dixon, pastor of the Indianapolis Baptist Temple and secretary of the National Moral Majority, a 1980s organization involved in political lobbying with an evangelical Christian agenda; the Reverend James Gentry, pastor of St. Mark's United Methodist Church of Bloomington, Indiana; the Reverend John Hosler, pastor of Lifegate Baptist Church; and Dr. Edgar A. Towne, a Presbyterian minister and Professor of Theology at Christian Theological Seminary. The Reverend Richard Davies, head of the Federation's Communications Unit, conceived of and moderated the discussion.[3]

Community Concerns

The complexity of urban life in the Hoosier capital presented additional challenges for the Church Federation to adapt its mission of outreach and ecumenism to the city. One of the most pressing problems dealt with police-community relations. Since the 1970s there had been several incidents of controversial police shootings, harassment, and complaints of excessive force. In November 1980 Indianapolis police shot and killed a fifteen-year old black male who was fleeing an officer. In response, Mayor William H. Hudnut III appointed the Tanselle-Adams Commission, which reviewed police firearms policy; Federation President Margaret S. Robbins was a member. Robbins was among those who maintained there had been excessive abuse of youths in the city jail. The Federation's Denominational Concerns Committee issued a statement requesting that the police "observe more stringently the directives related to the use of firearms," the appointment of a civilian review board, and that the department must "weed out at all levels the insidious cancer of racism."[4] At the end of 1981 Executive Director McClure wrote in his annual report:

We continue to be concerned for the loss of life in our community because of the use of firearms. Our society seems to condone the settling of conflict by gunfire and it seems we have not found a way to enforce law except by gunfire.

Consequently, the Federation vowed to maintain a careful watch on police actions and the availability of firearms in the years ahead.

The Urban Affairs Unit of the Federation, chaired by Roger Heimer, addressed a wide variety of social issues of the day. It worked with the Marion County Department of Public Welfare to provide food stamps to senior citizens and others in need for meals at local restaurants. In early 1983 the unit met with Mayor Hudnut in response to his call to assist low-income households with fuel, shelter, and food during the winter months. The Church Federation provided $10,000 from its Contingency Fund to assist. Executive Director McClure and the Reverend Carl Smith of the Presbyterian Synod met with denominational leaders to enlist their participation in the effort.

One of the most significant initiatives of the Urban Affairs Unit, achieved under chair Jo Ann Brandt, was working with churches to assist pregnant teens and address infant mortality and homelessness.[5] During the 1980s, Indianapolis had the highest rate of black infant mortality in the nation. After a task force studied the matter, Mayor Hudnut and the City-County Council established the "Indianapolis Campaign for Healthy Babies."[6] The initiative helped to develop the infrastructure to provide health care to low-income women and children, promote a city-wide Healthy Babies Month, remove the financial barriers to prenatal and pediatric care, and establish "Baby Depots" around the city where people could donate baby furniture. Working through Church Women United, Mary Lou Rothe and Julia S. Fangmeier helped to recruit volunteers to support this initiative.[7]

Chaplaincies

The Special Ministries Unit of the Church Federation continued the long-standing program of placing chaplains in public institutions. The unit was chaired by the Reverend Urias H. Beverly, chaplain at Methodist Hospital/Clarian Health and associate pastor of Mount Zion Baptist Church who had served as Marion County Jail chaplain in the late 1970s. In 1981 the Marion County Sheriff turned down the Federation's nomination of Reverend Luther Hicks to be jail chaplain. Hicks had been arrested twelve years earlier for assisting students at Shortridge High School in a demonstration over the school's dress code.[8]

In 1982, however, the Juvenile Court chaplaincy became a

full-time position. The Reverend Jacqueline (Jackie) Means was instrumental in securing a gift from St. Paul's Episcopal Church to support the Reverend William L. Parish as chaplain. Since the City-County Council refused to provide public funds for this and other chaplain positions, the Church Federation relied upon church contributions to sustain the program.[9] By the late 1980s, however, the Federation encountered some difficulties with this program. Judge James Payne of the Juvenile Court rejected four court chaplain finalists because he said they were not "sufficiently evangelical." The Federation decided to review the philosophy and purpose of a clinically trained chaplain with Judge Payne and begin the process again. The Reverend Janet Casey-Allen, a graduate of Christian Theological Seminary with clinical pastoral education training, was named the new Juvenile Court Chaplain. Funding for the first two years of her employment came from St. Paul's Episcopal Church with assistance of Rev. Means. It was during this time that the Federation also expressed its opposition to Indiana's law that allowed capital punishment for juveniles.

Serving the Hungry

Recognizing the growing numbers of local residents who were hungry and the regular disposal of unsold food at groceries and restaurants, local activists began to explore the feasibility of establishing a food bank, which would distribute food to food pantries, soup kitchens, homeless shelters, orphanages, and schools. The Whitewater Valley Presbytery sent Marian K. Towne of Indianapolis to Phoenix where the first food bank had been established in the late 1960s. There, she learned that an estimated "30-40 percent of food processed is dumped" and that something needed to be done to distribute food to those in need. On 3 March 1980, with "start-up" funds from the Federation's Contingency Fund and Towne as director, Gleaners Food Bank began to serve the local population. In its first year, Gleaners distributed 83,021 pounds of food to 35 agencies, such as food pantries, senior citizen centers, and food service centers.[10]

Seven months after its founding, Gleaners hired Pamela Altmeyer to be its President and CEO. The first Gleaners building, obtained for one dollar, was at the former "Our Market" located at 1718 West 10th Street. Volunteers labored throughout the summer to get the operation running within a year. Gleaners received funding for at least one year — $105,000 from the Community Service Administration of the federal government. In 1981 Gleaners received a USDA commodities grant for pantries, one of three test sites, which allowed expansion of the food bank program statewide. Additional funding came from the Lilly Endowment, the Indianapolis Foundation, Christ Church Cathedral's Lilly Memorial Trust, the Whitewater Valley Presbytery, and the C.A.P. Council of the U.A.W. The food bank eventually relocated to larger quarters on East 16th Street and became the hub for the Indiana Food Bank Network, which collects anc distributes millions of pounds of food to food pantries and feeding sites. By 1984 Gleaners Food Bank had grown significantly and distributed 3½ million pounds of food to 215 pantries and feeding sites that year.[11]

School Desegregation

When Judge S. Hugh Dillin of the Federal District Court of Southern Indiana found the Indianapolis Public Schools (IPS) guilty of *de jure* segregation (segregation from deliberate administrative acts) on 18 August 1971, public school desegregation became an issue that affected the entire Indianapolis metropolitan commanity. Judge Dillin ordered the immediate desegregation of single-race schools in IPS and added surrounding metropolitan school corporations to his desegregation order to address "white flight" to the surrounding suburban schools.

Given the growing concerns among IPS and suburban district parents, the Federation joined efforts of easing tensions throughout the county. On 5 May 1980 Federation executive director McClure met with Howard McKinney of the U.S. Justice Department to discuss the implementation of Judge Dillin's desegregation plan as sustained by the Seventh Circuit Court of Appeals. In fall 1980 the Reverend T.C. Lightfoot, a Christian Methodist Episcopal pastor and the Federation's Vice President, filled a vacancy on the IPS Board, thus providing the Federation with direct input into the desegregation process.[12]

By the fall of 1981, inter-district busing was fully in place, resulting in black elementary students and high school freshmen being bused to township schools. McClure and Federation leaders met with pastors in areas where problems had been noted and recruited them to assist in easing tensions. The Reverend Charles DuMond, pastor of Edgewood United Methodist Church, recruited pastors in each township to deal with differences and conflicts, noting that pastors might have a better opportunity to resolve problems than law enforcement officers or the National Guard.[13]

In a report to the Federation Board on 8 June 1981, Executive Director McClure commented on the successes of the Federation in addressing the desegregation issues. Citing James 2:4–18, McClure noted:

The Federation exists as an entity dedicated to putting into action the mandate of the Gospel as described in the Book of James. … It takes many forms. … School desegregation is taking place this Fall with the transfer of students within IPS and also from IPS to the six township school systems. The PRIDE Committee of Greater Indianapolis has been working quietly at first, but now very publically, in order to assure a smooth school opening this fall. There are still tensions to ease and problems to solve, but hopefully, "We will overcome." … The Police Community Relations Committee chaired by Your Executive Director is preparing a program for this summer for youngsters, 8–18 years of age. It will be in seven parks and staffed by IPD officers, County Sheriff's deputies, the Park Department and to police explorer posts. This is a continuing effort to build good relationships between law enforcement officers and the community.[14]

The Church Federation also partnered with the Human Relations Consortium, established by the Indianapolis Urban League, which worked with parents and students as the city prepared for and implemented school desegregation. The Federation also produced television programs in support of desegregation and broadcast them on its *Impact Indiana* program. In 1982 the Greater Indianapolis Progress Committee (GIPC) recognized the work of the Church Federation in assisting the city to deal with desegregation.

Radio and Television Ministry

The Communications Unit continued to be one of the most active and successful divisions of the Federation. In order to provide direction for its activities, the Federation, in 1980, developed a statement on the purpose of broadcasting. Noting that programming was considered a "service to the public" and not advertising for the Federation, it specified four distinct categories of programming:
- Illustrating the good and meaningful life – *Time for Timothy* and *Light of Life.*
- Understanding – *Impact Indiana* and *Focus on Faith*
- Information – *Lessons for Living* and *Religion in the News*
- "Sign off" meditations and *Hoosier Pulpit*

Time for Timothy, a puppet show originally called *Timothy Church Mouse*, remained popular for children. It was produced from 1957 to 1991 but continued airing through 1999. Dr. Alfred Edyvean, a professor of communications at Christian Theological Seminary, served as part-time director of the Communications Unit.[15]

Given the ongoing changes in broadcasting, the Church Federation began to explore ways of utilizing new media for its outreach. In 1981 the Federation participated in public hearings on access to cable television. The next year, it held a workshop for pastors on the use of cable stations that were open to them. The Federation's Congregational Concerns Unit also developed a monthly program broadcast on Indianapolis Cablevision, which addressed issues such as pornography, housing, and race relations.

In 1984 Richard Davies, who had served as Director of Communications since 1978, left the Church Federation due in part to reduced financial support for the Federation's radio and television ministry and became pastor of Grace Methodist Church on the city's east side.[16] James Steele of the Communications Unit reported on the success of the Federation program *Religion in the News*. Designed as a forum for diverse ministries, the program was broadcast on the radio in Kokomo, Vincennes, Fort Wayne, Columbus, Crawfordsville, Salem, and Indianapolis. Dr. Edyvean also reported that he was experimenting with five-minute spots on cable television, using Dr. Carver McGriff of St. Luke's United Methodist Church as host.

By mid-decade, Pat McClure, executive producer of *Time for Timothy*, which aired on WTHR Channel 13 locally, announced that the program was being broadcast in the Los Angeles area, New York City, St. Louis, Cincinnati, and Louisville. A Fort Worth, Texas station had also requested program tapes. Clearly, the Federation's children's program proved popular beyond the Indianapolis community. But, given the changing face of broadcast media, the program's years were clearly numbered.

Organizational Issues

In its 73rd year of existence the Church Federation decided to revise its constitution again. The revision eliminated the election of board members by congregational representatives and now allowed "denominational units" to elect the directors. Each denomination received one director for "each six congregations and 5,000 members" (as of 1985), thereby effectively transferring governance of the Federation to denominational rather than congregational leaders.

The Church Federation also established a long range planning committee. After Dr. Robert Koenig resigned because of a heart attack, Dr. Edwin Becker of Christian Theological Seminary became committee chair. The committee received a grant from the Lilly Endowment to expand the Federation's planning and development program for another two years.

On 23 March 1987 Marilyn Wilkes, the Federation's office manager, received a "Distinguished Award in recognition of outstanding performance in business and industry or professions" from the Leadership Development Center of the Indianapolis Chamber of Commerce. Wilkes had joined the Federation in 1967 to assist McClure with Special Ministries.

On 20 November 1989 the personnel committee hired the Reverend Roger Heimer to serve part-time as interim Social Service Director. Heimer had been very active in the Federation's ministries for many years and knew the territory well. His tasks included assisting the Urban Affairs and Special Ministries units. Robin Andres was appointed Development Director.

Financial Matters

Throughout its history, the Church Federation continued to experience financial uncertainties. The 1980s were no different. During the first half of the decade, some 259 congregations contributed to the Federation's budget. By 1983 the Federation was able, with funding from the Lilly Endowment, to hire Beverly Emmons as part-time development coordinator. They also established a development committee consisting of Margaret Robbins and the Reverend William H. Huber and chaired by Dr. Charles Taylor.[17] The committee worked to increase the congregational contributions to support the Federation budget. In 1984, local church contributions reached over $70,000, accounting for 45 percent of the Federation's budget.

With 1984 at hand, the Church Federation learned that the United Way had not reached its campaign goal for the year. Consequently, the Federation's allotment for the year would be $37,500, or $1,500 less than it had planned and budgeted for. Consequently, Federation staff was reduced. The Reverend Richard Davies, director of communications, was cut to half-time, while Dr. Edyvean agreed to help the unit as a volunteer. The Reverend Don Carpenter, head of the Urban Affairs and Special Ministries units and editor of the monthly *News-Notes* for pastors, saw his full-time salary cut. To reduce operating expenses, the Federation moved to a smaller office in the Interchurch Center, which McClure said would be "for a few years." With the financial distress, one board member resigned because of the Federation's debt and the liability of board members.

In an effort to modernize its operations, the Federation expressed its need for a computer to maintain its *Directory of Churches and Synagogues*. McClure also wanted to publish a newsletter. The Federation received a Wang computer from Indianapolis Life Insurance. In November 1984 the Federation secured liability insurance for all officers and directors. It also signed a contract with Church World Service to co-sponsor the annual CROP Walk, a community event organized by local congregations to raise funds to end hunger at home and around the world.[18]

As a way of increasing public awareness of its work, the Church Federation began in fall 1984 to sponsor Sunday afternoon tours of historic churches. Not only was this intended to raise the profile of its work, but also to secure additional funds for operations. By 1987, however, congregational contributions had declined further to 37 percent of the Federation's budget.

Public Issues: Housing

One of the central concerns of the Church Federation since its inception was adequate housing in the city. Earlier in the century, the Federation had supported slum clearance efforts and new federal public housing projects. In 1967 it participated in the creation of H.O.M.E. Inc., (Housing Opportunities Multiplied Ecumenically), a program to provide houses for the poor. By late 1984 McClure claimed that Indianapolis had more than 44,000 substandard houses and was experiencing an increase in homelessness. But, he reported to the Federation board that H.O.M.E. had been successful in providing many houses to the city's poor. He also cited the Federation's Contingency Fund, supported by the Lilly Endowment, which had granted "thousands of dollars for home repair." McClure reported that "one church in our city has laymen who have repaired homes for persons" and asked if it might be "possible that more churches can do the same?"

Public Issues: Labor

The Church Federation became involved in issues of social justice and labor rights. In 1982 the Farm Labor Organizing Committee (FLOC), a labor union founded in 1967 representing migrant workers in the Midwest, launched a boycott of the Campbell Soup Company. The union wanted to ensure human rights, self-determination, and social justice for migrant workers. The boycott centered on Campbell's responsibility to enforce its contracts with growers regarding worker housing and health conditions and to engage in mutually agreed upon negotiations in good faith with the union. The National Council of Churches supported the initiative as did the Federation's Urban Affairs Unit chaired by Roger Heimer. By the fall of 1985, Campbell's officials agreed to negotiate with FLOC.[19]

Public Issues: Lottery

In the mid-1980s the Indiana General Assembly began to explore ways of raising additional revenue to fund public education and general operations. Lawmakers began discussions about creating a state lottery. On 13 January 1986, shortly after the Indiana General Assembly convened, Church Federation executive director McClure recommended that the Federation take a public stand on the proposed lottery bill. Dorothea Green, director of the United Christmas Service and first woman president of the Indiana Council of Churches (1975-1977), also recommended that McClure make a statement affirming the position that the Federation had originally taken against the lottery. This was accepted with the proviso that several church leaders join McClure in signing the statement. The Federation sent a letter to the Indiana General Assembly expressing its concern about changing the state constitution to allow a lottery:

We are opposed on moral grounds because [the lottery] teaches you can gain financially without being a producer in our society... and because it is a very expensive way to raise money...and because it is regressive because it takes more from lower income persons.

209

That same year, Marian K. Towne announced her candidacy for the Indiana House of Representatives from District 49 on the northeast side of Indianapolis. She was encouraged by the board of Indiana Citizens Against Legalized Gambling to run for the office. The Reverend Richard Hamilton, pastor of North United Methodist Church, was especially persuasive with Towne. She won the Democratic primary handily by supporting issues of adequate funding for education, the Uniform Marital Property Act, an extension of Aid for Dependent Children-Unemployed Parent Act, and consumer and environmental protections. Characterized as a hard-working campaigner, Towne, however, lost in the general election.[20]

The Metropolitan Center

The Metro Center, short for Metropolitan Urban Center, had long been an issue for the Federation. In 1970 First Presbyterian Church, located at 1505 North Delaware Street near downtown, merged with Meridian Heights Presbyterian Church at 4701 Central Avenue. The Whitewater Valley Presbytery continued to operate the structure, built in 1903 with Tiffany windows memorializing President Benjamin Harrison, as a community center, child care center, and home to assorted social services and two congregations. In 1977 the Presbytery decided to deed the building to the Church Federation and offered to supply the Federation with $70,000 a year for five years to operate the facility. The Federation's executive committee accepted the offer in 1978 and established a commission to manage the building. Sister Antoinette (Toni) Ressino became the center's director.[21]

However, many problems arose and repairs were immediately required. The center, mortgaged to meet expenses by 1979, added Adult Day Care, which required remodeling for accessibility to elderly and handicapped persons. The Program for Independent Living was moved there. The center quickly became a drain on Federation funds. In October 1982 the Federation board decided to incorporate the Metro Center as a separate entity. Following two years of negotiations, Federation president Dorothea Green announced the sale of the Metropolitan Center, which led to the transfer of the property to the Indianapolis Foundation and the center's programs to Metropolitan Center, Inc. By this action, the Federation found itself out of debt for the first time since the spring of 1978.

75th Anniversary Celebration

As the Federation looked toward the celebration of its 75th anniversary in 1987, the Week of Prayer for Christian Unity in 1986 took on special significance. Roberts Park United Methodist Church, where the Federation had begun, featured the Indianapolis Symphonic Choir. Dr. Premen Niles of Singapore, Ecumenical Associate in the Division of Overseas Ministries of the Christian Church (Disciples of Christ), spoke on "You Shall be My Witnesses" (Acts 1:8). It was a colorful occasion with the leaders wearing their ecclesiastical vestments.

The 75th anniversary worship celebration of The Church Federation of Greater Indianapolis was held 18 October 1987 at Roberts Park United Methodist Church, the site of its birth. Dr. Martin Marty, Lutheran theologian from the University of Chicago Divinity School, spoke. Dr. Edwin L. Becker, Emeritus Professor at Christian Theological Seminary, read excerpts of his Federation history, *From Sovereign to Servant*. Dr. Keith Watkins, Professor of Practical Parish Ministry at Christian Theological Seminary, organized the liturgy for the service. The choirs of First Baptist and Second Presbyterian churches provided the music.

Worshippers celebrated the impact the Church Federation had made on the city. They heard about the Federation's four program units and their impact on all sectors of the city. They learned that 1,122 volunteers had devoted 19,706 hours in service to the Federation during the previous year. Attendees also applauded the continued popularity of the long-running television program, *Time for Timothy*. Most important, however, participants in the celebration service commended the Federation for seventy-five years of Christian service to the city of Indianapolis and its citizens.

The next month, on 11 November 1987, the Church Federation

sponsored a "Witness for Peace" gathering at Sweeney Chapel of Christian Theological Seminary. Presenters included Marian Towne, Annabel Hartman, and other Church Women United members. They displayed sections of the "Pieces to Peace" Ribbon, part of a nation-wide symbolic "tying a yellow ribbon" around the Pentagon, emphasizing the theme, "What I cannot bear to think of as lost forever in a nuclear war."

Transition in Leadership

1987 proved to be an eventful year for the Church Federation. In September 1987 the Federation joined in welcoming Pope John Paul II to Indianapolis. In October the organization celebrated its seventy-fifth anniversary. The Federation's four ministry units were busy administering their programs – Communications Unit producing radio and television programs; Congregational Concerns Unit supporting local churches; the Special Ministries Unit coordinating chaplaincy programs; and the Urban Affairs Unit responding to the social needs of the community.[22] As usual, the Federation continued to face financial struggles, requiring a $10,000 loan to finish 1987.[23]

The year also brought a major transition for the Church Federation. Executive director Paul McClure, who had worked for the Federation for more than twenty years, announced his retirement at the end of the year. The board appointed a search committee consisting of Monsignor Raymond Bosler; Presbytery executive Herbert Eggleston; Thomas King, president of the Indianapolis Chamber of Commerce; Marcia Levin; and chair Richard Christopher. Pat McClure also announced her retirement as executive producer of the long-running *Time for Timothy* television program.

On 16 November 1987 the Church Federation board of directors announced that it had selected the Reverend C. Bruce Naylor, Executive Director of the Evansville Council of Churches and a United Methodist minister who also was ordained by the Disciples of Christ, to succeed McClure.[24] Naylor, hired at a salary of $40,000 with moving expenses, began 1 January 1988, and his installation service was scheduled during the Week of Prayer for Christian Unity. Thus, the Church Federation entered a new period of its history.[25]

In his last report to the executive committee on 16 November 1987, the retiring McClure reflected on the developments of the Church Federation over the course of his tenure. But, one particular issue stood out. McClure reported, "My first few weeks on staff were spent, among other things, writing a report which turned into a book, *Religion in the Public Schools.* . . . This issue has been the most difficult to face in our country. . . . It is interesting that the issues facing us in 1966 are exactly the same in 1987."[26] With his retirement, Paul McClure completed fourteen years as the Federation's executive director and twenty-one years of service to the Church Federation, the longest of any Federation official to date.

Among Naylor's first actions as executive director was to pay tribute to the Reverend Grover L. Hartman, a Church of the Brethren minister who had recently died. Hartman directed the Social Service Department of the Federation for eight years and had a distinguished ministry of ecumenical service with the Federal Council of Churches, the Church Federation of Washington, D.C., and the Indiana Council of Churches.

Settling into his position, Naylor found the Church Federation at a crossroads and began to lead the organization through an evaluation of its mission and direction. Naylor visited federations in South Bend and Cleveland and later in Seattle, Portland, Louisville, and Dallas for ideas on how to improve the Indianapolis organization.[27] In June the Federation's Long Range Planning Committee submitted a report that identified major issues for the Federation to consider, such as whether the Federation should remain a Christian organization or become an interfaith group, how to increase minority participation, and how to improve the Federation's rocky relationship with the United Way of Central Indiana, which had provided a significant portion of the Federation's funding for years.[28]

In the fall of 1988 Naylor invited Dr. William Cate, president of the Church Council of Seattle, to help "delineate our mission and develop the Federation." Cate's report concluded that the Church Federation's board of directors needed more young people, women, and minorities; Federation programs should be more responsive to the pressing needs of the community; and the Federation needed renewal and a fresh evaluation of its leadership.[29]

Naylor quickly learned of the Federation's ongoing financial struggles. Deficits became a common last resort during the late 1980s and early 1990s. To make matters worse, the Church Federation's relationships with the United Way of Central Indiana grew increasingly tenuous. Since it did not generally provide direct services to the needy, the Federation had a constant problem meeting United Way criteria and keeping up with the paperwork and statistics that United Way required. Facing pressure from United Way to change or risk losing funding, the Church Federation's soul searching produced some results. Naylor appointed a Mission Statement Committee consisting of Mary Crow, Jim Rutherford, Edwin Becker, and himself. In March 1989 the board of directors approved a new mission statement, which stated the Church Federation "attempts to make visible God's gift of unity in Jesus Christ and the quality of community that God wills for the whole human family." The mission statement affirmed four programs areas —communication on behalf of local churches, coordination of local ministries, advocacy for the defenseless, and celebration of Christian unity.[30]

By late 1989, with United Way's assistance, the Church Federation reorganized and set quantifiable goals for their services. The result was the renaming of ministry units. A new board and new president set out to create a five-year business plan for the Federation. These changes, however, failed to satisfy United Way. By the early 1990s United Way had cut the Federation's allocations in half and the Federation's debt quickly soared to $50,000. The Church Federation seriously considered withdrawing from United Way by 1992, but decided against the move because it could not raise enough of its own support. The Church Federation's financial struggles continued.

214

Communications

While the Church Federation's governing board was re-evaluating the organization as a whole, the Communications Unit did some soul-searching of its own. Denominational grants to communications efforts dropped dramatically to $16,150 in 1986 after a high of $35,632 in 1972. In 1987 the Federation produced seven weekly television and radio programs.[31] In a matter of weeks, Robert Friedly, chair of the Communications Unit, reported that local stations had cancelled three of the Federations programs — *Lessons for Living*, *The Church in Marion County*, and *Light of Life* – and the Federation feared it would lose more.[32] One of the Federation's longest-running and most successful television shows, *Time for Timothy*, also was in particular peril.

By the late 1980s, the problems experienced by *Time for Timothy* illustrated the wider problems that the Communications Unit faced. Despite the show's nearly forty year history and large pool of viewers, the Communications Unit voted in February 1988 to suspend production of new shows because the show was out of scripts, which were written by volunteers. The unit hired Susan Zurbuchen to analyze the show and its audiences and make recommendations for the future.[33] Zurbuchen concluded that *Timothy's* problems stemmed from a lack of a clear organizational structure and over-expansion into syndication as well as live performances which exhausted its shrinking pool of volunteers.[34]

The problems for the Federation's Communications Unit were both external and internal. Television was changing. Since federal regulations no longer required TV stations to donate airtime to non-profit organizations, the bottom line now drove stations' decisions regarding whether to give the Federation airtime. The three main stations feared losing revenue to cable networks, which now had an astonishing forty channels, and VCR recording enabled viewers to fast forward through advertisements. Stations thought the Church Federation's programming had too little action and too many talking heads to attract audiences. Broadcasters also felt

Federation shows like *Impact Indiana,* which appealed to African American viewers, and *Focus on Faith,* which provided a Jewish voice, had too narrow an appeal to be profitable.[35] Though Comcast Cable Company claimed it canceled *Lessons for Living* and *The Church in Marion County* because evangelicals complained that the theologically liberal Church Federation received more airtime than they did, further investigation by the Communications Unit indicated that the need for revenue drove the station's decision more than anything else.[36]

Though the Church Federation recognized the external challenges early on, it did not deal with internal weaknesses until they threatened to collapse the communications program. For years, the Federation lacked adequate communications staff and resources to produce up-to-date programs. Longtime volunteers were nearly burned out and when key leaders stepped aside, there was no one to replace them.[37]

Fortunately, the Communications Unit had the wisdom to study its problems. What emerged from its evaluation was an increased commitment to Church Federation communications. Dr. William Fore's book, *Television and Religion,* strongly influenced Communications chair Bob Friedly and the committee. Fore, who spoke at the 1988 Church Federation Annual Meeting,[38] argued that television was becoming so pervasive in American society that it was essential for faith groups to have a television presence, not to evangelize, but to ask serious religious questions and point out religious truth.[39] Fore's thinking gave the Communications Unit a renewed sense of purpose for their work.

One project sought to make Federation programming relevant to the times. Sara Buchwald and Marian Towne approached the Church Federation to participate in an important program dealing with religious cults. They wanted the Federation to sponsor a video on the life of Catherine (Hyacinth) Thrash, an Indianapolis resident and early convert of Jim Jones who survived the mass suicide in Jonestown, Guyana, on 18 November 1978. The women argued that the video would help the Federation educate the public about how individuals got caught up in cult movements.[40]

216

In his 23 January 1989 report to the Church Federation board of directors, Friedly insisted on the importance of the Communications program to the Federation's mission and challenged the board to support the program by funding key staff.[41] Friedly's request produced desired results. In May 1989 Don Frick joined the Federation's staff as part-time Communications director.[42] Despite reorganization of efforts, the communications program never fully recovered and was not financially capable to keep up with the latest technology in broadcasting. The Church Federation never again produced the number of programs or had as much popularity as it had before the 1980s.

Social Service

The Urban Affairs Unit also experienced several major programming and organizational changes in the late 1980s. In November 1988 Don Carpenter, long-time Director of Social Service, became seriously ill and could not fulfill his duties.[43] It was not until 1990 that the Board of Directors hired Jim Morgan as a successor for Carpenter. As an African American and an ex-offender, Morgan brought more diversity to the Federation's staff.

In 1989 the unit received a new name and expanded mission. The committee was renamed Ministries in Society and expanded from a narrow urban focus to include rural and global concerns as well. The unit was to develop new task forces, act more independently, and recruit its own members. The Ministries in Society Unit responded by expanding its areas of interest to include domestic violence, elder care, and criminal justice.[44] One of its first initiatives under its new name was creating Interfaith Volunteer Caregivers with the help of the Visiting Nurse Association in 1989. The program trained volunteers to help elderly or homebound people for four hours per week by doing errands or providing companionship.[45]

The Church Federation also continued to serve the community through its Contingency Fund, established in 1970 to distribute money from the Lilly Endowment to start innovative religious projects or to help religious organizations minister to the community.

By 1987 the fund had completed 744 projects. In 1988 some of the causes funded included sponsoring a conference on economic justice, sending children of prisoners to camp, providing baby food and prescriptions, and repairing a woman's home heater which had been broken for two years.[46]

Special Ministries Unit

Under Naylor's leadership, the Special Ministries Unit, which later became Ministries in Specialized Settings, sought to support chaplains and others involved in ministries outside the local churches. The Church Federation had a long history of supporting chaplaincy programs for Indianapolis hospitals, law enforcement organizations, the juvenile court, and even a local Boy Scout camp.[47] The Federation continued this tradition by establishing a clergy identification badge program which provided clergy with official ID cards, making it easier for them to gain access to hospitals and other locations where they ministered.[48] At the annual meeting of the Federation on 22 September 1989, Executive Director Naylor reported that representatives of the Islamic faith had joined the Special Ministries Unit.

Metro Indianapolis Campus Ministries

In 1989 the Church Federation stepped in to save a ministry on the verge of dissolution. When Indiana University and Purdue University partnered to form a new campus in Indianapolis in 1969, the Church Federation helped ensure that the faith community had a presence at the new university.[49] By 1989, however, Metro Indianapolis Campus Ministries (MICM) was in crisis after the resignation of its chaplain, Wayne Olson.[50] Federation Executive Director Naylor determined that the Federation should assist the struggling organization. By the end of June 1989, MICM dissolved and turned its functions over to the Federation.[51] In response, the Federation created a task force on campus ministries and helped MICM reorganize and create a new board. After a two year hiatus, MICM returned to the IUPUI campus. The Church Federation continued to advise and manage MICM's finances through the early 1990s, thereby ensuring that ecumenical Christian churches would continue to have a voice on one of the largest college campuses in the state.[52]

Congregational Concerns Unit

The Congregational Concerns Unit was the arm of the Federation that supported the ministries of member churches. Later divided into an Education and Training committee and a Celebration and Unity committee, the unit provided education for pastors and united congregations in ecumenical services.[53] One of the unit's main tasks was organizing the annual Week of Prayer for Christian Unity. The Church Federation found a location for the service and invited ministers and musicians from a variety of denominations to attend.[54] The Federation also conducted a yearly New Pastors Orientation to the city of Indianapolis.[55] New efforts in the late 1980s included the creation of a Food Handlers Workshop to train church staff and volunteers in food safety and a Church Treasurers workshop, among other training events.[56]

Public Issues: Lottery

When the Indiana General Assembly began discussions earlier in the decade about creating a lottery to generate funds for public education and other initiatives, the Federation had expressed its opposition. Given the growing concerns over the social impact of lotteries and gambling, executive director Naylor endorsed the Federation's earlier stance and reported that he would assist the Indiana Citizens Against Organized Gambling with the development of bulletin inserts and airing a video, "What Kind of a State?" produced by anti-lottery citizens group. "Lotteries," said Naylor, "are viewed as a tax on the poor, and all who win will win at the expense of losers." Jane Fribley, Marian Towne, and the Reverend Scott Schieswohl, new director of the Indiana Council of Churches, spoke out on the importance of local action against gambling in Indiana. In the fall of 1988, voters went to the polls and considered the option: "Shall the Constitution of the State of Indiana be amended by removing the language that prohibits lotteries?" Despite several years of anti-lottery activities, Indiana voters approved the lottery referendum with a 62 percent approval in 1988. The Indiana General Assembly subsequently approved the measure in May 1989 and lottery sales debuted in fall 1989.

Conclusion

During the 1980s, the Church Federation continued to demonstrate two key themes that had been prominent since its founding in 1912 – its commitment to Christian unity and its firm rooting in faith. While these themes seem obvious, given the nature of being a "Church Federation," these themes gave the organization its distinctiveness. The Federation was not simply a social service or community organization, even though it administered a strong social service department and worked actively in the local community to serve the people of Indianapolis. The Church Federation, as a faith-based organization, demonstrated how it was possible to create and mobilize a network of Christian churches and people of faith to impact their city. Faced with a secular culture and pressing social problems, the Church Federation sought to transcend religious, racial, and cultural barriers that divide Christians and mobilize the faith community to address social needs.

Throughout the decade, The Church Federation of Greater Indianapolis faced a host of challenges – increased tensions between police and the African American community; a city divided by court-ordered desegregation and busing of children to township schools; high infant mortality, hunger, and inadequate housing; changes in technology which affected the Federation's communication outreach; the ever-present nagging financial issues; and a society that was becoming increasingly diverse, secular, and uninterested in the religious emphasis of the Church Federation. Nevertheless, while its programs and public outreach had evolved since its founding, the Federation remained truly committed to ecumenical Christian work to demonstrate the power of faith in the city.

Endnotes

1   Jan Shipps, "Religion," *The Encyclopedia of Indianapolis*, eds. David J. Bodenhamer and Robert G. Barrows (Bloomington and Indianapolis: Indiana University Press, 1994), 180.

2   Edwin L. Becker, *From Sovereign to Servant: The Church Federation of Greater Indianapolis* (Indianapolis: Church Federation of Greater Indianapolis, 1987), 119.

3   Tapes of these discussions are available in the Library Archives of Christian Theological Seminary, Indianapolis, Indiana.

4   Becker, 123-124.

5   Urban Affairs Unit Annual Report to Board of Directors, 1988; Minute of the Urban Affairs Unit, 17 November 1988, CF; Carol Elrod, "Churches Dealing with Teen Sex: Organizations Tackling Formerly Taboo Topic," *Indianapolis Star,* 21 March 1987.

6   "Campaign for Healthy Babies," *The Encyclopedia of Indianapolis,* eds. David J. Bodenhamer and Robert G. Barrows (Bloomington and Indianapolis: Indiana University Press, 1994), 382.

7   Minutes of the Urban Affairs Unit, 21 September 1989, CF; *Federation Forecast*, October/November 1990, Report of the Office of Special Ministries, 1-2.

8   Becker, 128.

9   Ibid., 129.

10 Comments from Marian K. Towne, December 2011.

11 For more information about Gleaners Food Bank, visit www.gleaners.org

12 Becker, 122.

13 Ibid.

14 Report of the Executive Director, 8 June 1981, Church Federation of Greater Indianapolis Records (hereafter CF), Indiana Historical Society, Indianapolis, Indiana.

15 See: Marian K. Towne, *Dreaming the Impossible Dream: The First Thirty Years of the Edyvean Repertory Theatre at Christian Theological Seminary.* (Freeman, S.D.: Pine Hill Press, 1996), 13-14.

16 Becker, 128.

17 Becker, 134.

18 For more information, visit www.cropwalk.org

19 See: W.K. Barger and Ernesto M. Reza, *The Farm Labor Movement in the Midwest.* (Austin, TX: University of Texas Press, 1994); "Migrant Workers Organize a Boycott of Campbell," *New York Times*, 2 July 1984.

20 Marian K. Towne, *That All May Be One: Centennial History of Church Women United in Indianapolis, 1898-1998* (Freeman, S.D.: Pine Hill Press, 1998).

21 Becker, 132-133.

22 Minutes of the Board of Directors, 31 March 1989, CF.

23 Minutes of the Board of Directors, 16 November 1987, CF.

24 Ibid.

25 Minutes of the Executive Committee, 4 January 1988, CF.

26 See: Paul McClure, *Religion and the Public Schools.* (Indianapolis: Church Federation of Greater Indianapolis, 1966).

27 Minutes of the Board of Directors, 21 March 1988 and 28 June 1988, CF.

28 Minutes of the Board of Directors, June 1988, CF; "Report of Long Range Planning Committee of Church Federation of Greater Indianapolis," 28 June 1988, CF.

29 Minutes of the Executive Committee, 1 December 1988, CF.

30 Minutes of the Board of Directors, 31 March 1989, CF.

31 Bob Friedly, "Communication Unit Report, 16 November 1987 to Board of Directors," CF.

32 "Report to the Executive Committee, Federation of Churches, 4 January 1988, from the Communications Unit," Minutes of the Executive Committee, 1988, CF.

33 Minutes of the Communications Unit, 25 February 1988, CF.

34 "Time for Timothy" Operational Records, 1975-1990, Problem Statement, CF.

35 "Report to Board of Directors, 21 November 1988 from Communications Unit," Minutes of the Board of Directors, 1988, CF.

36 "Report to the Board of Directors from the Communications Unit, 25 January 1988," CF.

37 "Report on 1988 and Plans for 1989," Communications Unit, CF.

38 Annual Meeting Program, 18 April 1988, CF.

39 Bob Friedly, "Communications Unit Report to Board of Directors, 16 November 1987, CF.

40 Catherine (Hyacinth) Thrash, as told to Marian K. Towne, *The Onliest One Alive: Surviving Jonestown, Guyana* (Indianapolis, 1995). A videotaped interview of Thrash was also made.

41 Bob Friedly, "Communications Unit Report to Board of Directors, 23 January 1989," CF.

42 Minutes of the Communications Unit, 19 May 1989, CF.

43 Minutes of the Executive Committee, 17 January 1989, CF.

44 Minutes of the Urban Affairs Unit, 21 September 1989, CF.

45 Ibid.; *Federation Forecast*, October/November 1990.

46 Annual Meeting, 1988, Contingency Fund Annual Report, 11 April 1988, CF.

47 Paul McClure interviewed by Amanda Koch, 10 June 2009, Franklin, Indiana.

48 *Federation Forecast*, October/November 1990, CF.

49 Paul McClure interviewed by Amanda Koch, 10 June 2009, Franklin, Indiana.

50 Minutes of the Special Ministries Unit, 14 March 1989, CF.

51 Minutes of the Executive Committee, 1 June and 20 June 1989, CF.

52 Minutes of the Executive Committee, 18 June 1991; *Federation Forecast,* November/December 1991, CF.

53 Minutes of the Congregational Concerns Unit, 1987-1988, CF.

54 Programs for the Week of Prayer for Christian Unity, 1985-1993, CF.

55 Minutes of the Board of Directors, 1988, CF.

56 Minutes of the Board of Directors, 1987, CF.

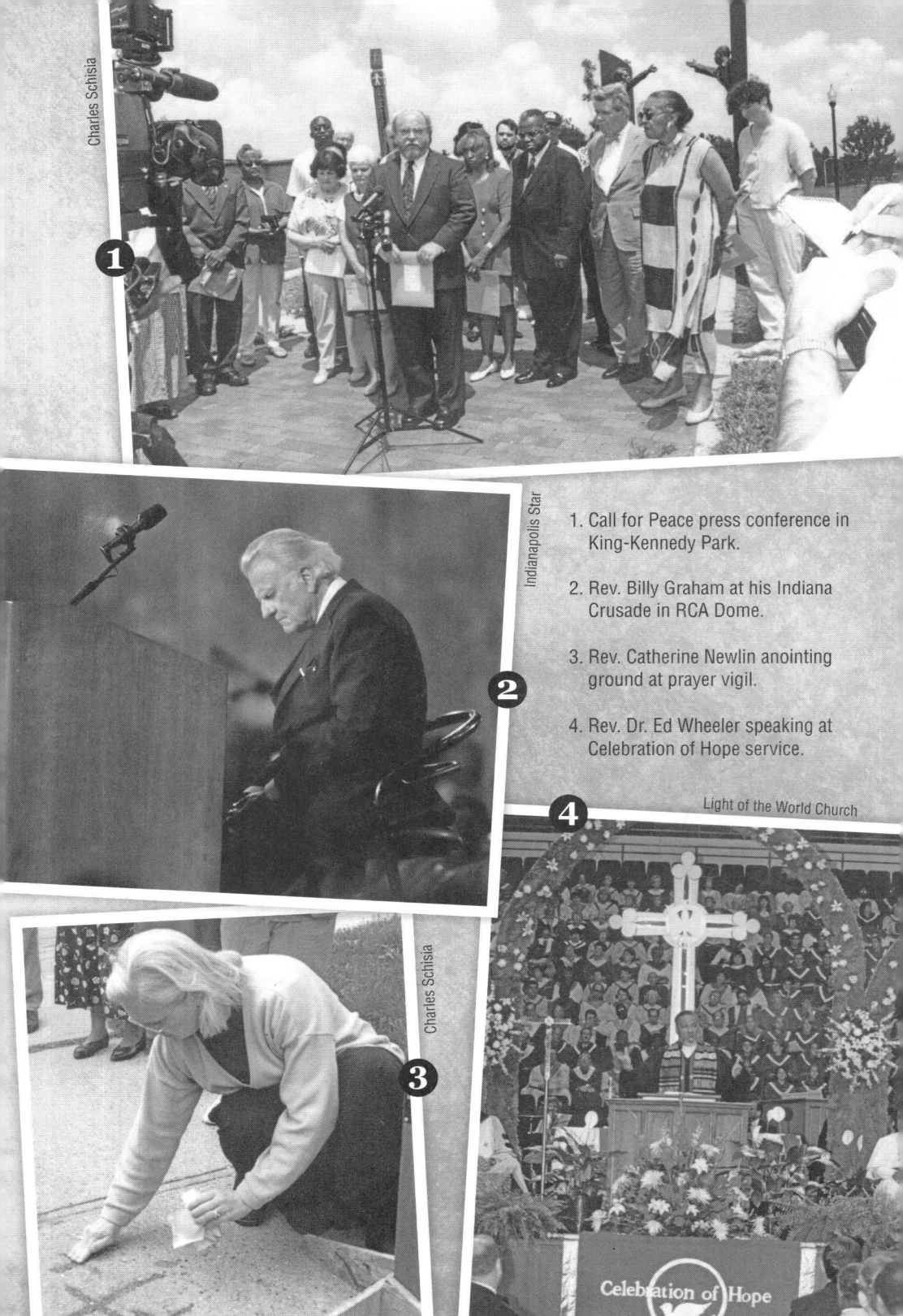

Charles Schisia

Indianapolis Star

Charles Schisia

Light of the World Church

1. Call for Peace press conference in King-Kennedy Park.

2. Rev. Billy Graham at his Indiana Crusade in RCA Dome.

3. Rev. Catherine Newlin anointing ground at prayer vigil.

4. Rev. Dr. Ed Wheeler speaking at Celebration of Hope service.

Celebration of Hope

1990s

Shalom

Amanda J. Koch

W HAT STARTED AS A SILENT PROTEST QUICKLY turned into a race riot on a hot July night in 1995. Craig Hughes, age twenty-three, led a march to protest the Indianapolis Police Department's alleged brutality against his friend, twenty-one year old Danny Sales, during a drug arrest the previous day. A search uncovered no drugs on Sales's person. Hughes and about fifty other people, mainly African Americans, gathered at College Avenue and 42nd Street in a silent demonstration in front of an Indianapolis Police Department station. But as their numbers swelled to 150, tempers flared and the crowd became unruly. The police responded with riot gear and tear gas. The next day violence broke out again, as angry young people threw rocks at cars and looted a nearby Revco drug store. The police again returned in riot gear to disperse the crowds. Though no one was killed in the violence of 26-27 July 1995, the incidents showed a city bitterly divided along racial and class lines. Some Indianapolis residents claimed police brutality was responsible for the violence; others argued that a reckless youth culture dominated by drugs and alcohol accounted for the area's problems. One thing that was clear was that the city of Indianapolis remained far from peaceful.[1]

As the violence of July 1995 demonstrated, the city of Indianapolis experienced significant and sometimes difficult changes in the 1990s. Like many urban areas around the United States, Indianapolis underwent spatial changes as wealthy and middle-class residents moved to the surrounding suburbs, leaving fewer and poorer residents in the cities. Historic urban neighborhoods such as Fountain Square and Martindale Brightwood lost population and saw poverty and crime increase.[2]

The remaining residents in these neighborhoods were often minorities and of a lower socio-economic status, and thus spatial changes furthered racial and wealth disparities, dividing the city and leading to the resentment that boiled over in July 1995. The 1990 Census showed that statistically Marion County's total population was racially diverse with a 77 percent white population and a 21 percent black population as well as smaller numbers of people of Asian, Native American, and Pacific Islander descent. Additionally, Indianapolis had a small, but growing number of Hispanic residents. Though people of Hispanic origin only accounted for about 0.01 percent of Marion County's total population in 1990, their numbers would grow rapidly throughout the decade, making the Hispanic community another important part of the area's demographics.[3]

While the city faced crises such as crime, poverty, and racial tension, The Church Federation of Greater Indianapolis faced one of the greatest crises in its history. Severe financial pressures, changing leadership, and doubts about the its continued relevance threatened to destroy the organization entirely. The Federation's board and member churches asked whether the group would survive the decade. And if it did, what could ecumenism possibly do to solve the city's problems of crime and poverty? What duty, if any, did member churches from the Indianapolis suburbs owe to the area of the city inside the I-465 loop? For both the city of Indianapolis and its Church Federation, the early 1990s were a time of insecurity and uncertainty about the future. "Shalom," the Hebrew word connoting peace, seemed impossibly far away.

Out of the chaos of the early 1990s, the Church Federation emerged, after serious questioning and soul-searching, with a renewed commitment to Christian ecumenism, a focus on diversity, and a desire to provide religiously-based services to the struggling inner city of Indianapolis. Ecumenism for the Federation in the 1990s meant accepting even more racial and ethnic diversity than before and reaching out to people of other faiths, such as the Jewish and Muslim communities, while remaining a Christian organization. By the mid-1990s, the Federation board decided to focus its efforts on three areas in which the city most needed help —crime prevention, education, and race relations. Thus, when the July 1995 riots broke out, the Federation was prepared to lead in helping the churches and the city address the anger and frustration of the area's young people. The Church Federation started several visible new ministries such as the Sanctuary Church Movement and its well-publicized prayer vigils (part of the response to the July 1995 riots), a Celebration of Hope to foster racial unity, and an education initiative with the Indianapolis Public Schools called "Loving our Children." The Federation eventually could look back on the last decade of the millennium with much to celebrate, but, at the beginning of the decade, these accomplishments seemed nearly impossible. It first had to confront a set of crises that threatened its very survival.

Impending Crisis

The Church Federation had already gone through a process of re-organization by 1990, but the start of a new decade presented serious challenges for the group. After the Reverend C. Bruce Naylor, a former Executive Director of the Evansville Council of Churches and a United Methodist minister, became executive director in 1988, he led the group through a re-evaluation of its mission and direction. His efforts included establishing a Long Range Planning Committee, drafting a new mission statement, which said in part that the Church Federation "attempts to make visible God's gift of unity in Jesus Christ and the quality of community that God wills for the whole human family," and focusing on four program areas—communication on behalf of local churches, coordination of local ministries, advocacy for the defenseless, and celebration of Christian unity.[4]

The Federation's situation in the early 1990s highlights a recurring theme for the decade: financial struggle. The Federation attempted to regain a solid financial footing in 1990, and a major grant from the Lilly Endowment brought a glimmer of hope. In order to restore the organization's financial health and create a development program that would secure future donors, the Endowment gave the Federation a $210,000 grant in 1990. By November of that year, the Federation hired Carol Blinzinger as director of development. While the Lilly grant provided the Federation with much-needed relief, the development program had only modest results and did not enable the group to become self-sustaining.[5]

The Church Federation underwent reorganization in part to satisfy United Way, one of its most important funding sources. The nature of the Federation's ministries, which involved coordinating and mobilizing churches to provide spiritual as well as social services to the community, did not easily fit the United Way's criteria for quantifiable progress. The Federation's reorganization in the late 1980s failed to satisfy United Way, and between 1991 and 1992 the United Way cut the Federation's allocations in half and the Federation's debt soared to $50,000.[6]

In spite of the Federation's financial turmoil, its program committees soldiered on. Though it lost three of its seven television programs within a few weeks in 1987, the Church Federation's Ministries in Media unit (formerly the Communications Unit) sought to reinvent its remaining shows for a changing television culture.[7] Don Frick joined the Federation's staff as part-time Communications director in May of 1989. United Way gave the Federation a grant in 1990 to produce a special episode of the popular children's show, *Time for Timothy,* to warn elementary school children of the dangers of drug use in 1990. The Federation updated the television show *Focus on Faith* in 1991 with a contemporary talk-show feel, including moderator, studio audience, and more diverse and relevant topics. The Federation started using desktop publishing to redesign and expand the content of its print publications, *Pastors News Notes* and *Federation Forecast*.[8]

The Ministries in Media Unit attempted to change with the times, but it lacked the resources to keep pace with the technological developments in television and the previously strong support of local stations, which no longer had to donate airtime to non-profit organizations. As a result, the Federation never again produced the number of programs or had as much popularity as it had before. One of the most telling changes to the Media Unit came in 1990 when it started a lobbying campaign to bring the religious cable station VISN to the Indianapolis market. This new project marked a change from producing original programming to trying to secure religious programming on the air in Indianapolis. The change was not necessarily a failure, but rather a realistic recognition of the state of television. Thus, the Federation did its best to ensure that the city had access to religious television.[9]

The Federation's second ministry area, formerly the Urban Affairs Unit and later named Ministries in Society, proved to be a spot of vitality for the Federation and many of the Federation's new ministries grew out of this unit. By the mid-1990s most of the Federation's work could be classified as social service. The Federation's Ministries in Society committee continued to support previous programs such as a city-wide Healthy Babies Month, which included collecting donated baby furniture, and Interfaith Volunteer Caregiver, which trained volunteers to care for the elderly or homebound.[10] Another continuing program was the Contingency Fund, renamed the Benevolence Fund in 1991, which provided money for innovative religious projects, such as St. Lawrence Catholic Church's utility assistance program and a grant for the outreach program at Jones Tabernacle AME Zion Church.[11]

Two new initiatives pointed to the Federation's direction for the rest of the decade. In 1991 the Federation launched the Family and Congregational Mentoring Program designed to help at-risk

229

families, mainly on the northeast side of Indianapolis. The program garnered significant community support and frequent attention from the *Indianapolis Star*.[12] With the help of a grant from the Lilly Endowment, the Federation welcomed the Reverend Dr. Angelique Walker-Smith, former executive director of the Trenton (New Jersey) Council of Churches who had recently moved to Indiana, to train volunteers for a women's prison ministry that same year. The goal was to unite member churches in helping prisoners re-enter society. Later that year the Endowment approved an additional criminal justice grant to enable Rev. Dr. Walker-Smith to continue her work for another eighteen months.[13]

Even as the Committee started exciting new programs, it struggled to find the right staff. Long-time Director of Social Service Don Carpenter resigned in November 1988 due to serious health problems, and it took more than a year for the Federation to hire a replacement. The organization chose Jim Morgan, an African American and "ex-offender," to head the social service division in part to add diversity to the staff. Morgan's time with the Federation was short and rocky though. At a June 1992 meeting, the board discussed "misconduct," "negative attitudes," and "temper" that meant that Morgan could no longer "fairly represent" the group. The Federation terminated Morgan soon after and remained firm in its decision even after Morgan appealed.[14] Morgan's departure was not the only one in 1992 that would darken the outlook for the Federation's future.

Even as the Federation reorganized its operations in the early 1990s, it managed to start important new ministries for the Indianapolis community, including a chaplaincy program at the Indianapolis International Airport. When an American Eagle aircraft crashed in 1994 after leaving Indianapolis, killing sixty-eight people, a group of Asian businessmen stood in the Indianapolis airport, confused and grieving. But, with the help of airport chaplain the Reverend Yung Chen, they were able to get reliable information and comfort in their early stages of grief and shock.[15] Crises like a major plane crash illustrated the need for spiritual guidance in specialized settings outside the church, and the Church Federation anticipated this need when it started a chaplaincy program at the airport in 1991. The program still exists as an independent organization called the Indianapolis Interfaith Airport Chaplaincy. Though, thankfully, chaplains do not deal with dramatic and tragic occurrences like plane crashes on a daily basis, they present the friendly face of Indianapolis for visitors by giving directions to lost travelers or providing support to those facing crisis by doing tasks like driving the wife of a heart attack victim to the hospital.

When the city of Indianapolis has needed spiritual guidance for organizations from hospitals to law enforcement agencies to the juvenile court, it has consistently looked to the Church Federation. The Federation did not disappoint in starting a vital new program at the airport that enhanced the city's image for travelers. Ministries in Specialized Settings, formerly the Special Ministries Unit, created another new initiative to aid religious work outside the walls of the church in 1991 by providing clergy with identification badges, making it easier for them to enter hospitals and other locations.[16]

The Congregational Concerns Unit was the arm of the Federation that supported the ministries of member churches. Later divided into an Education and Training committee and a Celebration and Unity committee, the Unit organized the annual Week of Prayer for Christian Unity and conducted a yearly New Pastors Orientation, along with other training programs for churches on topics such as handling food or training treasurers.[17]

Though financial and leadership challenges clouded the horizon, the Church Federation drew inspiration from its past during its 80th Anniversary celebration at the Indianapolis Zoo on 2 June 1992. In addition to an ecumenical worship service at Roberts Park United Methodist Church several days later, the Federation wanted a fun and casual celebration that could include families. After guests toured the zoo, had dinner, and listened to music, they enjoyed a program that honored various people who had played prominent roles in the Federation's past, such as former executive director Paul McClure, past president Margaret Robbins, friend and officer of the Federation Raymond Bosler, and Annabel Hartman, widow of Social Service Department director Dr. Grover Hartman.[18] As the Federation celebrated its past and looked to its future, its present remained uncertain. In spite of the laughter of children and the antics of the monkeys at the zoo on a beautiful June night, the next few months would bring major upheaval to the Federation that threatened its prospects for the next several years.

Despite the light-hearted anniversary celebration, June 1992 proved to be a trying month for executive director Bruce Naylor. In addition to the ordeal of Morgan's resignation, the Federation's financial situation had deteriorated to the point that even the Lilly Endowment, a faithful and significant supporter of the Church Federation, eventually opted to delay funding for the Family and Congregation Mentoring Project in 1992 out of concern regarding the Federation's long-term health and goals.[19] In spite of staff layoffs and reduced hours, the organization still needed $13,000 more for the year than it had received. The Federation and the cause of ecumenism were both struggling, and these factors weighed heavily on Naylor personally. As a result, Naylor finally made the painful decision to resign as executive director of the Church Federation at the end of June 1992 and return to local church ministry. In his resignation letter he wrote, "No one has agonized more or lost more sleep over the struggles of the Church Federation than I have. As the executive director, I certainly feel the burdens of our failures to accomplish all we have planned, yet I do not accept blame for all our ills. We have experienced the woes of many organizations in transition and of many ecumenical agencies at the present time."[20] Naylor served through the end of 1992, but he significantly reduced his activities.

In the wake of Naylor's resignation, the Church Federation seemed more vulnerable than ever. Several *Indianapolis Star* articles publicized the Federation's struggles and empty coffers, while noting that ecumenical agencies around the nation were facing similar circumstances as local churches faced budget constraints and thus had less money to give to ecumenical organizations.[21] By the end of the year, the situation was worse. The board of directors held an emergency meeting on 14 December to discuss staff cuts and finding new ministries that churches would be willing to fund. Fund-raising committee member Rev. Ray Bowden said pointedly, "The focus needs to be the kind of ministries that individual, big-steeple churches are willing to pull together and pay for." Federation president the Reverend Darin Moore of Jones Temple AME Zion Church said the group's first priority should be finding an interim executive director who could give new direction. The Federation made it through 1992 with a $50,000 Lilly Endowment grant, but its United Way funding for 1993 was in doubt and the Federation risked losing its programming.[22] The Church Federation faced an uncertain future in which everything, even its survival, was now in question.

New Vision, New Direction

The year 1992 found the Church Federation at an impasse without an executive director and with pressing financial problems. But even before Rev. Naylor tendered his resignation, the Church Federation's board began taking action. Early in 1992 the Federation requested advice from the Society of Retired Executives. In April 1992 consultants Mitchell E. Daniels and Jan Finney gave their report, advising the Federation to include more prominent business leaders on the board, make the board more active in daily operations, and improve fundraising in order to make the Federation more independent.[23] The executive committee attempted to implement the consultants' long-term advice, but, in the short term, it had to make major staffing cuts. This reorganization made Director of Development Blinzinger the interim executive director from December 1992 to March 1993.[24]

After Naylor's resignation, the Church Federation went through a year-long period of major re-evaluation of its mission, purpose, and activities. During 1993 the board's intense strategic planning process examined Indianapolis's needs, evaluated the Federation's place in the community, and questioned each aspect of its identity, including whether it should remain a Christian organization or become an interfaith group. To guide them through the planning process, the Federation board hired Rev. Dr. Angelique Walker-Smith as the part-time interim executive director for one year, starting in April 1993.[25] Walker-Smith had already provided training for the Federation's ministry to women in prison for several years and appeared on the Federation program, *Faces of Faith*. An ordained National Baptist minister with five years of experience as the executive director of the Trenton (New Jersey) Council of Churches, she graduated from Yale University Divinity School with a Master's in Divinity, and was the first African American woman to receive her Doctor of Ministry degree from Princeton Theological Seminary. Walker-Smith, who served as a part-time interim executive director while she completed her doctoral dissertation, became the first woman and first African American to lead the Church Federation of Greater Indianapolis.[26]

Walker-Smith's year as interim director was a challenging one. In one year, the Federation's staff had gone from ten to four people and its 1993 budget of $90,000 was less than half the previous year's amount.[27] As interim director, Walker-Smith did not start any new programs, but simply maintained the group's existing work. The Federation carried out little programming during 1993; most of its time was spent in the planning and evaluation process.[28]

After a long, intense year of discussion and planning, the Church Federation emerged with new clarity and direction for the future. The board, led by president Priscilla Savage and then Rev. Richard Moman, opted to maintain the Church Federation's identity as a Christian, rather than interfaith, organization and determined its mission should be to build bridges among Christian churches and between the Christian community and an increasingly multi-faith world.[29] The board of directors adopted a new strategic plan on 8 March 1994. Once the group decided on its identity and direction, it needed more permanent leadership to implement its goals. The Federation launched a nationwide search for an executive director, but after reviewing over one hundred resumes, the board voted to make Rev. Dr. Walker-Smith the Federation's permanent executive director.[30]

It had been a harrowing several years, but at Walker-Smith's installation service, the Church Federation had many reasons to celebrate. The Federation welcomed its first female and first African American leader. The 11 June 1995 service celebrated the new diversity that Rev. Dr. Walker-Smith brought to the Federation with a procession of nineteen church leaders, male and female, from various denominations and ethnic backgrounds. The Federation was optimistic as it celebrated and looked forward to a future of new ideas and ministries.[31] But only weeks after the Church Federation celebrated racial and religious diversity at the installation service, dramatic events in Indianapolis showed that the city still faced deep and dangerous divisions.

Seeking Peace in the City

Once the Church Federation decided on its direction and leadership, it needed to get programming started as soon as possible in order to regain credibility in the community after receiving harsh criticism from some of the public. After more than a year with limited programming, it was time to ramp up the organization's activity. While the Federation continued to struggle over the next several years and faced more staff reductions, it had a new focus and new leadership and was ready to anticipate the city's needs. As a result of the strategic planning process, the board decided that the Federation should focus on three areas—crime prevention, education, and race relations. It would not take long for events to unfold to prove just how pressing these needs were.[32]

Even before the Church Federation completed its strategic planning process and selected a permanent executive director, events in Indianapolis illustrated the city's needs for spiritual and civic leadership on the issue of race relations. Indianapolis received a distressing reminder of its state's troubled racial history when the Ku Klux Klan announced that it would march on the steps of the Indiana Statehouse on 16 October 1993. Alarmed at such a bold manifestation of the racism that they hoped their city had renounced years earlier, the Church Federation quickly joined other community groups and leaders, including Mayor Stephen Goldsmith, in organizing a counter-event that would celebrate the city's racial and religious diversity. Participants included many major religious denominations, the Jewish Community Relations Council, the Young Women's Christian Association, the National Association for the Advancement of Colored People, and the Indianapolis Urban League. Called Celebration of Hope, the rally called participants to a nonviolent celebration of diversity and rejection of hatred.[33]

Skirmishes broke out at the rally itself as about thirty-five Klan participants, hundreds of anti-Klan demonstrators, police, and some Klan supporters converged on the Statehouse. Also in response to the rally, the Federation welcomed the Reverend Johnny Lee Clary, a former imperial wizard of the White Knights of the Ku Klux Klan, as a guest on its local television program, *Faces of Faith*. Clary shared his story of how he repented from the sin of racism and became a pastor of the racially diverse Independent Assembly Church of Tulsa, Oklahoma.[34] The Klan rally demonstrated how persistent racial animosity was in Indianapolis.

Just a few months after the Federation hosted its first Celebration of Hope rally in response to Klan activities, two Federation member churches initiated a program of racial reconciliation that moved Celebration of Hope into one of the Federation's largest and most visible projects. The program grew out of conversations between Bishop T. Garrott Benjamin, Jr. of Light of the World Christian Church and Dr. William G. Enright of Second Presbyterian Church about the need for their two congregations to discuss race relations. In 1994 the two congregations held a joint worship service and in 1995 the partnership grew to include twenty Indianapolis churches in a huge worship service in Market Square Arena.[35]

The high point of Celebration of Hope came one Sunday morning in June of 1996 when more than 9,500 people gathered in Market Square Arena to seek racial reconciliation through Jesus Christ. The recent acts of firebombing, arson, and vandalism against sixty African American churches in southern states provided a disturbing reminder of the need for the service. Worshippers of various races and denominations joined together to transcend the barriers which had so long divided them. As the congregation sang, took communion, and made donations to rebuild the southern churches ravaged by the fires of racism and hatred, attendees began to receive a vision for what true Christian unity could look like. The message set forth a vision of racial harmony that could be possible if the Christian church was committed to it. Five hundred people responded to the message by pledging to join focus groups to discuss practical ways to overcome racism at the grassroots level.[36]

Celebration of Hope continued to hold spring and fall joint worship services, but the heart of the program was the dialogue that occurred at small race relations focus groups and in annual pulpit and choir exchanges. In 2000 the Federation declared that Celebration of Hope had moved from a partnership into a movement that emphasized building relationships between churches.[37] Celebration of Hope built two homes with Habitat for Humanity, organized pulpit exchanges, and held focus groups and prayer meetings to foster racial reconciliation. It continued the annual corporate worship services and added programs for youth and children. Celebration of Hope officially dissolved in 2007, but the Federation continued the work of racial reconciliation with programs like Sacred Conversations and the Hispanic/Latino Urban Forum.[38] Interestingly, Celebration of Hope was remarkably similar to the activities of the Church Federation's 1920s race relations committee. Celebration of Hope showed what was possible when the churches of Indianapolis united toward a common goal. Significantly, it was member churches who chiefly initiated the program; the Church Federation simply facilitated what individual churches were already committed to accomplishing. While the Federation and its member churches saw exciting things happen through its new programs, more local news events quickly showed how much work remained.

Reflecting on her first months as permanent executive director, Walker-Smith later said that the Spirit was at work, turning tragedy into an opportunity for the Church Federation to be of service to the Indianapolis community by addressing its second area of focus—

crime prevention. A little over a month after the Church Federation celebrated diversity at Walker-Smith's installation service, the city of Indianapolis experienced what many termed a race riot between police and primarily African American citizens over allegations of police brutality. Several Federation member churches had programs in the areas where rioting took place, and the Federation and its members saw an opportunity to mediate between community members and the city government. Walker-Smith put her community organizing skills to work and started listening forums after the unrest in which young people could express their concerns and anger to the churches in the community. Through the forums, young people expressed their frustration over poverty and continued gun violence, churches began to understand the concrete issues that their members faced, and the Federation started to propose ideas to address the problems.[39]

One of the concrete proposals to come out of the community forums was a plan to have prayer vigils at the site of every violent death in Indianapolis. One of the Federation's unique strengths was its recognition of the spiritual dimensions of every crisis and the need for prayer. Churches around the city could unite in prayer for the city's crime and race problems. Out of these realizations came the Church Federation's Sanctuary Church Movement, which sought to ensure that churches provided safe spaces for their community's young people. The Sanctuary Church Movement worked to prevent violence from occurring by starting a Youth Speakers Bureau and conducting twice yearly services of Remembrance and Peacemaking.[40] Prayer vigils became a vital part of the Sanctuary Church Movement, and starting in February 1996, Federation volunteers held vigils at the site of every violent death in the city within forty-eight hours of the occurrence. The sight of Christian services on the streets of some of the city's worst neighborhoods provided a powerful symbol of the Federation's commitment to the city. The prayer vigil ministry quickly became one of the group's most visible and publicized programs.[41] They received regular coverage in Indianapolis newspapers. The *Indianapolis Star*, for example, published a story on Julie and Bruce Madsen, a Cleveland couple who set out on a nationwide road trip "to write a book about hope, community and goodness in America." In Indianapolis the Madsens found hope and goodness among the prayer vigil volunteers who, as Julie put it, were "doing something most people wouldn't. They are trying to reconnect instead of being afraid."[42]

The Church Federation wanted to provide support for families of victims beyond a one-time prayer vigil. Thus, in 1998 the Sanctuary Church Movement started the Ecumenical Project for Reconciliation and Healing (EPRH). The Project trained mentors to provide support and referral to community resources for families who had lost loved ones to violence.[43] It had special significance for one Indianapolis mother who signed up to learn to be an EPRH mentor. Michelle Miller lost her three year old son when he found a gun in their apartment and accidentally shot himself. Three years later, Miller wanted to share her own experience with other families and help them overcome loss as well.[44]

One of the Federation's continuing programs also aimed to reduce crime and poverty by preserving families in low-income Indianapolis neighborhoods. The Family and Congregation Mentoring Program was already active in the Meridian-Kessler neighborhood, providing after-school tutoring and services for the elderly. [45] In 1997 the Federation helped open a Family Cares center in Martindale Brightwood, an African American neighborhood on the city's eastside that had struggled with increasing poverty and declining population since the 1970s. In 1999 New Birth Ministries in Fountain Square became an official Family and Congregation Mentoring site. Located in another historic Indianapolis neighborhood that lost population and jobs to the suburbs, New Birth Ministries provided a food and clothing pantry, child care, Christian counseling, and discussion groups.[46] The Family and Congregation Mentoring Program, renamed the Church and Neighborhood Partnership in 2002, continued supporting these sites in the next decade.

The Church Federation's last area of focus after its reorganization was education. The issue of education was intertwined with previous initiatives. The Federation observed that Indianapolis Public Schools

(IPS) increasingly grappled with racial issues as the city's population grew more diverse and as the Latino population grew. The board believed the Church Federation needed to become a stronger advocate for education.[47] One Federation initiative was a partnership with IPS, called "Loving Our Children." The partnership began in 1995 and sought to connect churches with schools that educated at-risk children. The Federation encouraged member churches to adopt an IPS school and provide tutoring, kids' clubs, parenting classes, and sports programs. A $30,000 grant from the Moriah Fund in 1997 fueled the program, and by 1999, the Federation had twelve sites around Indianapolis.[48] The Church Federation also started participating in an annual "Children's Sabbath" and other special events aimed at drawing attention to the needs of the city's children.[49]

The Church Federation's goals gradually came to fruition. The *Star* published an article that highlighted Rockea Bell and Lakisha Johnson, two Broad Ripple High School students who tutored elementary students at IPS School 14 every week. Bell and Johnson worked with First- Meridian Heights Presbyterian Church's program and both tutors said they experienced immense satisfaction not only helping the students' grades improve, but learning to appreciate others as individuals. Bell reflected, "This has taught me to respect other people's opinions. ... I respect what other people are trying to do with their lives. I want to help kids grow."[50] "Loving Our Children" began to improve education in the city and build relationships and respect among its residents.

Though an emphasis on crime, race relations, and education shaped the Federation's new programming in the latter part of the 1990s, the organization continued many of its older programs as well. The term "social service" has always been too narrow to cover the Federation's spiritual as well as physical ministries, but it captures many of the group's activities. The Benevolence Fund distributed money from the Lilly Endowment to faith-based ministries, especially new ministries. In the mid-1990s the Fund also started giving money to the CROP fund to be distributed to local food pantries.[51] The Federation had been involved in prison ministry since the early 1990s, and it expanded this work later in the decade. It also continued coordinating with chaplains at the Indiana Women's Prison and Rockville Correctional Facility to help inmates complete their sentences and re-enter society.

Despite a new executive director with communications experience and a background in television, the Church Federation's communications program did not see a major revival in the 1990s. Its programs *Faces of Faith* and *Religion in the News* continued broadcasting, though Faces of Faith later moved to the Internet.[52] In 1995 Channel 13 moved *Time for Timothy* from its main station and to its lower power station, Channel 27. Throughout the 1990s the Federation searched for new ideas for a children's show, but never created a new program. In 1995 the Federation hired Julie Foster as its new communications consultant and she focused on updating the Federation's logo and redesigning its print newsletter, the *Federation Forecast,* which the Federation produced until 2003. The group's new prioritization of education, crime prevention, and race relations made previously strong ministries like the Communications Unit a lower, though still important, priority. Combined with technological changes and the increasing cost of producing original programming, the Federation's communications program diminished in the late 1990s.

Other continuing Federation ministries sought to coordinate Indianapolis churches and ministries more effectively. Ministries in Specialized Settings continued to facilitate chaplaincy programs in Indianapolis, including the Indianapolis Police Department Chaplaincy.[53] The Indianapolis Interfaith Airport Chaplaincy continued its work for many years under the leadership of the Federation until it became an independent organization in 2003.[54] The Federation started a Clearing House Ministry in the late 1990s to help churches network with each other and with people in the faith community who could provide helpful services. The ministry no longer exists under that name, but the Federation's mantra today is "building faith-based networks," which it does through projects such as publishing its annual directory of churches and faith-based groups. The Clergy Badge Program continues to provide official identification for clergy to use when ministering in hospitals and other institutions.

In addition to its various programs, the Church Federation worked to fulfill its principal mission of uniting the faith community. One of its major projects in the late 1990s was helping to bring the Billy Graham Crusade to Indianapolis on 3-6 June 1999. The Federation worked to unite churches in organizing the massive event that saw an attendance of 193,500 over four days and received over 15,000 new believers. More than 20,000 volunteers helped put on the services.[55] The Billy Graham Crusade brought together Indianapolis churches and the community on a large scale and thus served as an appropriate final major event of the 1990s for the Church Federation. It embodied many of the themes from the Federation's history such as ecumenism, faith, and evangelism. The Crusade provided a fitting project for the Federation at the close of the decade and the millennium.

Conclusion

As the final calendar pages flew by in 1999, the nation looked to the new millennium with some trepidation. Fears about the ramifications of the Y2K computer bug had some people stockpiling food and water. Fortunately computer programmers successfully enabled most machines to display four digit dates, rather than two, and the nation avoided any Y2K related crises, but the transition to a new millennium still remained unsettling for many. The city of Indianapolis experienced prosperous economic times at the start of the 2000s and continued its long tradition of philanthropy and activism to improve the quality of life for its residents, of which the Church Federation was a part. But the problems the Federation worked on in the 1990s, including crime, race relations, education, and poverty remained. Still, as Indianapolis community leaders, including Walker-Smith, looked toward the future they remained optimistic about the community's ability to confront those challenges and find solutions.[56]

The 1990s had been a challenging decade for the Church Federation as it encountered financial and organizational challenges and watched the city of Indianapolis experience tumultuous events. Though the first years of the decade brought financial troubles and a leadership transition that seemed to threaten the group's existence, the Church Federation re-emerged from a year of reflection and evaluation with a new sense of direction and purpose. With Walker-Smith as the new executive director, the Federation focused on meeting what it viewed as the city's most pressing needs by focusing on crime, education, and race relations. Its recognition of the spiritual as well as the physical aspects of these problems made the Federation's responses unique among Indianapolis organizations. The group started new programs such as Celebration of Hope and the Sanctuary Church Movement that garnered significant participation from the community and public recognition. As the Church Federation carried out its programs, it embraced an even more expansive definition of ecumenism that was characterized by racial diversity and cooperation with people from faiths beyond Christianity. The Federation remained a distinctly Christian organization, but built relationships with other groups and the wider community. Through the Church Federation's fervent efforts and outpouring of compassion, the city of Indianapolis came closer to experiencing "shalom." Perhaps just as importantly, the Church Federation's many programs helped thousands of individuals experience peace in their own lives. And those thousands of individual transformations are what truly make the difference.

Endnotes

1   James A. Gillaspy and Sherri Edwards, "Silent Protest Sparks Violence," *Indianapolis Star,* 27 July 1995; Dan Carpenter and Mary Francis, "Residents Stand Divided over Cause of Problems," *Indianapolis Star,* 28 July 1995; Sherri Edwards, "Sporadic Violence Strikes Area," *Indianapolis Star,* 28 July 1995; Annette L. Anderson, "Suspect Accuses IPD Officers of Assault," *Indianapolis Recorder,* 5 August 1995.

2   *Martindale Brightwood Neighborhood, Indianapolis, Indiana: Timeline, 1872-1994,* The Polis Center at IUPUI, 1998; *Fountain Square Neighborhood, Indianapolis, Indiana: Timeline, 1820-1997,* The Polis Center at IUPUI, 1997.

3   Charles Guthrie, Dan Briere, and Mary Moore, *The Indianapolis Hispanic Community*. (Indianapolis: University of Indianapolis Press, 1995).

4   Minutes of the Board of Directors Meeting, 28 June 1988 and 31 March 1989, Church Federation Records (hereafter CF), Indiana Historical Society, Indianapolis, Indiana.

5   Bruce Naylor and Philip Amerson, Letter to Finance Committee/Board of Directors, 10 November 1989; Minutes of the Executive Committee Meeting, 20 November 1990, CF.

6   Mitchell E. Daniels and Jan D. Finney, "Society of Retired Executives Consulting Evaluation for the Church Federation of Greater Indianapolis," 24 April 1992, report submitted to 19 May 1992 Executive Committee Meeting.

7   "Report to the Executive Committee, January 4, 1988, from the Communications Unit," CF.

8   Communications Unit Meeting Minutes, 19 May 1989 and 25 January 1990; *Federation Forecast,* October/November 1990.

9   Share the Vision of VISN, 17 April 1991, CF.

10 Urban Affairs Unit Meeting Minutes, 21 September 1989, CF; *Federation Forecast,* October/November 1990.

11 Executive Committee Meeting Minutes, 18 June 1991; Contingency Fund Committee Meeting Minutes, 12 February 1991, CF.

12 Board of Directors Meeting Minutes, 28 January 1991, CF.

13 Executive Committee Meeting Minutes, 19 March 1991 and 27 August 1991, CF.

14 Board of Directors Meeting Minutes, 30 April 1990; Executive Committee Meeting Minutes, 16 June 1992; Board of Directors Meeting Minutes, 22 June 1992, CF.

15 Scott L. Miley, "Airport Chaplains Aid Victims' Kin," *Indianapolis Star,* 5 November 1994.

16 Paul McClure interviewed by author, 10 June 2009, Franklin, Indiana.

17 Congregational Concerns Unit Meeting Minutes, 1987-1988, CF.

18 Program for 80th Anniversary Celebration Worship, 7 June 1992, at Roberts Park United Methodist Church, CF.

19 Executive Committee Meeting Minutes, 15 September 1992, CF.

20 Executive Director's Report, 22 June 1992, CF.

21 Carol Elrod, "Financially Ailing Church Federation to Lose its Director," *Indianapolis Star,* 8 July 1992.

244

22 Gregory Weaver, "Money Woes May Alter Mission of Church Unit," *Indianapolis Star,* 2 December 1992.

23 Daniels and Finney, "Consulting Evaluation," 24 April 1992, CF.

24 Carol Blinzinger Report to Executive Committee, 13 December 1992 to 19 January 1993, CF.

25 Executive Committee Meeting Minutes, 22 February 1993, CF.

26 Angelique Walker-Smith interviewed by author, 27 September 2011, Indianapolis, Indiana.

27 Gregory Weaver, "First Black and Woman Chosen to Lead Troubled Church Group," *Indianapolis Star,* 23 February 1993.

28 Walker-Smith interview, 27 September 2011.

29 Ibid.

30 *The Federation Forecast,* Spring/Summer 1996, CF.

31 "Diversity Sets Stage for Installation of Church Federation's Executive Director," *Federation Forecast,* Fall 1995, CF.

32 Walker-Smith interview, 27 September 2011.

33 Gregory Weaver, "Religious, Civic Groups Plan Rally to Counter Klan Gathering," *Indianapolis Star,* 27 September 1993.

34 Andrea Neal, "Ex-Klansman Trades his Robe of Hatred for a Cleric's Garb," *Indianapolis Star,* 25 September 1993.

35 Pamphlet: "Celebration of Hope," Indianapolis co-chairs: Rev. Ivan Douglas Hicks and Dr. Kent Millard, no date, CF.

36 *Federation Forecast,* Fall 1996; Judith Cebula, "Forging Ties that Bind," *Indianapolis Star,* 24 June 1996.

37 *Federation Forecast,* Spring 2001.

38 2007 Annual Report, CF.

39 Walker-Smith interview, 27 September 2011.

40 *Federation Forecast,* Spring 1997, CF.

41 Walker-Smith interview, 27 September 2011.

42 Judith Cebula, "Hunters of Hope," *Indianapolis Star,* 19 September 1996.

43 *Federation Forecast,* Spring 1999, and 1998 Annual Report, CF.

44 Dianna Penner, "Mentors Will Help Families Coping with Violent Deaths," *Indianapolis Star,* 31 August 1999.

45 *Federation Forecast,* Spring/Summer 1996.

46 *Martindale Brightwood Neighborhood, Indianapolis, Indiana: Timeline, 1872-1994,* The Polis Center at IUPUI, 1998; *Fountain Square Neighborhood, Indianapolis, Indiana: Timeline, 1820-1997,* The Polis Center at IUPUI, 1997; *Federation Forecast,* Spring 1999 and Fall 1999, CF.

47 Walker-Smith interview, 27 September 2011.

48 *Federation Forecast,* Spring/Summer 1996; Spring 1997; Spring 1999, CF.

49 *Federation Forecast,* Spring 2000, CF.

50 John Bansch, "Program Has Lessons for Young Students, Tutors," *Indianapolis Star,* 20 December 1997.

51 *Federation Forecast,* Spring/Summer 1996.

52 2008 Annual Report, CF.

53 *Federation Forecast,* Spring 2002, CF.

54 2003 Annual Report, CF.

55 *Federation Forecast,* Fall 1999 and Spring 2000, CF.

56 Stephen Beaven, "City's Bright Future Includes Some Hard Issues, Observers Say," *Indianapolis Star,* 3 January 2000.

1. Race, religion and politics forum at St. Luke's United Methodist Church

2. Community prayer service for families of victims of violent death.

3. Executive Director Angelique Walker-Smith

4. Child participant at Faithfest, a multicultural festival of various expressions of faith.

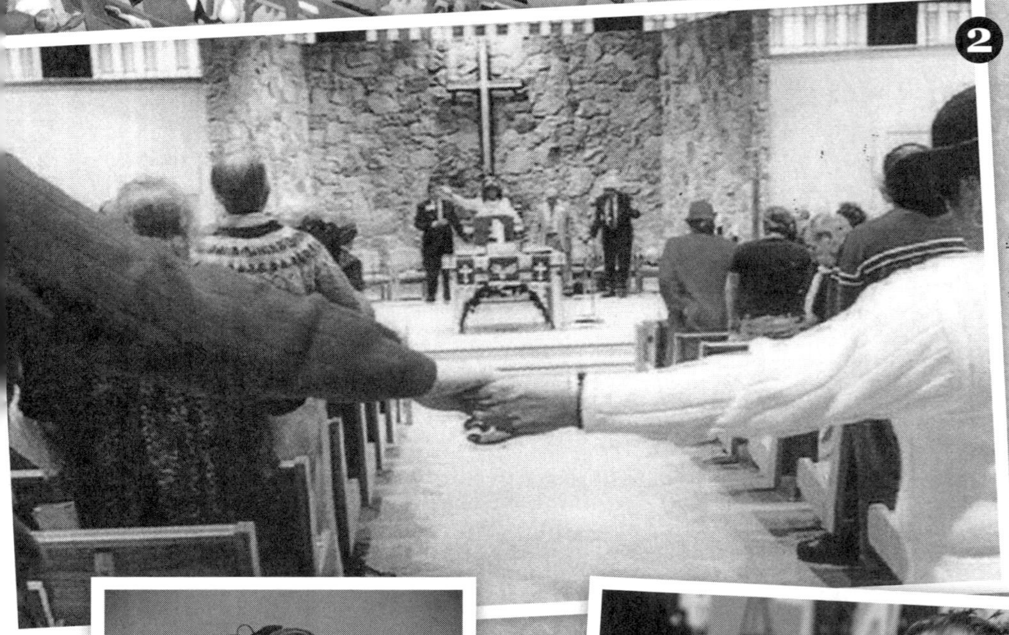

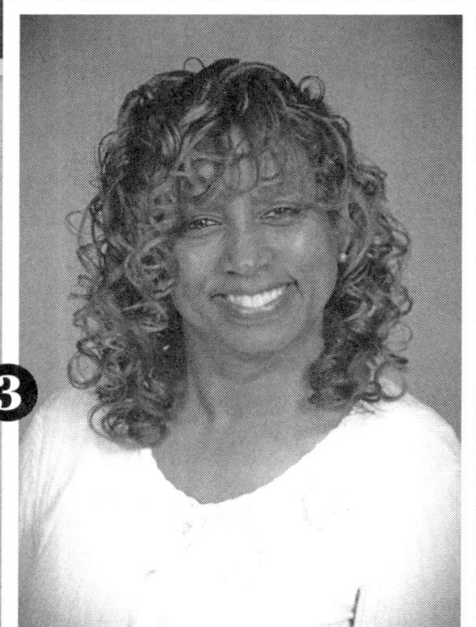

Olan Mills

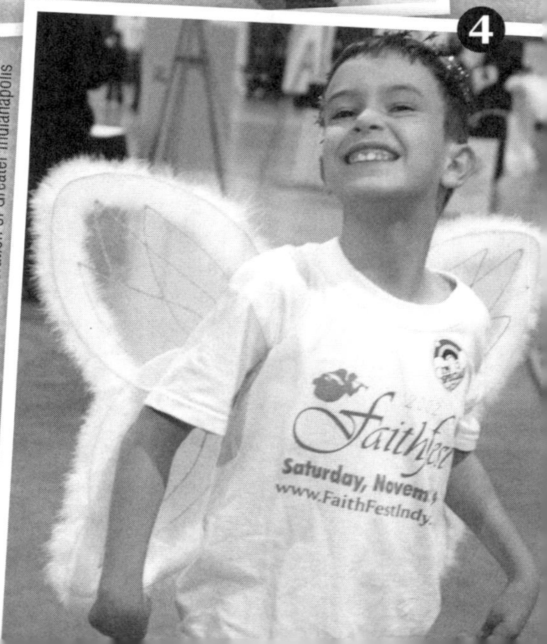

Faithfest

Saturday, Novem

www.FaithFestIndy.

2000s

The Church Federation in the New Millennium

Amanda J. Koch and John Warner

E ARLY IN HER TENURE AS EXECUTIVE DIRECTOR, the Reverend Dr. Angelique Walker-Smith refocused the Church Federation's efforts on three areas – crime, race relations, and education.[1] Emphasis on these three areas was more in keeping with service to the needs of the Indianapolis community rather than a reflection of the Federation's historical attempts to dictate to the faith community. Its struggles continued for the next several years after Walker-Smith's assumption of leadership in 1995. Staff reductions and budgetary concerns required more than the usual attention but optimism reigned. The Federation now had new focus, new leadership, and a new enthusiasm in anticipation of the upcoming millennium.[2]

The Church Federation of Greater Indianapolis entered the year 2000 with a new sense of direction and in a stronger financial position than it had achieved in years. The Federation adopted a new business plan, based on an external evaluation, to direct its work and resolved to retain only those programs that its membership valued. The external evaluation by the Executive Service Corps of

249

Indianapolis revealed what member congregations liked, disliked, and/or desired the Church Federation to be to the faith-based community of Indianapolis. From this analysis, the Federation derived a business plan predicated on linking the organization's members to maximize interrelationships. Captured in four succinct statements of intent, the Federation intended to implement the new plan by:

- Linking Resources & Referrals;
- Linking Relationships;
- Linking Stories; and
- Linking Voices.

The new business plan included strategies to support the shift in emphasis from a directed approach by the Federation on specific actions/activities to a more capstone mission of membership support. An increased focus on marketing, fund raising-development, and organizational transition/ restructuring sought to bring about change in the organizational philosophy. The end result of this change caused the elimination of some programs and only the programs "valued and owned by the membership" remained. By 2004 the plan's evolution began to meet earlier expectations "that [it] will lead to more effective delivery of member-based ministries and programs." As the Federation's executive director noted, "not-for-profits [organizations] need to learn to function on a business footing" in these times.[3]

Although this new business plan oriented efforts to establishing linkages, it did not automatically obviate the need for continuing earlier ministries that offered support to local needs but rather rethink those needs and develop strategies best suited to meeting them.

The Message via the Media

One of the continued ministries dealt with the communications to and within the faith community. Despite all efforts by the new executive director, the Church Federation's communications

250

program continued to languish throughout the early years of the new century. As local television stations changed their programming focus, the ability of the faith community to communicate through television programs continued to diminish. The Federation's programs *Faces of Faith* and *Religion in the News* now reached the community via the Internet.[4] The *Federation Forecast,* the organization's newsletter, remained in publication until 2003. Since that date, the yearly activities and successes have been captured in the organization's annual reports.[5] Now, the Church Federation invests less in video or print communications projects and instead focuses on its online Web presence. In September 2009 the Church Federation launched its new website, Indyfaith. org, with the goal of creating a communications hub for the Indianapolis faith community.

The Church in the Community

Rev. Dr. Walker-Smith's commitment to social service increased the number of ministries dedicated to that end exponentially. The Federation continued some of its existing programs. The Benevolence Fund continued to distribute money from the Lilly Endowment to faith-based ministries throughout the Greater Indianapolis area emphasizing projects such as church-related social services within neighborhoods. In the mid-1990s the Fund started giving money to the CROP fund for distribution to local food pantries.[6] As of 2010 the Fund continued to provide CROP-World Service and Lilly funds through grants to local churches, agencies, and food pantries in the community. In keeping with the new emphasis on community needs, the Benevolence Fund, in conjunction with local law enforcement agencies, gave a grant to a gun buyback program in order to get weapons off the streets and prevent gun violence.[7]

Another social service ministry, Family and Congregation Mentoring Program, aimed at preserving families in low-income Indianapolis neighborhoods. The program provided various programs to community centers in the Meridian-Kessler, Fountain

Square, and Martindale Brightwood neighborhoods.[8] The Family
and Congregation Mentoring Program maintained these centers
until 2002 when a new program, the Church and Neighborhood
Partnership, took over its mission in these neighborhoods.[9] The
Partnership, in support and with the support of low-income housing
residents, lobbied for hazardous waste cleanup in the Martindale
Brightwood neighborhood. At the Blackburn Terrace and Laurel
Wood low-income housing complexes, the Partnership worked with
residents to identify needs and other partnerships to be developed to
aid in neighborhood improvement.[10]

Since the last decade of the twentieth century, prison ministries
have been within the Federation's purview. The Federation
coordinated with chaplains at the Indiana Women's Prison and
Rockville Correctional Facility to help inmates complete their
sentences and re-enter society.[11] By 2000 the Federation's direct
involvement with the women's prison ministry decreased but
chaplains still visited the prisons. In the ensuing years, the
Federation launched a new program called "Faith and Fathers."[12]
This program sought to help incarcerated young men become better
fathers by providing mentors and parenting classes for inmates at
the Plainfield and Pendleton Juvenile Correctional Facilities. In
2006 the program shifted entirely to the Pendleton Facility, but the
Federation continues its mission to help young men find their faith
and live up to their responsibilities as parents.[13]

Chaplaincy programs, another of the ministries continued after
the reorganization, connected the community with the Christian
faith and offered assistance where possible. Ministries in Specialized
Settings continued to facilitate chaplaincy programs in Indianapolis,
including the Indianapolis Police Department Chaplaincy.[14] The
Indianapolis Interfaith Airport Chaplaincy continued its work for
many years under the leadership of the Church Federation until it
became an independent organization in 2003.[15] The Clergy Badge
Program, which provides official identification for clergy to use when
ministering in hospitals and other institutions, supplied badges to
90 pastors and other clergy in 2007.[16]

New Ministries to Serve the Community

As it sought to address the changing needs of an increasingly diverse metropolitan area, the Federation established new ministries under Walker-Smith's leadership and refocused the organization's ability to fulfill its mission and the linkages defined under the new 2001 business plan.

The Sanctuary Church Movement, started in 1995, evolved into the Prayer Vigils and Ecumenical Project for Reconciliation & Healing (EPRH). The Federation's original purpose under the aegis of this program concerned providing safe places where mediation could replace violence and churches could partner with community groups to build relationships and solve problems before they became crises.[17] As the need for more support to those left behind as a result of violent death to a family member or friend became apparent, the program expanded to a prayer vigil ministry at the sites of these deaths, an offering of mentors to counsel, and a training program for mentors. In 2006 the ministry conducted 120 vigils after a particularly violent year (153 deaths in all). By 2007 the program had 24 lay and clergy mentors active in the service of those in need.[18] The Sanctuary Church Movement also worked to prevent violence from occurring by starting a Youth Speakers Bureau and conducting twice-yearly services of Remembrance and Peacemaking.[19] In 2006 EPRH received a $50,000 federal Hope II grant to improve program capacity. In 2010 in response to local homicides (96) the Federation conducted 80 vigils to pray for the victims and their survivors. EPRH continues today to train mentors and provide hope for families facing personal loss.[20]

Loving Our Children is an educational initiative seeking to form partnerships between Indianapolis Public Schools and neighborhood churches to reach at-risk children in an environment that offers a variety of activities, such as sports, recreation, and tutoring. In 2006 St. Luke's United Methodist Church, one of the city's largest churches, adopted IPS' School 20, and made a three to five year commitment to tutor and mentor their students.[21]

Celebration of Hope, a program focused on racial reconciliation, became one of the Federation's principal worship and educational initiatives. Pulpit exchanges between black and white churches, pairings that became an integral part of the program, fostered relationships and understanding between various congregations through the auspices of their pastors. In 2001 F. Willis Johnson, Jr. became executive vice president of Celebration of Hope. Johnson raised the visibility of the program through his communications skills that included radio talks and a weekly column in the *Indianapolis Recorder*.[22] Throughout the life of this partnership between it, member churches, and the Federation, Celebration of Hope energized the various congregations involved in the program to seek better understanding of ways and means to counter the effects of racism. Even in its last year, Celebration of Hope brought 2,500 participants to its Spring Worship Service at Tabernacle Presbyterian Church.[23] The Celebration officially dissolved in 2007, but the Church Federation continues the work of racial reconciliation with programs like Sacred Conversations and the Hispanic/Latino Forum.[24]

A Pastors and Christian Leaders Summit in 2003 illustrated one result of this new direction strategy evolving from the new organizational/business plan adopted in 2001. The summit, entitled "Organize, Mobilize and Energize," brought together a who's who list of Indianapolis business and community leaders to discuss ways of creating links between faith and the community.[25] By creating these links the Federation sought to reestablish a long-diminished interconnectedness that once combined the efforts of local "movers and shakers" and the faith community. Now, much more inclusive of the disparate components of "community", this move harkens back to the pivotal role of local community leaders (primarily white and protestant at the time) who were instrumental in founding the Federation. The success of this effort to link business, community, and faith leadership continued to be apparent in 2009 as the Federation regularly partnered with various leaderships and the Indianapolis Chamber of Commerce during the year to discuss progress and future efforts, and to maintain channels of communication. Operationally, the Federation moved forward in implementation of its new motto, "organizing, mobilizing, and energizing faith-based networks." Implementation included seeking new ways to represent the faith community both in supporting its membership and within the larger community.[26]

The Church Federation's new plan continued some programs previously mentioned and pioneered several others during these years. In 2000 the organization hosted over 100 congregations and organizations and 1,000 people at FaithFest, an event designed to celebrate religious diversity and increase awareness of the Church Federation's mission. The first FaithFest was held 11 November 2000 at the Indiana State Fairgrounds. The event included live performances, children and youth activities, community services, speakers, and a cake walk. The day ended with a community prayer service and fellowship meal.[27] The Federation held the event annually through 2003. In 2004 FaithFest and a Federation-sponsored discussion group, the Greater Indianapolis Urban Forum, became part of the Federation's annual convocation and meetings. This Forum, co-sponsored by the Federation and the Indianapolis Athletic Club and inaugurated in 2000, provided (usually at a luncheon) a venue for discussions of community faith, public policy, and other broad issues.[28]

In the spirit of a growing national trend in environmental activism, the Church Federation established a short-lived, but highly visible program called Stewardship of Creation. The program sought to educate churches about the dangers of climate change and provide practical responses to it. The program collected signatures from faith-based groups on environmental petitions, conducted training sessions, and supplied faith groups with compact fluorescent light bulbs for use or resale for fundraising.[29] The program coordinated with the Indiana Faith-Based Climate and Energy Campaign at FaithFest 2002 to give away a hybrid car.[30] The program gained media exposure in local and church publications and on a CBS production on religion and environmental issues. Like other programs/ministries evaluated against the new 2001 plan philosophy this effort served a specific purpose, obvious through its title, but did not make the cut when compared to others programs vying for scarce resources.[31]

The early years of the new millennium brought better financial times for the Federation. In 2003 the Lilly Endowment once again supported a part-time Director of Development, Dr. J.C. Lasmanis.[32] Major grants from the Nina Mason Pulliam Charitable Trust and the Indianapolis Foundation also improved the financial outlook of the organization.[33] In the same year, local businessman and philanthropist P.E. MacAllister, chairman of MacAllister Machinery Corporation, spearheaded the Mustard Seed Campaign, a project aimed at securing major donors for the Church Federation. The effort raised an extra $100,000 per year for the next three years, an unusual period of time in the Federation's financial lifespan when income actually exceeded expenses.

Representing the Faith Community

The first decade of the millennium provided the Federation with almost too many opportunities to demonstrate its importance as a representative of the faith community. After the terrorist attacks on the World Trade Center and the Pentagon on 11 September 2001, the Church Federation helped unite the Indianapolis faith community in quelling anti-Muslim sentiment. On the afternoon of 11 September, the Federation and other religious organizations sponsored a prayer service in the garden of the Interchurch Center and took out a full-page advertisement in the *Indianapolis Star,* with other Indianapolis churches, against anti-Muslim violence or demonstrations. Four years later, in 2005, Hurricane Katrina's assault on the city of New Orleans energized the Federation to join with other Indianapolis groups to organize relief. The Federation sent two individuals to direct relief efforts and help some families relocate to Indianapolis.[34] The Federation continues annual memorial services in honor of both events.

Celebration of Hope's dissolution did not obviate the need for a forum for racial reconciliation. The Federation established the Hispanic-Latino Urban Forum in 2002. Fostered under a partnership between the Federation and the Indianapolis Athletic Club, this forum seeks to address issues important to the Hispanic-Latino and to promote dialogue between this rapidly growing population and the rest of the community.[35] The meetings grew to include "cultural immersion" trips to Hispanic and African American historical and cultural sites and celebration of Hispanic-Latino culture. The program also included meetings to discuss issues of race and diversity.[36] In 2005 a group of twenty-five African American and Hispanic pastors commenced meeting to discuss ways to bring their two communities closer together.[37] In June 2006 African American and Hispanic Christians held a joint worship service at St. Rita Catholic Church. The service had been planned for some time, but its timeliness and necessity became evident to all its attendees when less than twenty-four hours before the service a seven-member Hispanic family was murdered in their home. The Indianapolis police arrested several African American men as suspects in the crime. The incident created a potential racial confrontation between the two groups. The Reverend Felipe Martinez, a key leader in organizing the service, said the gathering allowed them to communicate and grieve together.[38] This program, along with Sacred Conversations, another Federation program designed to enhance race relations, continues to work to overcome racial and cultural barriers in the community.

A major new program of social service, the Loaves and Fishes Advocacy Network, signaled an effort to help member churches make the best possible use of a rare resource – their benevolence funds. The network seemed a natural fit for the Linking Resources & Referrals lobe of the new business plan instituted in 2002. A concurrent grant from the Nina Mason Pulliam Charitable Trust paid for a program director. The next year, the program held training workshops on diversity, case management, and grant writing.[39] In August 2004 Loaves and Fishes became operational at St. Lawrence Catholic Church and served 106 families with rent and utility assistance, spiritual support, and referrals to other agencies that could assist needy families.[40] By 2005, with benevolence funds pooled by nine churches, the Federation opened a second site at St.

Luke's United Methodist Church. In 2007 the program became the Caring Churches Network and serves the community through the auspices of Catholic, Presbyterian, and United Methodist churches in Indianapolis and Zionsville. By 2009 the ministry served over 300 recipients with assistance with housing and utilities.[41]

Numerous milestones marked this first decade of the twenty-first century for the Church Federation. In June 2002 the Federation celebrated its 90th anniversary with a program and play at the Indiana Historical Society where the Federation's historical records are stored.[42] Three years later, in 2005, the Federation welcomed its first Catholic President, Father John Beitans of St. Lawrence Catholic Church.[43] In 2007 the Federation honored the 50th anniversary of its children's show, *Time for Timothy,* with a program and activities at the Children's Museum of Indianapolis.[44]

Organizationally, the closing years of the decade reflected the continued focus of the Church Federation's mission of service to the faith community and the community of Greater Indianapolis. Specific mission objectives for the year 2008–2010 included making visible God's gift of unity in Jesus Christ and being a convener of church and church-based groups that respond to needs of the community; encouraging advocacy; and promoting service to others. Old and new ministries instituted under the aegis of the 2002-2004 business plan moved forward to extend help to the needy through the Caring Churches Network and the Hunger Fund Grants programs. Mentoring programs like Faith & Fathers continue to offer spiritual help to incarcerated young men; some are enrolled in parenting classes. Through various media such as *IndyFaith. org*, *Faces of Faith*, and *Religion in the News*, the Federation communicates with the local community. The Hispanic/Latino Forum built bridges between different cultural groups. Finally, the Ecumenical Project for Reconciliation and Healing worked to manage the sorrow attending violent deaths in the community and promote the healing process through vigils, mentoring, and various programs of remembrance.[45]

The Recent Past

The years 2010-2012 have been a period of increased and deepened relationships with old and new churches as well as with other faith-based partners through the planning of the Church Federation's Centennial observances. The process of planning started 2008 and has deepened the board's and staff's critical reflection on its past while providing renewed insights about the core values of the organization and its important roles of convener, collaborator, and catalyst. The specific projects of this centennial year have included a collaboration with Butler University's Center for Faith and Vocation focusing on "Global Christianity in the 21st Century"; a Week of Prayer for Christian Unity Lecture Series highlighting spiritual biographies in Greater Indianapolis done in partnership with Marian University, Crossroads Bible College, IUPUI, Franklin College, and Christian Theological Seminary; and a conference entitled "Vision of Faith in Greater Indianapolis" held at Martin University and featuring former mayors William Hudnut and Bart Peterson.

Other centennial events included an exhibit on the Federation's history at the Interchurch Center; a gala centennial celebration at the Indiana Roof Ballroom on 7 June that acknowledged the impact of the Church Federation and its benefactors; the unveiling of this centennial history publication on 9 June at the Indiana History Center; and a Sacred Walking Tour of the sites of downtown member churches and places where the Church Federation was born. Of great significance is the Centennial Village Build of ten homes in the Martindale Brightwood neighborhood in partnership with Community Resurrection Partnership, Habitat for Humanity, Martindale Brightwood Community Development Corporation, and Faith, Hope and Love, a project that has renewed the interest of the member churches and their partners. Finally, the Church Federation has been engaged in a consultative planning process to explore how the organization can advance its mission over the course of the next century.

259

Conclusion

The first decade of the twenty-first century witnessed more than a few changes in organizational philosophy mixed with operational housecleaning. With the acceptance and recognition that doing business "in the same manner" was no longer feasible or even mission-fulfilling, the leadership of the Federation adopted the new philosophy spelled out in the 2001 plan, took that plan and expanded it, and adopted a new plan for the period 2005-2007 and beyond to continue the momentum that will lead to more effective delivery of member-based ministries. Intertwined amongst and inseparable from these plans are the personalities and skills brought to the table by professionals and volunteers alike. In somewhat the same manner that "location, location, location" vocalizes a guiding principle for realtors, "development, development, development" became a guiding principle for new efforts by the Federation to insure its viability. The work of individuals such as Dr. J.C. Lasmanis, P.E. MacAllister, the Reverend Dr. Ray J. Marquette, and others who rendered their professional and often voluntary service to the Federation moved the organization from a not-for-profit, teetering on the edge of financial disaster, to a not-for-profit meeting its requirements and commitments to support its membership and continue to expand its capabilities to survive. Without this tenacity in its basic tenets, the Federation could not have provided for the faith and material needs of the Indianapolis community. During the past decade, the guidance, involvement, and support of the presidents and boards sustained an environment for change. This progressive approach to management allowed the operative element of the organization the freedom to adapt its efforts to meet challenges in support of the membership.

The Church Federation of Greater Indianapolis has a rich history that retains a solid foundation for future work. While remaining faithful to the themes of faith, Christianity unity, diversity, service, and education, the Church Federation continues its work and its commitment as it represents the faith community in Indianapolis at this centennial and in the years to come.

Endnotes

1   Rev. Dr. Angelique Walker-Smith, "Focus on the Federation: An Update From Your Executive Director," *Federation Forecast*, Fall, 1995, Issue 5, 2.

2   1996 Annual Report, *Federation Forecast*, Spring 1997, Issue 10, Church Federation of Greater Indianapolis Records (hereafter CF), Indiana Historical Society, Indianapolis, Indiana.

3   *Federation Forecast*, Spring, 2001 and 2000 Annual Report. Vol. 7, Issue 1; *Federation Forecast,* Fall, 2001. Vol. 7, Issue 2. *Federation Forecast*, Spring, 2002; 2001 Annual Report, Vol. 8, Issue 1; and 2004 Annual Report; Interview with the Executive Director on 19 March 2012., CF.

4   2008 Annual Report, http://churchfederationindy.org/images/2008AnnualReport.pdf. Accessed October 8, 2009.

5   Julie Foster, "A Message from Your Editor" *Federation Forecast*, Spring/Summer, 1996, Issue 7.

6   1995 Annual Report, pp. 4-5; 2008 Annual Report, CF..

7   *Federation Forecast*, Fall, 1999. Vol. 5, Issue 2; 2010 Annual Report, *The Church Federation*, Centerfold; "Just 1 Minute," *Indianapolis Star*, 30 June 2007.

8   1995 Annual Report, 4-5, CF.

9   2001 Annual Report, *Federation Forecast*, Spring 2002, Vol. 8, Issue 1, CF.

10 2004 Annual Report, CF.

11 1995 Annual Report, 4-5, CF.

12 1999 Annual Report, *Federation Forecast*, Spring 2000, Vol. 6, Issue 1, CF.

13 2005 Annual Report; 2006 Annual Report, CF.

14 2001 Annual Report, CF.

15 2003 Annual Report, CF.

16 *Annual Report*, 2007, Committee & Ministry Reports, 7, CF.

17 *Federation Forecast*, Fall, 1995, Issue 5.

18 *Annual Report*, 2006, Committee & Ministry Reports, 4; *Annual Report*, 2007, Committee & Ministry Reports, 4, CF.

19 *Federation Forecast*, Spring, 1997. Issue 10..

20 2006 Annual Report, 4, CF.

21 Russ Pulliam, "Church, School Build Lasting Relationship," *Indianapolis Star*, 10 December 2006.

22 *Annual Report*, 2002, 4, CF.

23 *Annual Report*, 2007, 7, CF.

24 2007 Annual Report, CF.

25 2002 Annual Report, *Federation Forecast*, Spring, 2003 and 2002 Annual Report. Vol. 9, Issue 1, CF.

26 *Federation Forecast,* Fall, 2001, Vol. 7, Issue 2, CF; Judith Cebula, "Faiths unite for peace - Different religions grieve as one," *Indianapolis Star*, 12 September 2001; Flyer for Service of Remembrance and Peacemaking on Anniversary of 9/11. Sunday, 8 September 2002, CF; Special Report 2009, *Mission & Ministry Successes,* The Church Federation of Greater Indianapolis, 3, CF.

27 *Federation Forecast*, Spring, 2001 and 2000 Annual Report. Vol. 7, Issue 1, CF.

28 2004 Annual Report, CF.

29 *Federation Forecast,* Spring, 2001 and 2000 Annual Report. Vol. 7, Issue 1, CF.

30 2002 Annual Report, CF.

31 2003 Annual Report, CF.

32 Ibid.

33 "$698,000 in Grants Aid Local Groups," *Indianapolis Star*, 13 April 2004; "Pulliam Charitable Trust Awards Grants Totaling $1.6 Million," *Indianapolis Star*, 15 November 2004; Rob Schneider, "Pulliam Trust Will Award $1.8 Million in Grants Today," *Indianapolis Star*, 20 March 2006.

34 2005 Annual Report; Blair Claflin, "A Faith Rewarded - New Orleans Pastor Finds a New Church," *Indianapolis Star*, 30 August 2007.

35 2002 Annual Report, CF.

36 2004 Annual Report, CF.

37 Robert King, "Two Communities United in Faith – Black and Hispanic Christians Hold a Combined Service," *Indianapolis Star*, 3 June 2006.

38 Ibid.

39 2002 Annual Report; 2003 Annual Report, CF.

40 2004 Annual Report, CF.

41 Annual Report, *Federation Forecast*, Fall 2001, Volume 7, Issue 2; *Annual Report*, 2007, Committee & Ministry Reports, 7 ; Special Report 2009, *Mission & Ministry Successes,* The Church Federation of Greater Indianapolis, 1.

42 Program for 90th Anniversary, CF.

43 Angelique Walker-Smith, "Pope Inspired Dialogue with Other Faiths, "*Indianapolis Star*, 11 April 2005.

44 2007 Annual Report, CF.

45 2010 Brochure "Our Successes 2010," CF.

Conclusion

Paul A. Crow, Jr., Richard Hamm, and Angelique Walker-Smith

T HE HISTORY OF THE CHURCH FEDERATION OF
Greater Indianapolis is a significant witness to the prayer
of Jesus Christ that "they [his disciples] all may be one."
(John 17:11, 20-26). In the Indiana part of the Church,
religious leaders and congregations have across the years committed
themselves to seeking and hopefully manifesting the unity for which
our Lord prayed. The chapters included in this volume have chronicled,
decade by decade, how the congregations, judicatories, and visionary
Christians in Indianapolis have sought to be a community that lives
out Jesus' prayer for "oneness." It is the biblical calling of all Christians
and congregations in Indiana and throughout the world. In truth the
scandal of our divisions harms the churches' proclamation of the Gospel
and makes our mission in Christ's name ineffective. The Church's unity
is given by God in Christ to be a sign to all people of the unity that God
has given to the human community. Hence, the unity of the Church is
part of the salvation of the world.

The essays in this volume have explained how Christians in this part
of the Church, have over the decades, sought to manifest the unity for
which Christ prayed and heal the divisions that tragically limit their

mission and even diminish the power of the Gospel in American society. If we are to be faithful to our Lord Jesus Christ, the search for Christian unity must be centrally integrated into the priorities and mission of the individual churches. The gift of unity which God has given us cannot be the calling of only scholars, bishops, and leaders of the churches.

Some historians have entitled the twentieth century as "the Ecumenical Century." This label is partially true. But, in reality the twenty-first century is also "the Ecumenical Century."

For today the ecumenical mandate given by our Lord Jesus Christ is incomplete. We have reconciled some of the divisions that shame the churches throughout the world, but alienation and brokenness are still visible to the world and severely divide the people of God. Surely, we are called afresh, in this place known as Indianapolis, Indiana, to be reconciled and show forth the unity God has given to all people.

In order to do this, this biblical mandate must be engaged with its particular relevance and timelines in a given season in which it is lived out. The stories found within these covers demonstrate the faithfulness of the churches, individuals, and groups over the last one hundred years. Federation historian Edwin Becker, in his book *From Sovereign to Servant*, recounted the first seventy-five years of faithfulness as expressed through The Church Federation of Greater Indianapolis. He argued that over the decades the Federation moved from a posture of being a "Council of Churches" that acted in a way that was "sovereign" to one of becoming a "servant" of the churches and the local faith community, thus demonstrating by its Seventy-fifth Anniversary the relevance and timeliness of The Church Federation in Indianapolis. Another indicator of this evolution of the organization was the varying locations of the Federation – from downtown to mid-town to the north side – and a name change that reflected the decentralized movement of the churches in Greater Indianapolis. Now, a new landscape shift in Christianity is occurring in Indianapolis and elsewhere in the world at the Centennial moment of The Church Federation of Greater Indianapolis.

This landscape shift includes the following as identified by the Reverend Dr. Richard Hamm, Executive Director of Christian Churches Together in the USA, the latest and most broadly inclusive national body promoting Christian unity and mission with many of the national churches and faith-based groups.[1]

1. We are experiencing a multi-generational moment with varying assumptions about institutional life. Studies show that those who came to adulthood after 1968 (Boomers and beyond) typically distrust institutions. People who came to adulthood before 1968 tend to experience God primarily through institutional life, while those coming to adulthood after 1968 tend to experience God primarily through relationships with individuals and in small groups.

2. Younger people tend to think of institutions as necessary evils and so the smaller the boards and the more streamlined the committee work the better since hands on mission *work* is preferred to *talking* about mission. Older folks tend to think about what is meaningful and then look for something to do about what they thought, while younger folks tend to do something and then think about what it means.

3. Before 1968, there was a "mainline culture" that had been driven primarily by white males. After 1968, "mainline culture" rapidly disintegrated so that today there is no one predominant culture.

4. Since 1968, we have seen a rise in the numbers of people who are of faiths other than Christian or of no faith at all. The cultural hegemony enjoyed by American Christianity before 1968 has been lost so that the culture is not only no longer carrying the language and concepts of Christian faith but is at best neutral toward Christian faith and often downright hostile toward it.

5. Since 1968, we have seen the "flattening" of the world, as Tom Friedman puts it, as hierarchical systems of all kinds have been collapsing, replacing pyramids with pancakes. Thus, *formal* power and authority that used to be granted by office has given way to *informal* power and authority that are granted, or

withheld, at the will of the people. Parents, teachers, pastors, and even bishops increasingly must prove themselves *worthy* of trust and authority.

6. Younger people grant authority not because someone has a title, but because they see how a leader genuinely cares and operates with integrity. This often threatens older people who have been used to honoring "formal power and authority" and who expect to be honored now that they are older just because they are older.

7. Information, and misinformation, now travel at the speed of light via the Web, Facebook, and Twitter. We expect the latest word instantly, accompanied by video. The constant flood of information overwhelms democracy, which moves at a snail's pace and slower because the hard work of dialogue, debate and compromise to create effective legislation takes time, and because individual politicians are playing to their own political base rather than doing that hard work.

8. Before 1968, the fundamental building block of world community was national sovereignty. After 1968 and the advent of satellites, two new building blocks were added: mass communication and the market.

9. The giving patterns of older and younger persons are starkly different. People over 60 were taught to tithe and to give regularly to religious and civic causes. Those under 60, typically less interested in institutions and their needs, tend to give sporadically and more often to specific appeals rather than in a regular ongoing way. This has already seriously weakened congregations, denominations and ecumenical organizations. At the same time, the economic fabric of the Western nations has been undercut by financially disastrous wars.

10. The ensuing financial crisis has not only resulted in massive unemployment and government deficits, but has reduced the resources available to churches and other non-profits, partly because of reduced contributions and partly because of the decimation of endowments and other invested funds.

11. The Internet has connected us in amazing ways, making it possible for people on several different continents to play games on line in real time and to share personal information at will. But, in spite of such virtual connection, people often feel isolated, anonymous and disconnected. We have become high-tech and low-touch.

12. We see at once people of all colors and ethnicities and generations sharing life and work in previously unknown ways in this country, yet we also see a kind of re-tribalization occurring in the face of the anxiety generated by change and the fear of what might be coming.

13. We see people living within generational bubbles that isolate us from one another: you can hear radio stations aimed at your own demographic only; you can watch TV specifically aimed at your demographic; you can shop in stores and attend public events and concerts aimed at your demographic only; each cruise line tends to appeal to specific demographics; even our religious experience and our congregations have been dividing along generational lines.

14. And we see these kinds of polarized dynamics not only between various groups, but within our very selves as individuals.

While he admits that these developments might be somewhat depressing and bad news, Hamm states that "there is good news, too; *great* news":

1. The work our churches and our church organizations (including our organizations promoting Christian unity and mission) are called to do is *as important as ever*. *Every* generation needs to know Jesus Christ and the post-modern world is as much the subject of God's mission as any previous era ever was!

2. God is still with us! God has not turned God's back on us! We just feel deserted sometimes because of our own anxiety and the resulting rigidity and fear which causes us to be blinded to God's presence and the new things God is trying to do among us. We

must again "Be transformed by the renewal of our minds," as Paul says in Romans 12:1.

3. We don't have to change everything, just the things that are killing us!

4. We can do what needs to be done, but to do it we must open ourselves anew to the Holy Spirit, and stop making institutional survival the mission. Jesus said, "Whoever seeks to save his life will lose it, but whoever loses his life for my sake will find it." It is as true for institutions as for individuals: mission is not something you do when you get the institution straightened out, when you get attendance and giving up. Mission is the life blood of the church, mission is *how* we get our institutions straightened out![2]

It is in light of this that The Church Federation has engaged an envisioning planning process while developing its Centennial Observances. Dr. Hamm has assisted The Church Federation in reflecting anew about its future. The Centennial projects of the Centennial Habitat Build with churches throughout Greater Indianapolis, Habitat for Humanity, Martindale-Brightwood Community Development Corporation, Community Resurrection Partnership, Faith, Hope and Love, and others has brought in new partners concerning this initiative and truly demonstrated the whole purpose of the Federation. The Week of Prayer for Christian Unity was observed with approximately six colleges and universities. The Federation also recognizes that its outreach has morphed beyond the boundaries of the "old city" into Central Indiana and that it must deploy a more limber organizational model with agile programs to meet the needs of churches and people.

The collaborative model that has occurred in these projects has increased participation and leadership of youth and young adults and is making The Church Federation more task-oriented versus old approaches of committee and other hierarchical modeling of being together in faith. A renewed model of collaboration with churches and faith-based and community groups that includes old and new churches as well as including more evangelical and immigrant churches and small churches is evolving. The Church Federation is discovering renewed language that encourages the particularity of its Christian identity and yet promote hospitality to all God's people, including a deepened understanding and dialogue with our multi-faith neighbors.

This shift is seeking to find ways to bring into closer relationship the fruits of programs, ministries, and churches born in the past with both as a joint collaborative approach that can serve as a catalyst of togetherness for greater impact of our mission still rooted in John 17:20-23.

The board of directors has approved the following for the future of The Church Federation of Greater Indianapolis. We hope and pray that it will be a tribute to the past and the present and faithful to an effective future direction for and with its beloved community of Greater Indianapolis.

Living the Gospel Together

A Shared Vision and Mission for the Second Century of
The Church Federation of Central Indiana

2012

Our Vision

The Church Federation:
A Catalyst for Working Together as the Body of
Christ for Service, Unity and Reconciliation

In our second century of service to the people
of central Indiana we commit to:

1. Seeking to build bridges between diverse Christian denominations and faith based groups
2. Responding to evils and injustice in our culture with a Christian response that promotes healing and justice
3. Reaching out to diverse cultural groups with initiatives that promote peace and harmony among peoples
4. Partnering with youth and young adults to maximize their energy and imagination to make a difference in our city through faith based ministry
5. Serving as a catalyst to lead individual congregations and faith based groups to minister in effectively meeting the needs of people in our city
6. Bringing together clergy, laity, churches and faith based groups for fellowship, encouragement, and networking to promote oneness in Christ and shared mission efforts
7. Celebrating and promoting unity in Christ through existing and potential prayer and worship events
8. Connecting churches and faith based groups with local civic leaders and institutions to impact our city for the good of all people

9. Promoting chaplaincy programs to civic and service organizations
10. Creating and maximizing training and in-service opportunities for member churches, organizations, and constituents

1   Dr. Richard Hamm, "The Changing Landscape" for the Executive Committee Retreat, The Church Federation of Greater Indianapolis, 21 February 2012.

2   Ibid.

Appendix I

The Church Federation of Indianapolis
Financial Contributors in 1916

Editor's Note: While historical tradition notes that there were "40 congregations" that were involved in the formation of The Church Federation of Indianapolis in 1912, no documents have yet been discovered that list those "founding/supporting congregations." However, through the research efforts of Dr. James J. Divita, professor emeritus of history, Marian University, we have the earliest known list of financial supporters for The Church Federation of Indianapolis. Not only does it reveal the distribution of denominations, but also the earliest known financial support from member congregations as well as their locations in the city of Indianapolis.

Denominations	Contributions
Presbyterians	$1,565
Methodists	1,460
Baptists	660
Disciples	610
Quaker	200
Evangelical	140
Reformed	80
Congregational	70
United Brethren	35
United Presbyterian	30
English Lutheran	30
Unitarian	25
Methodist Protestant	15
Universalists	10

Congregations: [1]

Contributions of $500

Central Avenue Methodist, northeast corner, Central and 12th [2]

First Baptist, northeast corner, Meridian and Vermont

Contributions of $400

Meridian Street Methodist, northwest corner, Meridian and St. Clair
First Presbyterian, southeast corner, 16th and Delaware
Second Presbyterian, 36-38 E. Vermont
Tabernacle Presbyterian, northeast corner, 11th and Meridian

Contributions of $200

Central Disciples,[3] northeast corner, Delaware and Walnut
First Friends, southeast corner, Alabama and 13th

Contributions of $100

Broadway Methodist, corner, Broadway and 22nd
Roberts Park Methodist, northeast corner, Delaware and Vermont
Memorial Presbyterian, 722 E. 11th
Fourth Presbyterian, northeast corner, 19th and Alabama
Downey Disciples, southeast corner, Downey and Julian
Third Disciples, southwest corner, 17th and Broadway
First Evangelical [Association], southeast corner, New York and East

Contributions of $50

Capitol Avenue Methodist, northeast corner, Capitol and Vermont
Irvington Methodist, 27 Layman Ave., Irvington
St. Paul Methodist, southwest corner, Rader and Eugene
Grace Presbyterian, northeast corner, Capitol and 32nd
North Park Disciples, corner, Kenwood and 29th
Seventh Disciples, 877 Udell, North Indianapolis
First Congregational, southwest corner, Delaware and 16th

Contribution of $30

South Street Baptist, southwest corner, Fletcher and Noble

Contributions of $25

East Tenth Methodist, southwest corner, 10th and Keystone
Edwin Ray Methodist, southwest corner, Woodlawn and Laurel
Hall Place Methodist, 126 W. 16th
Home Presbyterian, 960 W. 31st
Irvington Presbyterian, corner, Johnson and Julian
Seventh Presbyterian, 828 Elm
College Avenue Baptist, 1501 College
Woodruff Place Baptist, southwest corner, Michigan and Walcott
First English Lutheran, northeast corner, Walnut and Penn
Evangelical [no specific name given]
Butler Memorial Reformed, E. 10th and Oakland
St. John's Reformed, southeast corner, Merrill and Alabama
First United Brethren, 741 Park
Unitarian [All Souls], 1455 N. Alabama

Contributions of $20

Immanuel Reformed, northeast corner, Prospect and New Jersey
Tuxedo Baptist, 29 Garfield Ave.
University Place Baptist, southeast corner, Meridian and 33rd

Other congregations:

Contributions of $15

Maple Road Methodist
Tuxedo Methodist
Meridian Heights Presbyterian
Brookside United Brethren
First United Brethren

Contributions of $10

East Park Methodist
Fletcher Place Methodist
Traub Presbyterian
Germania Baptist
Centenary Disciples

Englewood Disciples
West Park Disciples
Grace Evangelical
Universalists

Contributions of $5
Barth Place Methodist
Beech Grove Methodist
Blaine Avenue Methodist
Brightwood Methodist
Broad Ripple Methodist
First German Methodist
Grace Methodist
Fountain Street Methodist
Heath Memorial Methodist
King Ave. Methodist
Merritt Place Methodist
Morris Street Methodist
Nippert Memorial Methodist
Trinity Methodist
Wesley Chapel Methodist
West Washington Street Methodist
Woodside Methodist
Sutherland Presbyterian
West Washington Presbyterian
Westminster Presbyterian
Beech Grove Baptist
Calvary Baptist
Immanuel Baptist
Garden Baptist
River Ave. Baptist
Thirty-First St. Baptist
Beech Grove Disciples
Bismarck Disciples
Columbia Place Disciples

Hillside Disciples
Olive Branch Disciples
Sixth Disciples
West Morris Disciples
Second Evangelical
Brightwood Congregational
Trinity Congregational
Union Congregational
Peoples Congregational
St. Mark's English Lutheran
Mansur Park Methodist Protestant
Hoyt Ave. Methodist Protestant
Villa Ave. Methodist Protestant
Central Ave. Reformed
First Reformed
Woodruff United Presbyterian
University Heights United Brethren

Endnotes

1   Typed list of names of congregations found with executive committee minutes for 20 June 1916 in Church Federation archives, Box 1, Folder 2, Indiana Historical Society.

2   Addresses of the congregations are taken from the "Churches" section in the Indianapolis City Directory for 1916.

3   All congregations listed as "Disciples" are grouped under "Christian" in city directory.

Appendix II

Executive Secretaries/Directors of The Church Federation of Greater Indianapolis

Rev. Morton C. Pearson	1913-1919
Rev. Charles H. Winders	1920-1924
Rev. Ernest N. Evans	1925-1939
Rev. Dr. Howard J. Baumgartel	1939-1954
Rev. Laurence T. Hosie	1958-1966
Rev. Robert W. Koenig	1966-1972
Mr. Paul E. McClure	1973-1987
Rev. C. Bruce Naylor	1987-1992
Interim Period	1993-1994
Rev. Dr. Angelique Walker-Smith	1995-

Appendix III

Presidents
of The Church Federation
of Greater Indianapolis

Vinson Carter	1912-1913
Caleb S. Denny	1913-1918
Thomas C. Day	1918-1923
Earl R. Conder	1927-1928
Marshall D. Lupton	1928-1933
Thomas C. Howe	1933-1934
C.L. Harkness	1934-1937
Eugene C. Foster	1937-1940
Henry R. Danner	1940-1943
Rev. Ellis W. Hay*	1943-1945
Charles A. Breene	1945-1947
Jerrus M. Bryant	1947-1950
C. Oliver Holmes	1950-1952
Allan C. Miller	1952-1953
Dr. Ozie D. Pruett	1953-1955
Harold F. Brigham	1955-1957
Russell R. Hirschman	1957-1959
Theo Fisher	1959-1961
Lester Irons	1961-1963
Rev. Clinton M. Marsh**	1963-1964
I. Lynd Esch	1964-1965
Joseph Coffin	1965-1967
Rev. Dr. F. Benjamin Davis***	1967-1970
Leon Lawhead	1971
Shirley (Mrs. Beauford) Norris****	1971-1973
Dr. J. Ralph Beaty*****	1973-1975
David F. Rees	1975-1977
James R. Bradley	1977-1979
Margaret S. Robbins	1979-1981
Rev. William H. Huber	1981-1983
Dorothea S. Green	1983-1985
Rev. Dr. Harry N. Huxhold	1985-1987
Rev. Dr. Philip Amerson	1989-1990
Rev. Darin Moore	1991-1992
Priscilla Savage	1993
Rev. Dr. Richard Moman	1994-1995

Rev. Dr. James Lemler   1996-1998
Rev. Dr. Ernest Newborn   1998
Rev. James Clark   1999
Rev. Dr. Richard Clough   2000-2C02
Rev. Dr. John Wantz   2003-2004
Father John Beitans******   2005-2007
Rev. Dr. Al Goertemiller   2008-2010
Maria Pimentel-Gannon   2011-

*first clergyman president

** first black president

*** first president from non-founding denomination

**** first female president

***** first denominational executive president

****** first Catholic president

Contributors

Rev. Dr. Thomas F. Best, a pastor of the Christian Church (Disciples of Christ), taught in the Religious Studies Department at Butler University (1972–1983) and was Director of the Institute for the Study of Early Christianity, Tübingen, Germany (1980-1981). He was seconded by his church in 1984 to the Faith and Order Commission of the World Council of Churches in Geneva, Switzerland, a position he held until retiring in 2007. He has written extensively on the ecumenical movement (including articles for *The Oxford Dictionary of the Christian Church* and *Die Religion in Geschichte und Gegenwart)*, and served as editor of *The Ecumenical Review*. His most recent publications include *Baptism Today* (Liturgical Press) and "Ecclesiology and Ecumenism" in *The Routledge Companion to the Christian Church* (2008).

Rev. Dr. Paul A. Crow, Jr. (Ph.D., Hartford Seminary) is a distinguished leader, scholar, and statesman in the worldwide Ecumenical Movement. During the last half of the twentieth century, he has given formative leadership to all expressions leading towards Christian Unity. He has served as a campus pastor, minister of Disciples congregations, and professor of church history and ecumenical studies at Lexington (KY) Theological Seminary, Princeton Theological Seminary, and Christian Theological Seminary in Indianapolis. For decades, Dr. Crow served in various capacities with the World Council of Churches. He was among those leaders who shaped and directed the historic Consultation on Church Union (COCU), serving as its first General Secretary. He has written and spoken extensively on the topic of Christian Unity.

Dr. James J. Divita (Ph.D. University of Chicago) taught European history and political science for 42 years at Marian College (now University). He was longtime president of the Indiana Religious History Association. His research interests are Indiana religious and ethnic history, and his work has appeared in a dozen Catholic congregational histories, *The Encyclopedia of Indianapolis* and other encyclopedias, major publications of the Indiana Historical Society, *Indianapolis Ethnic Settlement Patterns*, and journal and newspaper articles. In 2011 he prepared papers on Friedrich

Wyneken, second president of the Lutheran Church Missouri Synod.

Dr. Jeffrey Duvall (Ph.D., Purdue University) is an Indianapolis-based independent historian. A specialist in late nineteenth/early twentieth century U.S. social history, Duvall has written on rural life in the Ohio River Valley. He served as research assistant and contributor to *The Encyclopedia of Indianapolis* (1994) and contributor to *The Governors of Indiana* (2006). He also has published in the *Register of the Kentucky Historical Society.*

Rev. Dr. Richard L. Hamm (D. Min., Christian Theological Seminary) is the Executive Director of Christian Churches Together in the USA, a forum dedicated to expanding fellowship, unity, and witness among the diverse expressions of the Christian faith. He also is senior consultant with The Columbia Partnership. He was a congregational pastor for many years, served as the General Minister and President of the Christian Church (Disciples of Christ) for ten years, and for several years served on the World and National Council of Churches. He has spoken and written on church renewal and church leadership in the post-modern age.

Amanda J. Koch (M.A., Indiana University, Indianapolis) is a Ph.D. student in history at Indiana University, Bloomington. She holds a master's degree in U.S. history from Indiana University-Purdue University Indianapolis. Her research interests include religion, gender, activism, philanthropy, and Indiana history. During the summer of 2009, Amanda served as an intern for The Church Federation of Greater Indianapolis. Her duties included helping plan the centennial celebration and updating the Federation's history. She is currently an editorial assistant at the *American Historical Review.*

Dr. Jason S. Lantzer (Ph.D. Indiana University) is a native Hoosier who holds a B.A, M.A., and Ph.D. from Indiana University. His research and writing interests center on the intersection of religion, politics, and law in American history. He is the author of *"Prohibition is Here to Stay": The Reverend Edward S. Shumaker and the Dry Crusade in America* (University of Notre Dame Press, 2009) and *Mainline Christianity: The Past and Future of America's Majority Faith* (New York University Press, 2012).

Mary Risher (photo researcher) Photography has been Mary's passion for as long as she can remember. She is happiest when tasked with commissioning, researching and editing images for a photo essay on the Everglades, a travel feature on Tuscany, or history book on the Battle of Gettysburg. She has been developing and honing her skills for more than sixteen years and can't think of a better way to spend her days. Some of her clients include Virtuoso Life, AARP, Outside's GO, National Geographic School Publishing, and the Globe Pequot Press. When not glued to her monitor, Mary is in the field working on a personal photography project documenting Indiana's rural cemeteries.

Dr. Scott Seay (Ph.D., Vanderbilt University) joined the faculty of Christian Theological Seminary in 2005 after teaching in the religion departments of two undergraduate colleges. A specialist in colonial and early national/ New England religion and culture, Seay has focused most recently on the global history of the Christian Church (Disciples of Christ) and related denominations. In addition to his work in theological education, he is an ordained minister and has served several Disciples and Presbyterian congregations in Ohio and Indiana as pastor, consultant, and Christian educator.

Rev. Dr. Raymond R. Sommerville, Jr. (Ph.D., Vanderbilt University) serves as Associate Professor of the History of Global Christianity at Christian Theological Seminary in Indianapolis. He came to CTS in 1994 from Fisk University in Nashville, Tennessee. Strongly rooted in the African American church tradition, he approaches church history from a Pan-African and ecumenical perspective. A native of Philadelphia, PA, he is a third generation minister in the Christian Methodist Episcopal Church. He has published articles in *Notable Black American Women* and *Encounter*. His current research projects include a study of Black Methodists in a global perspective, religion and conflict resolution in Africa, and the prophetic art of James Baldwin. He is the author of *An Ex-Colored Church: Social Activism in the CME Church, 1870-1970* (Mercer University Press, 2004).

290

Marian Kleinsasser Towne was born a Hutterite Mennonite on a farm in South Dakota but became a Presbyterian after marriage to Dr. Edgar A. Towne, a pastor, professor, and theologian. She was educated in a one-room rural school, in two Mennonite schools, the University of Chicago, and Christian Theological Seminary. She taught English, Speech, and Drama in high schools and colleges in the Midwest. She is the author of seven books, including: *Bread of Life; The Onliest One Alive; Jacob Hutter's Friends;* and *A Midwest Gardener's Cookbook*. She is active in religious and civic organizations.

Dr. David G. Vanderstel (Ph.D., Kent State University) is the Vice President of Institutional Advancement, Sponsored Programs, and Government Relations at Martin University in Indianapolis. A native of Grand Rapids, Michigan, Vanderstel has been a resident of Indianapolis since 1982. He is a specialist in immigration history, museums and public history, and Indianapolis history. Vanderstel was a Senior Research Associate at The Polis Center at IUPUI (1990-2002) where he served as the assistant editor of *The Encyclopedia of Indianapolis* (Indiana University Press, 1994) and Senior Research Associate for the Project on Religion and Urban Culture. Vanderstel was the executive director of the National Council on Public History (1994-2005). He serves as the Marion County (IN) Historian, a position appointed by the Indiana Historical Society and the Indiana Historical Bureau since 2000, and also continues as an adjunct professor of history at IUPUI.

Rev. Dr. Angelique Walker-Smith (D.Min., Princeton Theological Seminary) serves as the Executive Director of The Church Federation of Greater Indianapolis, one of the oldest Council of Churches in the world, founded in 1912. She is the first African American and first woman to serve in that position. Raised in Cedarville and Springfield, Ohio, Walker-Smith graduated from Kent State University with a degree in telecommunications, Yale University Divinity School with a Master of Divinity, and Princeton Theological Seminary where she was the first African American woman to graduate from the program. She was ordained at

Convent Avenue Baptist Church in New York City. Walker-Smith has made many national television appearances and received a number of awards and recognitions, including the 2008 Indiana Governor's Award for Recognition in Religion.

John Warner (M.A., Indiana University, Indianapolis) is a 1993 graduate of the Public History program at Indiana University Purdue University Indianapolis (IUPUI). As a professional historian, he has been involved in researching and writing portions of many books, conducting field work, and writing reports in support of Section 106 actions pursuant to the National Historic Preservation Act. He has researched and authored over 30 nominations for historic districts and private resources seeking placement on the National Register of Historic Places.

Index

A

African Americans 42, 44, 52, 53, 54, 55, 74, 75, 78, 102, 121, 122, 123, 137, 144, 146, 151, 153, 154, 158, 160, 161, 167, 168, 169, 178, 181, 199, 216, 217, 220, 225, 230, 234, 235, 236, 238, 239, 257, 290, 291
Alcohol 30, 58, 59, 67, 92, 225
Anti-Saloon League 26, 39, 60, 83
Artis, Lionel 77, 106

B

Bader, Jesse M. 85, 86, 94
Barton, John J. 153
Baumgartel, Howard J. 91, 92, 96, 97, 98, 99, 100, 103, 104, 112, 113, 118, 127, 137, 138, 139, 282
Becker, Edwin L. iii, ix, xii, xv, xvii, 43, 62, 63, 90, 93, 94, 113, 114, 115, 137, 138, 139, 140, 163, 181, 193, 194, 195, 206, 211, 214, 221, 222, 266
Bell, Joseph E. 28, 40
Benjamin, T. Garrott 160, 236
Bethel African Methodist Episcopal (AME) Church 53, 54, 229, 233
Beverly, Urias 177, 201
Blackburn, Cleo 76
Black Manifesto 161, 164
Blankenbaker, Richard 175
Blinzinger, Carol 228, 233, 245
Boetcher, Walter C. 76
Bosler, Raymond 139, 198, 212, 231

Bradley, James R. 180, 183, 185, 194, 284
Broadway Methodist Church 77, 90
Butler School of Religion 106, 162
Butler University 76, 77, 80, 99, 104, 119, 132, 179, 259, 288

C

Cadle Tabernacle 37, 47, 87, 125, 133
Campus Ministry 175, 179, 194
Carpenter, Don 207, 217, 230
Carter, Catherine 144
Catholics 4, 25, 33, 36, 52, 53, 56, 97, 122, 125, 143, 158, 159, 163, 173, 183
Celebration of Hope 224, 227, 236, 237, 243, 245, 254, 256
Chaplaincy 176, 231, 241, 252
Christ Church Cathedral 101, 114, 173, 203
Christian Theological Seminary 116, 133, 144, 146, 155, 159, 162, 170, 174, 200, 202, 205, 206, 211, 212, 221, 259, 288, 289, 290, 291
Church Women United 73, 93, 190, 201, 212, 222
Clutton, Ulysses S. 47, 48
Comity Committee 31, 32, 33, 44, 51, 52, 69, 81, 110, 111, 115, 124, 126, 144, 162
Communications Unit 184, 185, 200, 205, 206, 212, 215, 216, 222, 223, 228, 241, 244
Communism 119, 148
Conder, Earl 37, 44, 284

G

Gambling 27, 58, 84, 197, 210, 219
Gavisk, Francis H. 33, 37, 85
Gleaners Food Bank 196, 202, 203, 221
Goodwill Industries 71
Graham, Billy 117, 118, 129, 133, 134, 135, 136, 139, 146, 147, 191, 224, 242
Great Depression, The 61, 69, 70, 92, 93, 97, 109
Greek Orthodox 51

H

Habitat for Humanity 237, 259, 270
Hamilton, Richard 153, 184, 210
Hartman, Grover L. 112, 232
Healthy Babies 201, 221, 229
Heimer, Roger 200, 207, 209
Herod, Henry L. 54, 77
Hispano-Latino Urban Forum 237, 256
Holy Week 26, 84, 85, 86, 143
Hosie, Laurence T. 116, 128, 132, 134, 135, 139, 140, 143, 145, 148, 149, 150, 151, 152, 154, 155, 156, 159, 116, 282
Hospitals 48, 144, 186, 231
Housing 36, 42, 54, 71, 75, 76, 78, 105, 108, 123, 124, 127, 152, 153, 154, 159, 162, 179, 180, 205, 208, 209, 220, 252, 258
Housing Opportunities Multiplied Ecumenically, Inc. (H.O.M.E.) 159, 179, 208

Hudnut, William H. III 196, 200, 201, 259
Hunter, Gilbert T. 144

I

Immigrants 25, 36, 52, 59, 271
Indiana Council of Churches 120, 133, 152, 155, 156, 159, 174, 209, 213, 219
Indiana General Assembly 75, 84, 90, 180, 209, 219, 220
Indianapolis 500 172, 186
Indianapolis Council of Church Women 69, 73, 126
Indianapolis Hebrew Congregation 33, 37, 85, 139, 187
Indianapolis Ministerial Association (Ministers Association) 23, 46, 69, 80, 83, 100, 186
Indianapolis News 25, 26, 28, 35, 39, 40, 41, 63, 64, 121, 137, 138, 139, 193
Indianapolis Police Department 29, 124, 176, 177, 178, 204, 225, 241, 243, 252
Indianapolis Public Schools 77, 79, 109, 128, 183, 203, 204, 227, 239, 240, 253
Indianapolis Recorder 18, 42, 75, 93, 131, 142, 243, 254
Indianapolis Star xvi, 37, 39, 40, 41, 44, 62, 63, 64, 65, 66, 71, 84, 91, 92, 93, 94, 99, 114, 137, 138, 139, 148, 163, 177, 193, 196, 221, 224, 230, 232, 238, 243, 244, 245, 246, 256, 261, 262, 263